KAMIKAZE

KAMIKAZE
Japan's Suicide Gods

ALBERT AXELL and HIDEAKI KASE

To die voluntarily in the prime of life is unnatural.
The very thought of death is unbearable for any
person who is sound of mind. But these youths
were sound of mind . . .

The authors

Longman

An imprint of **Pearson Education**
London · New York · Toronto · Sydney · Tokyo · Singapore · Hong Kong · Cape Town
New Delhi · Madrid · Paris · Amsterdam · Munich · Milan · Stockholm

PEARSON EDUCATION LIMITED

Head Office:
Edinburgh Gate
Harlow CM20 2JE
Tel: +44 (0)1279 623623
Fax: +44 (0)1279 431059

London Office:
128 Long Acre
London WC2E 9AN
Tel: +44 (0)20 7447 2000
Fax: +44 (0)20 7240 5771
Website: www.history-minds.com

First published in Great Britain in 2002

ISBN 0 582 77232 X

British Library Cataloguing in Publication Data
A CIP catalogue record for this book can be obtained from the British Library

Library of Congress Cataloging in Publication Data
A CIP catalogue record for this book can be obtained from the Library of Congress

10 9 8 7 6 5 4 3 2 1

Set in 10/13pt Galliard
Typeset by Graphicraft Limited, Hong Kong
Printed in China

The Publisher's policy is to use paper manufactured from sustainable forests.

CONTENTS

LIST OF MAPS AND PLATES

MAPS

PLATES

ACKNOWLEDGEMENTS

The authors wish to express their gratitude to the following people for their kind assistance and support in the preparation of this book: Takeo Tagata and Hichiro Naemura, both former flyers and instructors of Kamikaze pilots, who supplied us with original material and photographs; Shigeru Tominaga, son of Lt. General Kyoji Tominaga, who allowed us to quote copiously from his father's unpublished papers and provided exclusive photographs; Taizo Kusayanagi, biographer of Admiral Onishi, who let us use material from his book; Lt. Commander (ret.) Nobuo Fuji, who told us the story of the 'Red Dragon Fly'; and also Masakatsu Shinkai, President, National Institute for Defence Studies; Shingo Oyama, chief librarian at Yushukan, Yasukuni Shrine's war museum; Lt. Col. (ret.) Mitsuo Takai; Toshio Sasaki; Hideyuki Ono; Ms. Maki Shirai; Ms. Ari Shoji; Ms. Rumiko Kanzaki; Mike Wallington; Nicholas Gibbs; Martin Blakeway; Janet Q. Treloar; John Hale-White; Eddie Grenfell; Ronald James Wren; David Monk; Festus McCann; Barry Holmes; Phillip Knightley; and Penelope Allport.

We also wish to thank Casey Mein, Anna Vinegrad and the London editorial staff of Pearson Education for their helpful suggestions and close attention to detail.

NOTE TO READERS

The name Kamikaze ('Divine Wind') derives from the thirteenth century when Kublai Khan's Mongol warriors – actually Mongol-Koryo (Korean) allied forces – twice attempted to invade Japan in 1274 and 1281 but failed when Mongol fleets were destroyed by what appeared to be heaven-sent typhoons – or Kamikaze on both occasions. In fact the first demand for Japan's capitulation was brought by Koryo royal messengers before the first attempted invasion. The word Kamikaze gained further currency after October 1944 when a Special Attack, or Kamikaze, Corps was created to destroy an Allied fleet east of the Philippine Islands, and later against American and British naval forces in the Okinawa area. The full name was 'Divine Wind Special Attack Force'. Tokko or 'Special Attack' is an abbreviation for *tokubetsu kogeki* and is a euphemism for suicide attack. Strictly speaking, the only real Kamikazes were the crash-dive pilots first organized in the Philippines by Vice Admiral Takijiro Onishi in October 1944. But the name was later applied to other Japanese suicide units. On these pages, the word Kamikaze is used for both Army and Navy suicide units and is sometimes replaced by the words Special Attack Force, or simply *tokko*. Actually, the name Kamikaze was pronounced *Shimpu* by the Navy when the first series of crash-dive attacks were launched. In the Japanese language, the *kanji* (or Chinese characters) can be pronounced different ways. Thus, *kami* is also pronounced *shin*. *Kami* is old-style Japanese while *shin* was an adoption of the ancient Chinese pronunciation. Ditto *kaze*. In 1960s Japan, Kamikaze became a metaphor for daredevils, reckless taxi drivers and breakneck skiers.

Taiwan and Kyushu figure prominently on these pages. During the war there were key Kamikaze bases on Taiwan and even more dotting the island of Kyushu, considered the cradle of Japanese civilization. Taiwan and Kyushu are roughly the same size, each being slightly larger than Belgium or equal in size to the US states of Massachusetts and Connecticut combined.

PREFACE

After the terrorist blitz on America in September 2001, the human race was forced to confront the most radical face of fanaticism – suicide. In this case, making use of human weapons. The shock was greater because commercial jets loaded with passengers were turned into manned missiles. People everywhere, confronted with a primal fear, wondered if a replica of the Kamikaze crash-dive zealots of the Second World War had suddenly appeared to threaten the peace of civilized states.

The reaction of Western experts to suicide hijackers and youthful suicide bombers in the new millennium was similar to that of Anglo-American witnesses to Kamikaze crashes in the Pacific: 'We haven't seen something like this before!'

But stereotypes of the Kamikaze had earlier come to the fore, in May 1972, when three members of a suicidal terrorist group calling themselves the Japanese Red Army landed at Tel Aviv's airport and opened up with sub-machine guns, killing some 25 and wounding about 80, mainly Christian pilgrims on a visit to the Holy Land. (Two of the assassins were fatally shot.) Ten years later a suicidal Muslim driving a truck full of explosives crashed into a US Marine billet in Lebanon, killing over 200 Marines. It was viewed by many as a Kamikaze-style mission.

Even the Russians, burdened by the ongoing Chechnya problem, spoke of their nemesis as Kamikazes. Example: an article in the *Moscow Times* of July 15, 2000, citing a suicidal incident in Chechnya, said that 'the Kamikaze driver' had crashed his truck loaded with explosives through a barrier, killing 40 policemen and wounding 74 others.

It is therefore no surprise that some experts claim that today's suicide bombers are the direct heirs of Kamikaze ideology and spirit. After the 'Nine-Eleven' attacks in America, many Japanese citizens bared their resentment against Western newspapers who equated the suicide hijackers with America's (and Britain's and Australia's) *bête noire* of the Pacific War: the Kamikaze ('Divine Wind') flyers. 'Kamikaze Terrorist

Attacks' and 'Kamikaze Blitz on the USA', screamed headlines in Europe and America, evoking images of the death-rain caused by suicide planes diving against Allied naval armadas in the Pacific. Other newspapers spoke of 'The Faces of Kamikaze Terrorists' and published photos of suspected hijackers. Eminent Japanese, including those critical of sending pilots on suicide missions in the Pacific War, protested, saying it was groundless to make these comparisons. They were correct: the real Kamikaze flyers were far from being terrorists. In the first place, the intended victims of Kamikaze sorties had an equal opportunity to defend themselves. Second, many US warships not only defended well but, with radar giving advance warning of danger, took countermeasures that worked so well that masses of Special Attack – or Kamikaze – planes were shot out of the sky, causing sailors to liken many an encounter to 'a turkey shoot'. (But all told, the skill and effectiveness of Kamikaze missions created a deep psychological shock among Allied forces.) Third, thousands of Kamikaze pilots, many of them novices with only a few hours' flying experience, missed their target altogether, ending up in a watery grave.

There were some superficial parallels between Japan's Kamikaze flyers and the Al-Qaeda activists willing to sacrifice themselves. Both volunteered to die for their sacred beliefs. Both shared a vision of self-righteousness and divine punishment to enemies. Both meditated on the carnage to come. Their preparation for the mission in hand involved both physical and spiritual means and the strength of each lay in their enthusiastic seeking of death. A survey has shown that, like the superior education level of many Kamikaze pilots, a high percentage of Al-Qaeda faithful, perhaps as many as 80 per cent, have attended college or university. And (also like the Kamikaze) there has been no shortage of volunteers.

More striking was the existence of written instructions, some of them beatific in tone, guiding the faithful of each organization step by step to the final aerial death-dive. The following excerpts from these writings are given consecutively, the Kamikaze entries taken from a top-secret manual for pilots that is hardly known in the West;[1] the parallel entries are taken from hand-written documents found in the luggage of one of the zealots of September 2001:

■ 'When diving into the enemy, shout at the top of your lungs: "*Hissatsu!*" (Sink without fail!)'

■ 'When you strike, shout "Allah is great" because this shout strikes terror in the hearts of the infidels.'

*

■ 'Be always pure-hearted and cheerful. A loyal fighting man is a pure-hearted and filial son. . . . Do your best. Every deity and the spirits of your dead comrades are watching you intently.' [All Kamikaze pilots were told they would become gods at death.]

■ 'Purify your heart and clean it from all earthly matters. . . . Remember the verse that if God supports you, no one will be able to defeat you.'

*

■ 'To live and be surrounded by Imperial blessings. To die and become one of Japan's guardian deities and, therefore, receive special honours in the temple.' [A choice that was presented to Japanese pilots.]

■ 'Everybody hates death, fears death. But only those, the believers who know the life after death and the rewards after death, would be the ones who will be seeking death.'

Psychologists, commenting on the events of September 2001, said the framework of war was a very common reaction in America; that to make sense of something so incredible one had to compare it to something familiar. In the USA exclamations such as 'It's just like Pearl Harbor!' were often heard. The explosive shock of Pearl Harbor on December 7, 1941 had been followed by another – the sinking of the British heavy cruiser *Repulse* and the allegedly unsinkable battleship *Prince of Wales* in the South China Sea a few hours later. A survivor, Sub-Lieutenant Geoffrey Brooke, who was aboard *Prince of Wales* when it was fatally hit by bombs and torpedoes, said the shock waves caused by Pearl Harbor and the sinking of the two warships 'equalled' that felt by the loss of thousands of human lives in the World Trade Center in New York on September 11, 2001, and the hundreds killed and injured at the Pentagon.

In fact, though, this parallel is flawed. At Pearl Harbor one nation's armed forces had bombed those of another, thereby widening a war that Adolf Hitler had begun.

Among Japanese citizens who were offended by the comparisons of the Kamikaze with the hijackers were many war veterans, including two pilots who had themselves volunteered to join Kamikaze units in their youth but survived when the war ended and all suicide missions halted. Both men said that after the media comparisons of the September 11 events, they wished to correct some misunderstandings.

Takeo Tagata, who was 86 years old in the second year of the new millennium, became an instructor of Kamikaze pilots before he himself in the last days of war decided to join their ranks. During dogfights he had often outwitted less experienced American and British pilots whom he encountered in the skies, mainly over China and Taiwan. He is categorical: 'Tokko [Kamikaze] flyers did not kill a single non-combatant. They fought in the air, man to man.'

Hichiro Naemura, an entrepreneur in the Osaka area, is a former Army pilot, who is five years younger than Tagata. He was upset by what he termed 'hurtful comparisons' between Japan's Kamikaze volunteers and those who destroyed New York's World Trade Center towers. Naemura, like Tagata, a former instructor of Kamikaze pilots, declared: 'The Special Attack [suicide] pilots did not in any way violate international law or the Geneva War Convention. They were absolutely not terrorists.'

We have met these hardy survivors and some of their wartime exploits are recorded in these pages.

Other citizens, who vented their dissatisfaction with the Western media in its references to the Kamikaze phenomenon included the Governor of Tokyo, Shintaro Ishihara, who is also a popular novelist and con-troversialist. In defending the Kamikaze pilots, the governor offered a contentious analogy of the September events, saying that the use of atomic bombs in August 1945 against Japan was a terrorist act. Here is a quotation from Ishihara, well known for the bluntness of his speech. (He was once chided by US Senator Max Baucus for being an 'America-basher'): 'The September 11 terrorist attacks with their in-discriminate massacre of civilians did not resemble at all the Kamikaze attacks in the Pacific War; they resembled the indiscriminate nuclear attacks on Hiroshima and Nagasaki.'

On the other hand, some observers in the West claim that only by using extreme measures could Japan be forced into surrender. Britain's Bertrand Russell contended that it was the samurai code of Bushido – one of the engines of Kamikaze education – that saw surrender to the enemy as ignominy; that this was also a reason why Japan never ratified the Geneva Prisoner of War Convention of 1929.

Professor Emeritus of Tokyo University Keiichiro Kobori agreed with the Governor of Tokyo, saying that the West often viewed the Kamikaze pilots unfairly. 'The Pearl Harbor attack, like the Kamikaze attacks,' he said, 'was strictly limited as to targets: warships and milit-ary facilities.' He added: 'I can say with authority that the personal lives of the Kamikaze pilots were consonant with Kishido [Western-style chivalry].' By which he presumably meant that members of the Kamikaze corps, a large number of whom were college-educated, were of a higher order of warrior.

Finally, the authors have attempted in this book to provide readers with some uniquely Japanese perspectives on war, culture, suicide and religion.

Field Marshal William Slim, who was wartime Supreme Allied Commander SE India, said of his opponents: 'Everyone talks about fighting to the last man, but only the Japanese actually do it.' After the Pacific fighting was over, Imperial Navy Captain Rikihei Inoguchi, who was a key participant in drawing up the initial strategy for suicide attacks, told US interrogators: 'If our wish is for a peaceful world, it would be well to study the spirit of the Kamikaze pilots . . .'

NOTE

[1] See Chapter 6, The Suicide Manual.

Map 1   The Philippines and South-east Asia

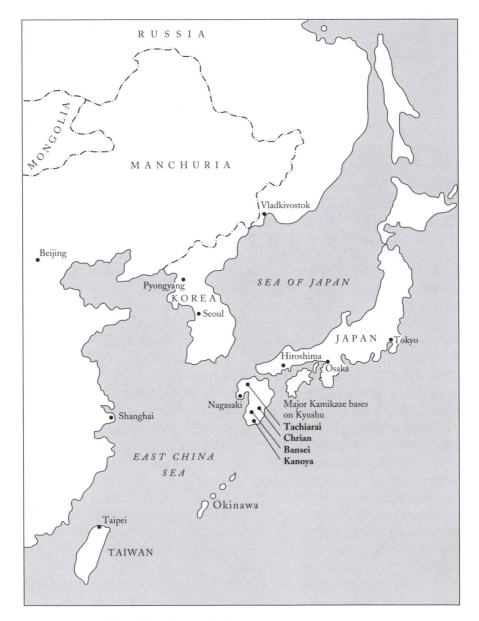

Map 2 Key Kamikaze bases in Japan

INTRODUCTION

JAPAN: THE NAKED TRUTH

The foreigner visiting Japan today is astonished at how seriously the Japanese take the work ethic, even the idea of punctuality. The latter amounts to a national obsession. For instance, trains run on time, the average delay in the year 2001 being less than 60 seconds. The population of Japan is receptive to such lofty principles as character-building and education-throughout-life which in the work place is expressed by such slogans as 'Don't spare yourself!' and 'Exercise self-control!'

Certain character traits stand out that are impressive and seem entirely fitting for a swollen population hemmed into four relatively small islands. Self-discipline, compulsory for a society to function properly, is evident. So is the pursuit of consensus and the shunning of loud and boisterous public behaviour. This is combined with lusty involvement of citizens in social activities like attendance at traditional festivals. All of this together ensures order within communities, deepens a sense of togetherness and, not least, eases daily stress. Since the Japanese enjoy a longevity that is according to United Nations statistics the highest in the world (in 1998 the average lifespan for men was 77.6, for women 84.6);[1] since contemporary Japan is sometimes called a well-oiled machine; since Japanese society has been described by experts as being 'subversion-proof' – there would seem to be good reason, if not to take the Japanese as a model, at least to learn more about them.

Is consensus perhaps the key to understanding Japan's post-war accomplishments? Whatever, in the spring of 2002, the well-known peacemaker and former president of Finland, Martti Ahtisaari, seeming to take a page from Japan's success story, called on the USA to build a 'true multilateral consensus' among leading nations in order to prevent new Nine-Elevens and other forms of global terrorism, not to mention solving the problems of economic inequality and environmental degradation.

An American expert has called Japan 'the largest mononational State in the world'.[2] This has advantages. There are no insurgent minorities flaunting exclusivity, nor aggressive religions that may cause a cleavage in society. Japan's economic wizards have an addiction to long-term planning. Some overseas visitors are shocked to learn that the portfolios of Japanese officials are crammed with detailed blueprints, many of which stretch 20 years into the future – or longer. Of no minor importance, Japan enjoys universal literacy and its citizens are (despite a flood of mind-numbing distractions, similar to Western nations) voracious readers.

Most generalizations about Asia stop at the Japanese border. Within it, the people have been unique in the capacity of retaining an individuality and a social system set up many centuries ago. An anonymous observer is probably near the truth in describing Japan as a combination of 'benevolent paternalism and an innate communal line of thought'. Such people are not easily cowed, or pushed into accepting alien imports, whether they be ideologies or religions. An example is Christianity which has tens of thousands of followers in Japan but has been unable to make more significant inroads despite the vigour of missionaries. But the Japanese are equally unlikely to be tempted by left-wing ideologies such as 'communism' – if anyone can say in the new millennium exactly what this means.

Over a century ago the Reverend W.E. Griffis made this observation about the Japanese: 'In moral character, the average Japanese is frank, honest, faithful, kind, gentle, courteous, confiding, affectionate, filial, loyal. Love of [blunt] truth for its own sake, chastity, temperance, are not characteristic virtues.'

The European editor of the *Japan Mail* noted, also a century ago, that the Japanese had a penchant for nicety of detail, being meticulous to a fault. When that editor was travelling through various provinces in Japan, he noticed that the distances along roads were given not only in feet, but also in inches. Such exactitude has disappeared on Japan's roads. But many traditional characteristics remain.

It is no secret that the qualities that have helped make Japan a world economic power and plucky trading partner – such as energy, precision, commitment, discipline, daring – were also those that made Japan an implacable opponent at war. (British Major-General Julian Thompson, says in a review of *The Full Monty: Montgomery of Alamein*, published in London, that during the war 'the Japanese were man-for-man more formidable than the best of the Germans'.) If there is a blot on the Japanese landscape it is probably the level of work-related stress. Studies show that one in 12 suicides are work-related, that on average there are over 30,000 suicides annually.

With the passage of time, historians, journalists and film makers – many of them conservative in their thinking – have taken up the war theme, with the result that films of a provocative nature have been produced, including some which challenge the verdict of the International War Crimes Tribunal that in 1948 passed sentence on Japan's defeated national leaders. And – an indication of the new era – in recent years a number of well-appointed museums have opened, dedicated to the memory of Kamikaze pilots. In the process, a number of Kamikaze survivors (those whose sorties were cancelled when the war ended) have become sought-after speakers on the domestic lecture circuit.

The Kamikaze, in the words of one British naval witness, were 'unlike anything that was known' in all the wars of the Western world. In addition, there were the 'human bombs' called *Ohka* ('Cherry Blossoms') and the manned torpedoes known as *Kaiten* ('Reversing Fortune') – pitiless weapons that sentenced their users to untimely death.

For the younger generation, the Kamikaze phenomenon is a curiosity from the past; to the older it is a reminder of a cruel epoch. In retrospect, there was probably a bad conscience on the part of the High Command in organizing and carrying out Special Attack – or suicide – operations. In fact, training and execution were left to front-line units. Moreover, there was little top-level guidance until the late spring of 1945, some six months after the Kamikaze sorties were begun. Meanwhile, in today's Japan, not a few citizens who winced at the squandering of the lives of thousands who joined the Special Attack units now feel free to regard the fallen pilots as selfless heroes.

A Kamikaze sortie was different from the usual battle scene in which a doomed soldier, fighting for his life, is surrounded by an enemy and determines to die in their midst. In a crash-dive attack, a flyer took off from a base far from the pandemonium of battle. Before doing so he had time to write final letters and, usually, a farewell poem. He may even have left a lock of hair and nail cuttings as mementoes for his family. Then, inside the cockpit, he forgot himself as he aimed his craft at a target and shouted imprecations before impact. Many of the letters and diaries of members of the Special Attack units reveal a different story from that given to the public in wartime as well as the early post-war years. Not everyone was heroic; some were less than enthusiastic about taking leave of the world. The writings of the pilots are not a confused jumble but the outpourings of sane, often highly rational and literate beings. Some of the letters combine a strong spirit of independence and self-discipline.

Despite the passage of many years, the older generation can remember the time when the entire nation was called upon to 'Display the Kamikaze Spirit!' – to be ready to give up one's life for nation and throne without a murmur. In the schools all students read about samurai ways, of Bushido (the Draconian 'Code of the Samurai'), of the ritual of seppuku (or hara-kiri). Life after all was transient and what was more consoling than to believe that after death one's spirit would 'continue to live with the living and the dead'? The introduction of Kamikaze tactics in the Pacific War, as a desperate measure to 'bleed the enemy white', was considerably less of a shock for Japanese than for Westerners.

A Japanese military doctor captured by the Americans during the war, when describing the difference between Western and Japanese philosophy, said the former tells a person how to live, the latter how to die.

The word suicide, it becomes clear, does not have the immoral connotation in the Japanese language that it has in English. In Japanese there are various words for suicide and they have subtle differences. For example: *jisatsu* (translated as 'self-killing') carries a negative, even sinful connotation, as the word suicide does in many Western cultures. But *jiketsu* (literal translation, 'self-determination' but actually meaning 'suicide') and *jisai* (literally 'self-judgement' but also meaning 'suicide') suggest an honourable or laudable act done in the public interest; for example, an act carried out to protect the honour of the one who commits suicide. Unlike Judeo-Christian morality, there is no ethical or religious taboo against suicide in Shintoist Japan.

Some Japanese make an earnest attempt to prove a difficult premise: that the Kamikaze deaths were not suicides. For instance, Saburo Sakai, an ace pilot and author of the book, *Samurai*, attempts to show that what looked like suicidal acts to Americans – when pilots chose to kill themselves by aiming their aircraft at the decks of Anglo-American ships – was not self-killing in the conventional sense of suicide because the overwhelming majority of the Special Attack, or Kamikaze, pilots never thought they were 'throwing away their lives'. For Sakai it makes all the difference if those who take their own lives (in this case Kamikaze pilots) do so cheerfully and for the most patriotic reasons.[3]

The nonchalant way a prominent family reacted to the loss of their son, a Kamikaze pilot, in the latter stages of the Pacific War, is typical of a deep-rooted stoicism in confronting death. In early 1945 Lieutenant General Kyoji Tominaga, a former Vice Minister of War who was now in disgraced forced retirement (he would later be recalled to duty), was informed by telephone at his Tokyo residence that his son, Yasushi, had lost his life when he sallied forth on a suicide mission. Yasushi, who had been a college boxer and was a collector of butterflies, had the reputation of being a bright, vivacious, if slightly mischievous youth, who loved the English language (he promoted English-language speech contests) and was an avid fan of Hollywood films, especially westerns like John Ford's *Stagecoach*. On the tail of his *Hayabusa* (peregrine falcon) suicide plane he had painted a skull and crossbones, apparently borrowing the idea from watching a US film. On learning the news, the general, clad in kimono and standing in his tatami-matted room with Western-stye furniture, simply uttered 'Is that right?' (*So deska?*) and thanked his informant, Lieutenant General Michio Sugawara, a close friend who commanded the Sixth Air Army on Kyushu. Then, turning to his wife, he said, 'Yasushi's gone.' She held his hand but both showed no emotion in the presence of their seven-year-old son. The general and his wife maintained 'stiff upper lips'.

Western experts on Japan have recorded some profound observations on the Japanese. On the idea of death, Professor Basil Hall Chamberlain, who taught Japanese and philology at the Imperial University of Tokyo in the late nineteenth century, explained that the Japanese had 'less high-strung nerves than Europeans'. He even classed 'indifference to death' among Japanese physical characteristics, because he argued that nobody could doubt that a less sensitive nervous system must tend in that direction. He conceded, though, that 'opinions and beliefs had some influence in the matter. Buddhism,' he went on, 'is a tolerant, hopeful creed, and promises rest at last to all, even though it may have to be purchased by the wicked at the price of numerous transmigrations. Christianity, on the other hand, with its terrible doctrine of the final and hopeless perdition of the immense majority of the human race, may have steeped in a still more sombre hue the naturally excitable and self-questioning European mind.' The professor added that the Greeks and Romans appeared to have braved death with a commendable indifference to which few moderns could attain.

On the nature of religion, Professor Chamberlain quoted a useful passage from a distinguished seventeenth-century German explorer and surgeon, Engelbert Kaempfer: 'The Japanese profess a great respect and veneration for their gods, and worship them in various ways. And I think I may affirm, that in the practice of virtue, in purity of life, and outward devotion, they far out-do the Christians. They are careful for the Salvation of their Souls, scrupulous to excess in the expiation of their crimes, and extremely desirous of future happiness. . . . Their Laws and Constitutions are excellent, and strictly observed, severe penalties being put upon the least transgression of any.'

Another quotation: in the 1850s Royal Navy Captain Sherard Osborn visited Japan and made this perceptive comment: 'Our day's observations led us to a conclusion which every hour in Japan confirmed – that the people inhabiting it are a very remarkable race, and destined, by God's help, to play an important role in the future history of this remote quarter of the globe.' The good captain could not of course have foreseen the genie-like explosion of Japan's economic and financial influence in all four quarters of the globe.

In the late nineteenth century, Lafcadio Hearn, an American, Greek-born authority on Japanese subtleties, who taught English literature at the former Tokyo Imperial University (he later became a Japanese citizen), looked for the source of Japanese stability and concluded that two awesome religions, Shinto and Buddhism, were 'the creators and preservers' of Japan's moral power. While Buddhism helped train citizens to master disappointment and sorrow, show composure in the face of adversity, and accept the impermanence of the universe, Shinto inculcated reverence for ancestral memory and devotion to Emperor and country, placing them ahead of family or self. Hearn, in a memorable work entitled *Kokoro*, describes the deep emotion of a boy visiting a Shinto shrine who bursts into tears because he is conscious of the 'prodigious debt' of the present to the past, and of the 'duty' of love and respect for the dead.

A further word on the Japanese worship of ancestors. From ancient times the people of Japan believed that the soul of the deceased remained behind to be celebrated by their descendants. It was believed that the soul would watch over the 'good fortunes' of these descendants together with the ancestral gods, or *kami*, who protected the livelihood and prosperity of the people from antiquity, remaining unchanged into future generations.

Finally, deep in the hearts of the Japanese people is the faith that the souls of the deceased dwell in the quiet and lofty place of one's birth from where they watch over the family, and will respond if called upon.

During the conflict in the Pacific, countless speeches and writings mentioned the modern warrior's debt to Bushido and the Code of the Samurai. Centuries-old Japanese letters advised that discipline for warriors, pared down to its fundamental component, meant readiness for death. The image of the valiant feudal warrior is presented in *Hagakure* (translated as *Hidden Behind the Leaves*), no doubt the most influential of all the samurai writings, authored by an eighteenth-century monk from Hagi Han – presently Saga Prefecture on Kyushu. It says that Bushido, or the Code of the Samurai, teaches the warrior how to die with nobility. Honour means fighting to the bitter end, surrender is equal to dishonour. Further, it is only at the instant when one determines to die that a man attains purity. Also from *Hagakure*: 'Calamity, when it occurs, is not so dreadful as was feared. It is foolish to torment oneself beforehand with vain imaginings.'

In feudal Japan, Shintoism and Buddhism, with an infusion of Confucianism, made important contributions to Bushido, the obligatory way of life of the warrior class, with emphasis on self-discipline, courage and loyalty. Bushido taught one 'to bear and face calamities and adversities with patience and a pure conscience'; that 'true honour lies in fulfilling Heaven's decree and [that] no death incurred in so doing is ignominious'. Followers of the code were called upon to fight on 'until one's sword was broken and one's last arrow spent'. In Inazo Nitobe's readable classic, *Bushido: The Soul of Japan*, the author says that the teachings of Confucius are the most prolific source of Bushido. Confucius is quoted as saying, 'A man must live in such a way that he is always prepared to die.'

Today, nearly all Japanese perform periodic Shinto rites even if they do not consider themselves to be Shintoists. Moreover, all Japanese Shintoists are concurrently Buddhists.

A fact worth remembering in this brief discussion of Bushido is that Japan had lived in uninterrupted peace for more than 250 years (there is no parallel in world history) from 1615 – except for a Christian rebellion on the island of Amakusa, off the coast of Kyushu, in 1637–38. (Protestant Dutch gunboats helped suppress this Catholic rebellion.) The samurai, often stereotyped as 'fierce warriors', turned into pen-pushing bureaucrats while harbouring the ideal of the samurai way of life. Because of this long period of unbroken peace, the code of Bushido began to be regarded as something idealistic, metaphysical and romantic.

Nitobe again: 'What Japan was [he was writing in 1905] she owed to the samurai. They were not only the flower of the nation, but its root as well. All the gracious gifts of Heaven flowed through them. Though they kept themselves socially aloof from the populace, they set a moral standard for them and guided them by their example.'

And what does the cult of Bushido say of women? Again, Nitobe: 'Bushido . . . praised those women most "who emancipated themselves from the frailty of their sex and displayed an heroic fortitude worthy of the strongest and the bravest of men".' Incidentally, while Nitobe's work has been highly praised, it has not escaped the rebuke that the author tends to romanticize the samurai. But the *Hagakure* has also been held up to criticism. Shigenobu Okuma, a samurai from Hagi Han and the founder of Tokyo's Waseda University who served as foreign minister and prime minister in the Meiji era, in a memoir strongly criticized Hagi Han's bible, *Hagakure*, as romantic nonsense. In much the same way, many Japanese regard Bushido as a set of highly romantic values.

If life, according to Buddhism, was but a temporary state, Buddhism also promoted the vision of a better life to come. The idea of a placid, perhaps even a blissful afterlife is contained in a litany of Buddhist proverbs as the following testify:

■ Human life is like the morning dew.

■ The world is only a resting place.

■ Only by reason of having died does one enter into life.

■ The future life is the all-important thing.[4]

It would, of course, be erroneous to think that only in Japan did there exist harsh exhortations on duty, loyalty, and self-sacrifice. Here, for instance, is what a French philosopher-priest, Félicité Robert de Lamennais (1782–1854), wrote: 'Human society is based upon mutual giving, or upon the sacrifice of man for man, or of each man for all other men; and sacrifice is the very essence of all true society.' And, confronting the growing emphasis on self, another Frenchman, Ferdinand Brunetière, said over 100 years ago: 'Individualism is the enemy of education, as it is also the enemy of social order.'

During much of the first half of the twentieth century, a time when the Army played a large part in shaping Japanese decisions on many questions of foreign and internal policy, Shinto and Buddhism helped imbue youth with patriotism and loyalty. The part this played in nurturing a first-class, resilient soldiery is obvious. Apart from the martial dimension, these religions, then as now, helped mould the Japanese character.

The Western reader with even a cursory knowledge of Japan can be in no doubt that 'honourable suicide' and 'death on the field of battle' have a commanding place in Japanese history and literature. It was a long-established belief in Japan that to die for Emperor and country was the greatest glory, even sometimes a religious duty. In the Second World War, the suicide charge became a 'weapon of choice'. Japanese soldiers were imbued with a 'sacred mission' to die for the *Tenno* (the Emperor). They were taught that to turn one's back on the enemy and flee was a breach of honour. Being taken prisoner was a humiliation as well as a danger; if captured the men (they were told) would be tortured and killed, the women raped and killed.

The following 'code of battle ethics' was distributed at the behest of War Minister General Hideki Tojo to all officers and men of the Japanese Armed Forces on January 8, 1941. The code, with apparent borrowings from *Bushido*, said:

> Do not stay alive in dishonour. Do not die in such a way as to leave a bad name behind you. . . . A sublime sense of self-sacrifice must guide you throughout life and death. Think not of death as you push through with every ounce of your effort, fulfilling your duties. Make it your joy to do everything with all your spiritual and physical strength. Fear not to die for the cause of everlasting justice.

Referring to this martial code, one commentator remarked: 'Suddenly the unwritten code of the samurai became the compulsory way of all servicemen.'

But earlier twentieth-century history had shown that Japanese civilians, too, could be driven to heroic suicide prompted by humiliation and dishonour. Following the London Naval Conference in 1930, when there was seething anger among Japanese military circles who felt the USA and Britain had insulted Japan by giving her a smaller quota of certain warships than the other major powers, one staff officer belonging to the Japanese delegation that had attended the conference committed ritual suicide in a railway carriage, using his officer's sword. One account of the incident said the officer had thereby redeemed himself.

In 1924, in a little-known incident, after the US Senate passed an Immigration Bill which discriminated against persons of Japanese ancestry, a young student sat down outside the gates of the American Embassy in Tokyo and disembowelled himself.[5]

But the most sensational suicide in Japan (actually a mass suicide) occurred in 1703 and is told in *The Story of the 47 Samurai*. A national epic, it has even now an incomparable hold on the Japanese mind. It is a rambling story of pent-up humiliation and desire for revenge, of absolute loyalty and, in the end, acceptance of ritual suicide for all. The idea of acceptance is correct because hara-kiri, or belly-cutting, was a form of execution carried out by the hereditary military governors (or Shoguns) of the time. In order to protect the honour of the samurai class, as it were, the 47 samurai were obliged to commit suicide in the prescribed manner. However, the obligatory nature of the self-killing of the warriors suggests that the word suicide in their case may be open to interpretation.

Lavishly retold in novels, plays and the cinema, the tale caught the eye of a famous British novelist and a young American who later became the 26th President of the United States.

Robert Louis Stevenson, author of *Treasure Island* and *Dr Jekyll and Mr Hyde*, was so impressed with this complex and classic Japanese story of a vendetta that when he read about it in Mitford's *Tales of Old Japan*, he commented: '[In Mitford] I learned for the first time the proper attitude of any rational man to his country's laws – a secret found, and kept, in the Asiatic [i.e., Japan's] islands.' Incidentally the story was also published in the *Fortnightly Review* of London in 1870.

Stevenson, stirred by the high level of patriotism in Japan, added: 'It is a case of competition of duties, and the continued triumph of the superior duty, the duty to the clan, that the tale has been considered by many writers. Our duties here in England weaken as they get further from the hearth, until patriotism is but a fitful and tepid consideration, and honesty to the State a stretch of Quixotry. To these Japanese, on the other hand, the Clan comes before the family.'

Also captivated by this tale was a youthful American named Theodore Roosevelt who, twenty years later, was elected President. To the vibrant, adventure-seeking young Roosevelt, the actual historical incident of the 47 samurai aroused his enthusiasm and his growing interest in things Japanese so much that he sought out all available literature on Japan, in the English language. He learned that a unique moral code called Bushido, or 'the way of knighthood', had existed in Japan. At once the young Roosevelt hired an instructor to teach him judo, the 'Japanese art of self-defence'. Years later, at the end of the Portsmouth Peace Conference in America (it was hosted by Roosevelt and ended the Russo-Japanese War), when a Japanese diplomat visited the President at the White House he heard from Roosevelt's lips that, after reading about *The 47 Samurai*, he had acquired 'an inspiration and admiration for your country'.

But feelings of admiration were not mutual. Instead, for many years up until the Pacific War the Japanese had suffered from revelations of persecution from the West, dating from the bombardment of the city of Kagoshima by the British fleet in July 1863 (after several British citizens were murdered by a few angry samurai), as well as a series of humiliating unequal treaties imposed on Japan. Nor did the bellicose manner of US Commodore Matthew Perry – who, arriving with his 'black ships', forced Japan to open her doors to the West in 1859 – help create a friendly image of the West. Perry had threatened to firebomb the Japanese capital unless Japan agreed to his demands. Among other things, Perry demanded that the Shogunate government supply wood and water to America's whale-catching fleets which sailed in Japanese coastal waters.

Meiji Japan (named after the Emperor Meiji who ascended the throne in 1867) sought to revise and eventually eliminate the unequal treaties imposed by Western powers. This, and preserving Japan's independence during the heyday of Western imperialism, was a national goal. This was also a time of foreign concessions in Japan where Japanese jurisdiction did not apply. In order to show that Japan was a 'civilized' nation, so that the unequal treaties could be rescinded, the Japanese leadership made a serious and often comical effort to 'assimilate' into the 'civilized Western world'. To date, the Emperor never wears Japanese clothes in public (except for Shinto rituals). At state banquets hosted by the Emperor, French cuisine is served. The government directed the people to wear black at funerals instead of white, so as not to appear barbaric. Incidentally, the last unequal treaty was revised after Japan's signal victory over Russia in 1905.

Thousands of new words were coined after the 'Meiji restoration' to facilitate the translation of Western writings. Examples: *Kojin* (an individual), *Hoken* (insurance, as in life or property), *Enzetsu* (oratory), *Seito* (political party) and *Shakai* (society). Another new word was *Shidosha* (leader) which comprises three Chinese characters: *Shi* (finger-pointer), *Do* (to guide), and *Sha* (person). A singular trait, the Japanese then (as now) considered consensus above leadership in the hands of a single person as necessary in bringing about a decision, unlike Western culture based largely on Judeo-Christian foundations.

Patriotism and loyalty were put to the supreme test when Japan was cornered after the Americans invaded the Japanese-occupied Philippine Islands at the end of 1944. With a minimum of dissent, the desperate idea of using human weapons against the invasion fleet was put forward and adopted; and thousands of men instantly volunteered to become suicide pilots and die for Emperor and country. The utter desperation in entering war against overwhelming odds goes far to explain the tragic saga of the Kamikaze.

The nation's leaders, schools, and propaganda organs had performed their duty well, teaching young and old their sacred obligations. Many of the final letters written by youthful suicide pilots, or their public statements as recorded by the press, reveal how they viewed these obligations. Here are a few examples:

Army Captain Ryoji Uehara, a graduate of Keio University's School of Economics, wrote (in a letter to his parents shortly before he undertook a suicide mission in May 1945): 'In Japan, loyalty to the Emperor and filial piety are considered one and the same thing; and total loyalty to the nation is a fulfilment of filial piety.'

First Lieutenant Takamisu Nishida died on May 11, 1945, taking off from Kanoya for Okinawan waters piloting a Zero fighter on a suicide mission. Just before takeoff, he was interviewed by war correspondent Sohachi Yamaoka. Nishida explained why he was giving up his life: 'I studied at a higher learning institution. Therefore, I know that Japan cannot easily win this war. If we should lose the war, what will happen? I am dedicating my life so that the country can seek more favourable conditions for restoring peace. My act will help the Japanese people's path after the war. It will bolster the nation's honour.' Nishida was 22 years old when he died. In less formal language, he wrote the following in his diary just before his mission: 'The morning of May 11 has dawned. In five hours from now I will smash into an enemy vessel. I bid farewell to everyone. [I ask you to] finish what I failed to accomplish. Dad, Mom, I am sallying. This is my last brushwork.' He added a few more words, in the style of poetry, no doubt thinking of (and praying for) the divine intervention, in the form of typhoons, that had saved Japan from an invasion in the thirteenth century: 'A divine thunder falls and the enemy fleet is eradicated.'

Navy Ensign Teruo Yamaguchi, a graduate of Tokyo's Kokugakuin University wrote (in a last letter to his father; his mother was deceased) before his crash-dive mission, also in May 1945: 'The Japanese way of life is indeed beautiful, and I am proud of it, as I am of Japanese history and mythology. . . . The Imperial Family is the crystallization of the splendour and beauty of Japan. . . . It is an honour to be able to give my life in defence of these beautiful and lofty things.'

When men were inducted into Japan's armed forces they knew that if they fell on the battlefield they would instantly become *kami*, or 'gods', and join the guardian spirits of the nation at the Yasukuni Shrine in Tokyo. In Shinto, everyone becomes *kami* after death. Therefore at a Shinto funeral for Taro Suzuki (the Japanese John Doe), the deceased would be called 'Suzuki Taro no Mikoto'. Mikoto means a person attaining the rank of *kami*. It was common among members of the Kamikaze corps, as well as all servicemen going into battle, to say farewell with the catch-phrase: 'I'll meet you at Yasukuni Shrine!' This Shinto shrine, built in 1868, was from the beginning known as the 'guardian shrine of Japan' and impressed everyone with its great bronze *torii*, or sacred gateway, the broad, paved approach to the shrine that is lined with cherry trees, rows of stone lanterns and statues of national heroes. Increasingly, the people's attitude to Yasukuni became a yardstick of patriotism.

Periodic deification rites were held to honour servicemen who had fallen on various fronts.[6] Typical of many was one held in October 1944, led by the Chief Priest. A reporter gave this brief description of the rites: 'Kneeling by the main path of the Shrine as the Holy Ark bearing the spirits of those to be enshrined was drawn slowly through the darkness toward the Inner Sanctuary were many kith and kin of the Japanese officers and men who had paid the supreme sacrifice.' The reporter added: 'For these persons, the moment the Holy Ark passed before them was one to be forever cherished in their memory for they were seeing their dear ones on their way toward becoming gods to aid in the nation's defence.'

At first, Yasukuni Shrine was known as the *Tokyo Shokonsha*, and was the place for worshipping the 'divine spirits' of those who died in the service of their country. The word *Shokonsha* (also *Shokonjo*) signifies a holy site where are invited the 'divine spirits of those who have made the great sacrifice'. The present name, Yasukuni Jinja, or 'peaceful-country shrine', was bestowed by Emperor Meiji in 1879 and, says a shrine brochure, 'This implies that, owing to the meritorious services of the spirits of the Deities [i.e., the departed war heroes] who are worshipped, the nation of Japan enjoys peace and security.'

A few years later, in 1882, Prince Hirobumi Ito, an outstanding political leader of the Meiji epoch, visited Germany and met Otto von Bismarck, the statesman who elevated Germany into a political and military powerhouse in the heart of Europe. (He did much to consolidate Germany and had formed the Triple Alliance with Austro-Hungary and Italy in 1882.) Bismarck was very impressed with the Shinto creed, and suggested that it could be effectively turned into a national military cult; that it should be taught in every Japanese school. Ito, who gratefully accepted Bismarck's advice, is regarded as the statesman who laid the foundations for the later Japanese Empire. After some years had passed and Japan had adapted to a number of European institutions, a German expert said that 'from an innocent animal in its lonely paradise, [Japan] became a tiger amongst tigers'.[7]

What makes Yasukuni unique for the Japanese is that virtually all of Japan's fallen soldiers and sailors have been registered at Yasukuni, a fact that conveys apotheosis. Because this deification cum glorification extends also to controversial figures like wartime leader General Hideki Tojo, the shrine has been a target of criticism by liberal and leftist politicians and intellectuals. Tojo was indicted as a war criminal by the International Military Tribunal for the Far East and hanged in December 1948. There were protests when he was among those deified at Yasukuni. Nevertheless, the number of annual visitors to the shrine has increased rapidly and, in the new millennium, has already surpassed 10 million.This growing number, says the official brochure, 'demonstrates how highly the Deities worshipped here are revered by the people of Japan'.

It is a curiosity that when a group of senior Japanese military leaders and politicians were put on trial in 1947–48, accused of war crimes, the main thrust of their defence was that they had acted to turn the tide of Western colonialism in East Asia; and this, say many experts, is not an argument easily dismissed. America, Britain, and other European powers had for many decades looked upon the East as fair game for their territorial acquisitions. In any case, there are some revisionist scholars who see the Tokyo trials as having been hastily prepared and poorly conducted, even regarding the trial itself as illegal under international law.

A question that continues to arise, especially with the publication in the West of new historical works on the Pacific War, is that of the degree of involvement of Emperor Hirohito in the war. Was he the constitutional monarch who entered the political arena only twice in the first half of the century – once to stop an attempted coup by young officers in 1936, and once to enforce Japan's capitulation in August 1945? Or was he, as some dissident Japanese claim, a player in the policies that led to the Pacific War and defeat? Hirohito played an important role in directing the war by not commanding but offering 'suggestions' from time to time. Admiral Heihachiro Togo, hero of the Battle of Tsushima (1905), and General Maresuke Nogi, hero of the seizure of Port Arthur (1905), were among Crown Prime Hirohito's tutors in military strategy.[8] In the Pacific conflict, Hirohito believed that Japan was fighting a 'just' war. Without doubt he was a 'player' in the war to a certain degree. At war's end, Hirohito was exempted from trial; and General Douglas MacArthur, the Supreme Commander of Allied Forces in the Pacific (SCAP), upheld Japanese tradition – that Japan must always have a line of Emperors, 'unbroken through ages eternal', to quote from a pre-war Japanese Constitution. MacArthur, who under the US occupation of Japan attempted to impose American populist-style democracy on the Japanese, also believed that Japan would be viable as a nation only if Hirohito remained as Emperor.[9] (A later chapter gives a close-up look at the Emperor in his palace bunker during an air raid on Tokyo.) No doubt, a large majority of Japanese citizens agreed with Prime Minister Prince Haruhiko Higashikuni who, when he met Western journalists on September 18, 1945, a month after the war ended, spoke about the role of Hirohito in these words: 'I firmly believe that the Emperor is not a war criminal.' Higashikuni did his best to defend the throne, knowing that if Hirohito were indicted, continuation of the Emperor system would be imperilled with unpredictable consequences. Investigations begun by SCAP supported this view.

From early childhood, citizens were taught that their Emperor was divine, that he was the spiritual head of the nation; in short, he was both divine and absolute. Japan's Emperor (the English translation of *tenno* means heavenly lord) is actually a priest-king. Thus, one of the two roles the *tenno* must play is that of head Shinto priest in the performance of a number of Shinto rituals. (The other role involves the composition of stylized poems, called *waka*.)[10]

With the stringent wartime controls over the conduct of citizens and the thorough indoctrination of both civilians and military, were there individuals with the courage to speak their minds, to be critical, for example, of the use of suicide as a military weapon? Could the commander of an air wing forbid his men from participating in tactics he considered a sheer waste of pilots? The answer to both questions is yes. They were in a small minority but there were a few strong-minded individuals who did speak out in opposition to the general line.

According to a memoir written by Ensign Kazuo Tsunoda, a pilot attached to the 201st Naval Air Wing, some commanding officers opposed the suicide flights with vigour. (Tsunoda said he himself was given 24 hours in which to 'volunteer' as a Kamikaze pilot. He agreed, but says that in his case he volunteered neither for country or Emperor. Rather, he'd been teaching others to be ready to die for the country, and simply he felt he had a duty to do the same.) The ensign related the following incident which he said he witnessed:

> Lieutenant Commander Okajima, the head of the 303rd Combat Squadron, adamantly opposed *tokko* [i.e., suicide] tactics and at a base in the Philippines engaged Flight Leader Tadashi Nakajima of the 201st Air Wing in a heated discussion at the officers' lounge. Okajima said: '*Tokko* is impermissible! We should take our men back to the mainland and rebuild our strength and fight the enemy head-on. I will not allow a single plane to take part in *tokko* from the 203rd Air Wing.' The exchange almost developed into a quarrel. Deputy Wing Commander Tamai, learning of the dispute,

thought it over and the next morning, the 203rd Air Wing was transferred to the Japanese mainland and left on transport planes.

The first officially approved suicide mission took off from a Philippine airfield led by Lieutenant Senior Grade Yukio Seki, a Naval Academy graduate. Admiral Takijiro Onishi, whose 'brainchild' was the Kamikaze corps, wanted a Naval Academy graduate to lead the first Kamikaze sortie, which consisted of a squadron carrying high-explosive bombs. Seki was chosen for the historic mission. But he did not volunteer for the one-way mission, having been put into a position where he could not honourably refuse the suggestion of his superiors.

In fact, although we are told that every single member of several Air Groups volunteered for the new Kamikaze units with spontaneous elation, Seki, who is called the first volunteer, actually dissented, but privately. Before his flight the ill-fated pilot confided to a journalist: 'Japan's future is bleak if it is forced to kill one of its best pilots – myself. I am confident that I can deliver a 500 kilogram bomb on the flight deck of an enemy aircraft carrier and come back alive!'

The veteran pilot also distanced himself from the conventional rhetoric about dying for flag and country. Before sallying he said: 'I am not going on this mission for the Emperor or for the Empire. I am going for my beloved wife. I am going because I was ordered to. Should Japan lose the war, only the gods know what the enemy would do to my dear wife. A man dies for the lady he loves most. That's glorious.'

The shock and pathos of one domestic suicide (it had a Kamikaze connection) caused Japan's Home Ministry to order an immediate ban on reporting it. Almost nothing, it seems, was said about it during the post-war years, the document having been buried in the Ministry's archives. But given such a well-publicized slogan as *Ichioku Sotokko* ('All 100 million for *Tokko*'), which was repeated in one wartime speech after another and which was embellished to mean, 'Every Japanese has the spirit to enable him to become a member of the Kamikaze Special Attack [Tokko] Corps' – what follows was probably predictable.

Hajime Fujii had joined the Army as a private and rose to the rank of lieutenant. After he became an officer, he switched from the infantry to the air force. He then volunteered as a Kamikaze pilot three times but was rejected on the grounds that he was a family man with two children.

On December 4, 1944, Fujii returned to his residence located near the Kumagaya Army Flying School in Saitama Prefecture, adjacent to Tokyo, and found a letter left on the table. The letter was written by his wife, Fumiko, and was addressed to her husband. It said: 'I know that because of us, you cannot exert your utmost for the country. Therefore allow us to take leave of the world before you join us. Please fight with nothing weighing on your mind.' The next morning the Kumagaya Police Station informed Fujii that his wife and two children had been recovered from the Arakawa River.

Fujii and the men from his company rushed to the site near the Arakawa Bridge. There they found Fumiko, carrying her one-year-old daughter, Chieko, on her back, and her four-year-old daughter, Kazuko, firmly tied by a rope to her mother's hand. They were dead. The two girls were wearing their best dresses. According to Master Sergeant Naganuma, who accompanied Fujii, the distraught husband and father wept profusely while removing by hand particles of sand from his wife's feet.

The Home Ministry's ban on reporting the suicide of Fujii's wife and daughters remained in effect throughout the war. The order said that no stories should appear either 'concerning the wish of Lieutenant Fujii to join the Special Attack Forces' or 'the suicide of the lieutenant's wife with their two young children'.

Five months later, Lieutenant Fujii, leading nine twin-seater fighters, took off from Kyushu's Chiran Air Base at dawn and executed a Kamikaze attack on an American task force in Nakagusuku Bay, on the east coast of Okinawa. The nine planes, carrying a total of 18 flyers, had landed the day before from the Ozuki Air Base in Yamaguchi Prefecture, close to Hiroshima. Each plane carried two 250-kilogram bombs.

The squadron was designated *Kaishintai* ('A Spiritually Satisfied Unit').

NOTES

[1] By comparison, the average lifespan for the USA: men 73.8, women 79.5; for Britain: men 74.8, women 79.7.

[2] Professor Edwin O. Reischauer of Harvard University who was US Ambassador to Japan in the 1960s. He also said that Japan, 'being well unified, displays the terrific power of rushing toward a single purpose'. But he wondered uneasily if Japan had acquired 'a seclusionist mentality', a 'narrow-minded pursuit of its own national interests, instead of acquiring a spirit of international co-operation and open-mindedness'. He advised Washington to 'handle Japan with care', saying that America 'must walk forward with them [the Japanese] or see them walk off in a different direction'.

[3] Sakai was the most celebrated Japanese Second World War Navy pilot. He flew 200 combat missions and shot down 60 Allied planes.

[4] In Japanese, respectively: *Tsuyo no inochi*; *Kono yo wa kari no yado*; *Shindar eba koso ikitare*; *Gosho wa daiji.*

[5] Suicide protests are not unique to Japan. In the summer of 1919, for example, an American anarchist, using dynamite, blew himself up outside the Washington DC home of Attorney General A. Mitchell Palmer.

[6] In Japan there is a Shinto shrine called Gokoku Jihja ('Defend the Nation' shrine) in every prefecture except Tokyo, which has the Yasukuni Shrine. Every member of the Self-Defence Force (Japan's post-war Army, Navy and Air Force) who dies while on duty is deified and enshrined at the Gokoku shrine in the prefecture they come from. This network of shrines was apparently set up at the time Yasukuni was inaugurated.

[7] *The Tokyo Trial and Beyond*, by B.V.A. Rolling and Antonio Cassese, London, 1993.

[8] Admiral Togo and General Nogi were deified after their deaths. Togo died at a ripe old age while Nogi committed suicide with his wife, Shizuko, when Emperor Meiji died. This was reminiscent of samurai who committed suicide out of loyalty to their masters who had departed to 'the other world'. There is a shrine for Togo (Togo Jinja) in Harajuku, Tokyo, and one for Nogi (Nogi Jinja) in Nogizaka, Tokyo.

[9] As a junior member of a visiting US Naval squadron in Japan shortly after the end of the Occupation, Albert Axell saw a sign inside a remaining US Navy base that tried nobly to remind US servicemen and women of their spiritual roots: 'You have entered Japan, a sovereign country. You are an American. Act like an American!'

[10] The form of poetry, called *waka*, has not changed in over 2,000 years. The first recorded *waka* appears in the *Nihon Shoki*, annals of history compiled after *Kojiki* (AD 712). *Nihon Shoki* records some 100 *waka* poems. They were orally transmitted throughout the days the Japanese did not have letters. The *waka* is still the most popular form of poetry in Japan.

1

THE FRAGILE PEACE

Peace in the Far East in the 1930s was as fragile as semi-transparent porcelain. One incendiary incident followed on the heels of another. Some reports speak of 300 Sino-Japanese flare-ups in those years, many involving fatalities. There were, to name a few: the Manchurian Incident (1931), the Shanghai Incident (1932), the Charhar Incident (1934), the Peking Railway Incident (1935), the Langfang Incident (1937) and the Lukouchiao ['Marco Polo Bridge'] Incident (also 1937).

After an incident near Mukden, the capital of Manchuria, in September 1931, Japanese forces, accusing the Chinese of blowing up a stretch of the railway outside Mukden, seized many of the principal cities and towns throughout Manchuria. Part of the job of the so-called Kwantung Army was to protect the South Manchurian Railway from acts of sabotage. Given the obscure locale of many of these conflicts, the absence of foreign observers, and the wildly contradictory accounts of the circumstances of each clash, to assess responsibility for what happened was often an impossible task. These outbreaks were part of the rugged landscape of 1930s East Asia: years of fighting, assassination, duplicity and disinformation, not to mention the shadowy intrigues of clandestine organizations.[1]

Meanwhile, there was a sad deterioration of relations between America and Japan, not helped by awkward situations like the Japanese bombing (accidental, it was said) of a US warship in Chinese waters. In such an atmosphere, fuelled in part by nationalist fervour and imperialist rivalries, a book, *If Japan and America Start a War*, by retired General Kohiro Sato, could appear in the 1930s. Possessed of a lively imagination, the author was sure that in the event of war with America the 'Bushido spirit' of the samurai would prevail over the 'weakling' Yankees whom he blithely dismissed as having been perverted by the Golden Calf. Referring to an ancient folk tale about 50 doughty swordsmen from Japan who had allegedly conquered ten Chinese provinces, the old soldier said that if a 'few thousand samurai' disembarked at, say, San Francisco, 'the result would not be disappointing'. There were at the time, in the 1920s and 1930s, in both the United States and Japan many sci-fi-like books about an imaginary war between the two countries. One book published in London and New York, *Gabriel Over the White House*, describes an Allied fleet being sunk by a 'Divine Wind' (or Kamikaze), off the Cape of Good Hope.

But while the general's imagination seemed comical, in December 1941 a Japanese fleet struck the main US naval base at Pearl Harbor, in the Hawaiian Islands, and within minutes put the United States Pacific Fleet (including 8 battleships and the whole of Army aviation in Hawaii) temporarily out of commission.

In August 1931, a Japanese intelligence officer and a companion were murdered in Manchuria, causing anti-Chinese demonstrations in Japan. A month later a Japanese brigade entered Manchuria from Korea, setting off the 'Manchurian Incident'. The capture by Japanese troops of the city of Mukden (Shenyang) in September 1931, was an event that marked the beginning of the Japanese occupation of Manchuria. Later, General Jiro Minami said that in occupying Manchuria and taking over parts of China, Japan's strategic aim was to 'stem the tide of Bolshevism' in the unstable climate of that country. The Dutch jurist, B.V.A. Rolling, who was a judge at the International Tribunal for the Far East, held in Tokyo at the end of the war, himself stressed the 'Red angle': 'In Japan there was in the first place the fear of Communism in China', he said in an interview. 'The Japanese were convinced: if we don't interfere, China will become Communist, and if China becomes Communist, then Japan is bound to become Communist.'

In short, Manchuria's role was to serve as a buffer between Japan and Russia. At the same time, British Conservatives, viewing Japan as a guarantor of stability and order in the Far East, deemed it necessary to co-operate with Tokyo for the preservation of the British Empire. Meanwhile, the Kwantung Army became the pride of the

Japanese Empire, its main force on the Asian continent. It fielded several hundred thousand men, mostly mobilized from the Japanese homeland.

In July 1937, the situation in China took a turn for the worse when a shooting incident occurred at the Marco Polo Bridge, in Beijing's suburbs. The new incident brought on the quagmire of the Sino-Japanese War which continued until 1945. Meanwhile with the outbreak of war between China and Japan there occurred a whole series of international crises leading up to the Second World War.[2]

China remained a major source of Japanese-American contention up to the Pacific War, with Washington opposed to Tokyo's military activities on the mainland, and Japan irritated with the Roosevelt administration's massive aid provided to Chiang Kai-shek's regime while US Army Air Force pilots were fighting as part of the Chinese air force under the guise of volunteers. (These were the celebrated 'Flying Tigers' under General Claire Chennault.)[3]

Prior to Pearl Harbor, Japan and Germany had put their signatures on an anti-Comintern Pact, in November 1936, aimed at Stalin's Bolshevik regime. After the fall of Czarist Russia, the Japanese Army General Staff drafted new operational plans against the newly created Soviet Union. Following the first Soviet Five-Year Plan, launched in 1928, the Japanese armed forces gave serious attention to Moscow's Red Army as the major hypothetical enemy. For them the Plan meant that Moscow was expanding its total national defensive capability and, at the same time, was fully determined to develop the economic potential of the Soviet Far East. Russia's military preparedness began to impress the Japanese Army whose generals now saw a re-emergent Russian power in the East as a real threat to Japan's national policies on the Asian continent. In July 1938 Japan completed the occupation of the entire eastern part of China, the country's most economically developed regions. On November 3, 1938 Prime Minister Fumimaro Konoe announced the creation of a 'New Order in East Asia', which meant a policy of incorporation of vast areas. In reply, one after another, the United States, Great Britain and France, avowed their intention of opposing the establishment of this 'New Order'.

The US government, showing its impatience towards Tokyo's foreign policy, in July 1939 abrogated the US–Japan Commerce and Navigation Treaty, creating a severe shock to a trading nation like Japan. Relations between the two countries worsened, with the US imposing in July-August 1941 an embargo on scrap iron and oil to Japan, including a total ban on exports of aviation fuel. Japan vigorously protested. In July 1941 Washington froze Japanese assets in the US.

Clashes with Russia had seemed inevitable, and in July 1938 Japanese troops clashed with the Red Army near Vladivostok (the 'Lake Khasan Incident') and were repulsed. On May 11, 1939 a large force from the Kwantung Army fought a pitched battle with a mixed Russo-Mongolian army at Khalkin-gol (Nomonhan) in Mongolia. By late August the Japanese forces retreated with heavy losses.

On September 27, 1940, a Tripartite Pact was concluded in Berlin, between Japan, Germany and Italy. The alliance was an extension of the Anti-Comintern Pact – the so-called Communist International from 1919 to 1943 – which united the Communist parties of many countries. With its conclusion, Japan intended to strengthen her diplomatic position and thereby facilitate an early settlement of the 'China problem'. Some observers said that underlying Japan's signing of the Tripartite Pact lurked a fear of 'missing the bus' on the part of the High Command, which was dazzled by the brilliance of the Wehrmacht's successes at the start of the Second World War.

When, on April 13, 1941, Japan signed a Neutrality Pact with the Soviet Union (prior to this treaty, Britain and France had withdrawn their troops from China, with the outbreak of war with Hitler's Germany, in order to strengthen the defensive posture of the home countries), this left Japan with only two powers to confront in China – Russia and America. But after the conclusion of the Neutrality Pact with Moscow, the situation was further simplified. Now, only Japan and the United States confronted each other.

Antagonism towards America grew as many Japanese felt their country was being strangled economically due to America's export restrictions and the ban on all-important aviation fuel. Feeling the pinch, Japanese Foreign Minister Hachiro Arita declared in June 1940 that it was vital to create an 'East Asian Co-Prosperity Sphere' under Tokyo's leadership. At the same time there existed in Japan a widespread resentment of perceived racial inequality as practised by Western powers. (Japan had called for the principle of racial equality to be adopted at the Paris Peace Conference of 1919 but this was rejected by the Conference.) Arita declared: 'The countries of East Asia and the regions of the South Seas are geographically, historically, racially, and economically very closely related.' He said the uniting of these regions in a single sphere would ensure stability in the area. A number of Asian leaders believed wholeheartedly in Japan's good intentions, not hesitating to speak out in favour of Japanese policies.

The momentum of events increased when in September 1940 Japan without much ado got the French Vichy government to agree to its occupation of Indochina. The day after the Tripartite Pact was signed, the Japanese Cabinet began discussions of the country's foreign policy.

It was decided that the Greater East Asia Co-Prosperity Sphere was to include China, Indochina, Malaya, Thailand, Burma, the Philippines, British Borneo, and a number of islands in Oceania. A month later, at another closed-door meeting, the Japanese Cabinet adopted a special decision to add Indonesia to the Co-Prosperity Sphere.

Evidence exists that Adolf Hitler had a blueprint for Asian conquest, that the Führer harboured plans for capturing Iran, Afghanistan, India, Indonesia, and a number of other Asian countries before the Second World War began. As Herman Rauschning, a former Nazi leader says in his book, *Gespräche mit Hitler* (Conversations with Hitler), in the summer of 1933, at a banquet for an exclusive circle of his associates, the Führer shared his plans for a 'victory march' across Asia and the Pacific to recover the lost German colonies on various islands there. As the years passed this idea was not forgotten and, as SS Obergruppen-führer Walter Schellenberg, one of the chiefs of Nazi intelligence, remarked in his memoirs, Hitler had decided by the late 1930s to conquer a large section of Asia, including New Guinea. In November 1939 German officials began work drawing up operational and strategic plans for future theatres of war. By that time Berlin's agents had stepped up their activities in Egypt, Turkey, Iraq, Iran and Afghanistan and by the time Germany attacked Russia, the number of German agents in Iran had reportedly reached 4,000. A year after Hitler's invasion of Poland, the Shah of Iran had for the most part already lost control over the situation in his country.

In November 1939, General Franz Halder, the Chief of the General Staff of the German Army, wrote in his service diary that Hitler had given instructions that plans be drawn up for operations throughout the globe. Halder mentioned the following countries and territories: Afghanistan, Iran, Iraq, Syria, India, Burma, Tibet, Nepal, Ceylon and South China.

On December 16 Halder held a secret meeting at which the issue of sending a 'sabotage expedition' to Tibet was discussed. It was to be led by an experienced secret service agent and mountaineer, Ernst Schafer, who had visited Tibet on several occasions. Schafer was to use for this purpose a special team attached to a 'Hindu Kush scientific expedition' which had been in Afghanistan since 1935, supposedly to study the country's history, flora and fauna. The Schafer team was to reach Tibet through Kashmir and Ladakh at an appointed time and then enter India through Sikkim and make conditions ripe for penetration in the country's north-eastern areas. The idea was to draw British troops to the Himalayas, thereby making it easier for German troops to invade north-west India through the Khyber Pass.

In December 1940 Adolf Hitler signed Directive 21, known as Operation Barbarossa – the invasion of Russia. Two weeks before the invasion, Hitler endorsed secret Directive 32, which was codenamed Operation Orient. However, the capture of Iran, Afghanistan and India were never carried out. As German historians point out, the plans envisaged in Directive 32 were based on a whirlwind conquest of Russia.

Exactly ten years after the 'Manchurian Incident' America suddenly demanded on November 26, 1941 that Japan restore things to the state existing before September 18, 1931; that is, to renounce all territorial gains during those ten years. A few days earlier the Japanese Foreign Minister, Shigenori Togo, said a US-Japanese understanding was still possible if Washington would 'understand Japan's national requirements and her position in East Asia and consider the situation as it exists in the light of realities'.

But Togo did not want America to interpret this as weakness on Japan's part so he added: 'There is naturally a limit to our conciliatory attitude.' Incidentally, Foreign Minister Togo's wife was Jewish, which was said to be a source of much embarrassment to Adolf Hitler and his Nazi minions. Togo had married Editha de Lalande in 1929 in Berlin when he was 31 and she a year older. Editha, whose maiden name was Pitsschke, met Togo after the death of her first husband, a Jewish architect who designed the Japanese Governor General's chancellery building in Seoul, Korea. Togo, a Korean by birth – his Korean name was Park Mu Tok – had served as counsellor at the Japanese Embassy in Berlin before the war and had lived at the residence of the Pitsschkes. The Togos (Parks) adopted the Japanese surname, Togo, when Shigenori was five years old.

It is worth noting that despite Japan's friendly ties with Berlin, Japan sternly refused to adopt Hitler's psychopathic racial hatreds.[4] In fact, thanks to her open-door policy, 30,000 Jews were rescued by Japan immediately before the Nazis attacked Russia in 1941, a time when few countries in the West were accepting Jewish immigrants. These Jews travelled eastward on the Trans-Siberian Railway, armed with Japanese visas for Manchuria and the Japanese city of Kobe. Members of Japan's small Jewish community have a number of times publicly thanked Japan – including specific Japanese officials – for this timely humanitarian act. One official, Chiune (Sempo) Sugihara, has been described as 'the Japanese Oskar Schindler'.

Negotiations between Tokyo and Washington to adjust their differences had begun in March between Admiral Kichisaburo Nomura, Japan's Ambassador to Washington, and State Secretary Hull. The talks were conducted under a veil of secrecy. Later, a seasoned diplomat, Ambassador Saburo Kurusu, was sent to Washington, DC at the eleventh hour to help Nomura in the critical talks that preceded Pearl Harbor. The new arrival had served as ambassador in many countries, including the United States, Germany, Italy and China, and had signed the Tripartite Pact between Japan, Germany and Italy in 1940 in Berlin. (Kurusu had an American wife, two daughters and a son who was an Army fighter pilot. During the war, Kurusu's wife and daughters lived in Karuizawa in the mountains ouside Tokyo, from 1944, while Ambassador Kurusu stayed at their house in Tokyo. Their son, Ryo, a star rugby player and captain of his team at Yokohama Engineering High School, was born in Chicago and was nicknamed 'Bear' in English. He enrolled in 1941 at the Army Air Engineering School and became a test pilot, rising to the rank of captain. On February 17, 1945, Captain Ryo Kurusu took off in a fighter plane from Tama Air Base in Tokyo and was killed in action when he apparently tried to ram an incoming American B-29 Flying Fortress but was shot down over Tokyo Bay.)

Meanwhile Tokyo offered new and 'final' proposals to the US for settling mutual problems but these proposals were rejected by Washington, thus marking the end of the long efforts to negotiate a settlement. The proposals, in US eyes, were far from being conciliatory. The firmness of US Secretary of State Cordell Hull was shown in a November 26 demand which was made only 11 days before Japan struck at Pearl Harbor with devastating results. The Japanese have always interpreted the Hull Note as an ultimatum, totally out of context of the negotiations that had begun in the spring. Ambassador Kurusu in a speech made in Tokyo three years into the war (November 26, 1944) said that the few days preceding the receipt of the Hull Note were 'the momentous days that decided the fate of Japanese-American relations'. In the United States, he said, there were 'both jingoists and moderates' and the former group (which Kurusu said 'constituted the war faction') was before December 1941 'underrating Japan's national strength and scheming to drive her to the wall and compel her to appeal to arms'.

The Hull Note demanded that Japan abandon Manchuria and the Chinese government led by Wang Zhao-ming, Chiang Kai-shek's rival, in Nanking. The Note also asked Japan to rescind the Tripartite Pact with Berlin and Rome. Japan had no inention of abandoning the pact. How, Tokyo's leaders asked themselves, could a sovereign country break an agreement with nations it recognized?

Foreign Minister Togo wrote later, after reading the Hull Note: 'I almost fainted.' He added: 'There was nothing more I could do to prevent war.'

A number of Japanese historians assert that their country had no choice but to make war. This view has received some international support. For example, Indian Justice Radhabinod Pal, who was a member of the International Military Tribunal for the Far East, said in his dissenting verdict that even the tiny principality of Luxembourg would have resorted to arms, presented with 'a set of totally unreasonable demands' advanced by the Hull Note.[5]

Also, Sir William Flood Webb, who was Chief Justice at the Tokyo Trial, stated:

> During the thirty months in which I sat upon the bench in Tokyo [1946–48] , I was frequently struck by the solicitude and reverence of witnesses toward the Japanese monarch, and by their earnestness and sense of rectitude in pleading their case. I sometimes asked myself what right we had to condemn Japan for having resorted to belligerency in 1941. I perceived much justice and extenuation in the able arguments of Defence counsel that Japan was a tiny land of 90,000,000 and with 15 per cent cultivable soil, and that she had been subjected to severe trade restrictions and limitations from without. I pondered how the United States or Britain would have reacted in that situation, and indeed how their peoples would have wanted them to react.

Webb's conclusion: 'The United States and Britain in a situation like Japan's in 1941 might well have had recourse to war.'

General Douglas MacArthur, who was the Supreme Commander for the Allied Powers after Japan's surrender, gave his views to a US Senate hearing in May 1951 on why Japan entered into war with America: 'There is practically nothing indigenous to Japan except the silkworm. They lack cotton, they lack wool, they lack petroleum products, they lack tin, they lack rubber, they lack a great many other things, all of which was in the Asiatic Basin. They feared that if those supplies were cut off, there would be 10 to 12 million unoccupied people. Their purpose, therefore, in going to war was largely dictated by security.'

With growing tension in the Far East between America and Japan, Prime Minister Winston Churchill realized that a clash of the two Pacific powers' interests could lead to armed conflict. He also felt that in view of the alliance already existing between Tokyo and Berlin, the conflict would automatically give rise to a declaration of war between Germany and the USA. Churchill therefore did all he could to prompt the American government to take a tough line towards the Japanese.

At this time, while Britain was busy fighting in Europe, the possessions of occupied France and Holland were unprotected in the Far East. The only major obstacle for Japan in the Pacific was the United States naval fleet. As for a full-scale war with Moscow, the Japanese generals were mindful of the fighting spirit of the Russians shown in two hard-fought battles, at Lake Khasan, near Vladivostok (in 1938), and at Nomonhan (Khalkin-gol) in Mongolia (in 1939). But on the Russo-German front during the summer and autumn of 1941 Hitler's Wehrmacht appeared unbeatable.

Meanwhile, Stalin's master spy in Japan, Dr Richard Sorge, who was exceptionally close to the German Ambassador in Tokyo, Lieutenant General Eugen Ott, informed Moscow that Japan had made a decision to move south instead of north, against Russia. Then, on December 5–6, 1941 the Russians began a sudden counter-offensive at Moscow. And, on December 7, hundreds of Japanese planes roared off in the direction of Pearl Harbor.

Three months before Pearl Harbor, on September 7, 1941, an Imperial Conference was held at the Imperial Palace in Tokyo, attended by Emperor Hirohito and presided over by Prime Minister Prince Fumimaro Konoe. The Conference decided that Japan 'in order for self-preservation and in self-defence' would complete preparations for war against the US, Great Britain and the Netherlands by mid-October 'unless the on-going US–Japan diplomatic talks were concluded in Japan's favour'.

According to the minutes of the conference, Hirohito intervened and asked which initiatives – the preparations for war or the diplomatic negotiations – carried more weight. Hirohito was assured that the diplomatic talks took priority over the war moves. Thereupon he read out loud a poem by the Emperor Meiji, his grandfather:

> When I regard all the world
> As my own brothers,
> Why is it that its tranquillity
> Should be so thoughtlessly disturbed?

Konoe, in his diary, writes: 'Everyone was stunned. Silence followed for some moments.'

Then Admiral Osami Nagano, Chief of the Naval Staff, asked to speak. He uttered these words of bravado:

> According to the government, the nation would invite destruction should we accept America's demands, but fighting the war

may also lead the nation to destruction. We may face national destruction by waging a war. We will be doomed to destruction of the nation forever by avoiding the war; but even if we were to lose the war, if we were to fight to the end with a spirit to safeguard the nation, such a spirit will endure and our descendants will rise again and again. As I have already stated, the High Command wish to see our national goals achieved through diplomatic talks, but in the unfortunate event that the opening of hostilities shall be decided and the Imperial Order issued, we shall bravely unleash our swords and will fight to the last man.[6]

Meanwhile, Japan's stockpile of crude oil was shrinking day by day. The military calculated that they would not be able to fight a full-scale war beyond the spring or summer of 1942, thus depriving the nation of its claws.

Despite Japan's initial success in waging war against America, no one in Japan expected their country to 'win' – that is in the sense of conquering or subjugating the United States. Rather the majority of Japanese (in December 1941) saw a model for victory in the Sino-Japanese War of 1894–95 and the Russo-Japanese War of 1904–5. That is, these wars ended in a truce or a negotiated peace favourable to Japan. A similar truce or peace negotiations with America would be considered as a major victory.

General Hideki Tojo, who succeeded Konoe as prime minister on October 18, 1941, confided to an aide after the Pearl Harbor attack in December that, for him, 'the decision to go to war was like leaping from Kiyomizu Temple'. The temple, built in Kyoto in AD 798 and dedicated to the Buddhist goddess of mercy, stands on a high cliff with a wooden platform from which a panoramic view of the city can be had. Incidentally, there is a famous Buddhist 'miracle tale' about a boy who made a suicide leap from the platform of the temple, believing his act would restore the health of his bed-ridden mother. The boy's exemplary filial devotion enabled his mother instantly to walk again. The magic wand of the goddess also touched the boy who survived his death-plunge.

The Japanese naval command, having extensive knowledge of the disposition of American ships at Pearl Harbor and of the location of the means of defence, drew up a plan for a surprise attack on the big US naval base on the south shores of Oahu Island, 10 kilometres west of Honolulu. On November 26 a Japanese carrier task force consisting of 2 battleships, 6 aircraft carriers with over 350 planes, 9 destroyers and

3 submarines, under the command of Vice Admiral Chuichi Nagumo, left the Kuril Islands. At dawn of December 7 (the night of December 7, Tokyo time) the task force reached a strike area north of Oahu.

In addition more than 20 Japanese submarines had been deployed ahead of time in the vicinity of Pearl Harbor. Airplanes took off from the aircraft carriers in two echelons from different directions and for two hours (before 10 a.m. local time) made several successive strikes at American ships, airfields and coastal batteries.

Although war with Japan was anticipated and information on the impending attack on Pearl Harbor was available, the American command was caught by surprise. As a result the Japanese sank 4 battleships, 2 destroyers, and 1 minelayer, damaged 4 other battleships, 3 cruisers and 1 destroyer. They also destroyed almost 200 planes and killed 2,325 US soldiers, sailors and marines. A small number of civilians (about 60) also lost their lives.

The Japanese fleet lost 29 planes and 5 midget submarines.

On December 8 the USA and Great Britain declared war on Japan. The World War had spread to the Pacific Ocean.

Having seized the strategic initiative and gained naval supremacy, the Japanese armed forces launched active operations in a southerly direction and won great victories in Malaya (with its fortress, Singapore), the Philippines, Burma, Indonesia and New Guinea, thus capturing vast reserves of strategic raw materials in the South Pacific. They had crushed the US Pacific Fleet, part of the British Navy, and Allied air and ground forces and, having secured superiority at sea, in five months of war deprived the USA and Great Britain of all their naval and air force bases in the western part of the Pacific Ocean. Through a thrust from the Caroline Islands, the Japanese Navy seized part of New Guinea and the adjoining islands, including a large part of the Solomon Islands, creating a threat of invasion to Australia.

The first phase of the Pacific War, ending in May 1942, was one of undisputed triumph for Japanese arms. Tokyo had gained a temporary advantage. The armed forces of America, Britain, the British dominions and the Netherlands surrendered one strategic point after another. Singapore, whose excellently equipped garrison of 100,000 could have resisted for a least several months, surrendered without a fight. (When the island fell in February 1942 Churchill described it as 'the worst disaster and largest capitulation in British history'. Lord Moran, Churchill's personal physician, records that the Prime Minister was stupefied at the fall of Singapore; that he could not understand how

100,000 men – 'half of our own race' – could hold up their hands to the Japanese.) American experts on Asia, Theodore H. White and Annalee Jacoby, described the initial Allied campaign in the South Seas as 'a narrative of shame, disgrace and stupidity'.

In five or six months the Japanese had gained possession of 3,800,000 square kilometres of territory with a population of some 150,000,000, excluding the Chinese territory earlier taken over. But the scales of war began to tilt against Japan in the spring and summer of 1942.

The Battle of the Coral Sea which took place on May 5 and 6 was a huge naval and air engagement in which a US fleet turned back a Japanese invasion force that was heading for strategic Port Moresby in New Guinea. The four-day engagement was a strategic victory for the Allies, whose naval forces, employing only aircraft, never closed within firing range of Japanese vessels. So many Japanese planes were lost that the Port Moresby invasion forces, without adequate air cover and harassed by Allied land-based bombers, turned back to Rabaul from where the main invasion force had been launched.

In a second battle early in June 1942, Japan suffered a new setback west of the Midway Islands. From June 4 to 6, US land and carrier-based planes attacked a Japanese fleet approaching the islands, sinking 4 aircraft carriers, with the loss of many planes, and 1 heavy cruiser. The US lost one destroyer and the aircraft carrier *Yorktown*. The Battle of Midway was the first decisive US naval victory over the Japanese in the Pacific War. It crippled Japan's naval air power and ended Japan's attempt to seize Midway as a base from which to strike at Hawaii. Many experts believe Midway was the turning point in the Pacific campaign.

One after another, US forces captured Pacific islands from the Japanese, often with much loss of life. In many battles US Marines engaged in hand-to-hand fighting before subduing the enemy. The biggest battle in 1943 was fought in the Bismarck Sea, a trial of strength that diminished Japanese power in the south-west Pacific. In 1944 US forces invaded the islands of Saipan, Guam and Tinian, which were essential as bases for powerful air raids on Japan.

Despite continued advances by the Allies in the first half of 1945, the Japanese did not intend to capitulate and were preparing to give general battle on the territory of their homeland. Berlin's capitulation in May 1945 was a blow to the Japanese leadership even though, after big Nazi reverses in 1944, this had been expected. Previously, many Army officers were optimistic about Germany's chances. (Towards the end of the nineteenth century the Japanese Army was trained by German officers and the Navy by the British.) But from mid-1944 predictions about Hitler's defeat were being heard at official meetings in Tokyo.

Meanwhile, Japan's economy had not suffered drastically in the fighting. War production at home was still high. The Manchurian industries, an important military and economic base, had more than doubled in ten years and the production of iron had risen six-fold. War industries had been established in half a dozen cities. To escape air raids, many Japanese industrial plants had been transferred from Japan to Manchuria in the middle of the war. Japan also had built war industries in Korea where it had also moved some plants from Japan proper.[7]

This fact – that Japan still had untapped war resources – plus Japan's stiff resistance underlined by the advent of Kamikaze tactics, caused the American and British governments to expect the war against Japan to last possibly several more years.

NOTES

[1] Japanese historians point to incidents in which Japanese residents were massacred by Chinese troops. For example, more than 260 Japanese residents, including women and children, were killed in Tong, 20 kilometres east of Beijing, in July 1937. But Chinese were also victims. While Japanese military retribution against Nanking and other cities in 1937 is generally accepted as fact, many Japanese historians question such accusations.

[2] The crises include: the Spanish Civil War (although this began in July 1936, it soon became a war of foreign intervention); the 'Austria crisis' (it loomed larger until, in March 1938, that country was engulfed by Hitler's armies); Czechoslovakia, where the Nazis soon began to 'turn on the heat' so that, in September 1938, the Munich Agreement surrendered vital parts of that country to Germany whose troops took over the entire country six months later. Two bloody border clashes of more than local significance between Russian and Japanese armed forces in 1938 and 1939 may also be added to the list.

[3] The Japanese government throughout the Pacific War attempted to negotiate with Chiang Kai-shek's representatives, trying to sue for a separate peace with his Republic of China. The belief among Japan's leaders was that the USA and Britain feared that if Chiang dropped out of the war, it would be seen in various parts of the world that the war was being fought 'between whites and Asians'. It was believed in Tokyo that this was the reason why the US was showering the generalissimo with aid as well as greasing various palms.

[4] Hitler appears to have been irked by Japan's independent spirit. In a monologue to his generals at Obersalzburg on August 22, 1939, Hitler said

(according to a transcript preserved by the International Military Tribunal): 'I have found that Japan does not go with us without conditions.'

[5] Three of the 11 judges at the Tribunal submitted dissenting opinions. They were Judge Bernard of France, Judge Pal of India and Rolling of the Netherlands. Pal was considered the only expert on international law among the 11 judges.

[6] After the war Hideaki Kase interviewed Prince Takamatsu, Hirohito's younger brother, who was a naval officer. In December 1941, Prince Takamatsu was a naval commander assigned to the Imperial Naval Staff. Kase asked the prince how he envisioned the end of the war on the day of the Pearl Harbor attack. 'I anticipated in a very vague way, a decisive naval battle like the Battle of Tsushima [of 1905] would take place somewhere in the Pacific. And because of superior training, we would emerge victorious,' the prince reminisced. Unlike Tagata, the prince pictured a decisive battle between the huge battleships with their big guns, which view was the consensus of the naval leadership of that time. The Japanese Navy was trained to fight a big-gun battle against the US fleet. It is an irony that this Navy, by introducing the world's first carrier task force (six flattops for the Pearl Harbor attack), put paid to the era of the 'big guns'.

[7] The November 2001 issue of *Boei Kenku* (Defence studies), published by the National Defence College, says that in 1944 Japan produced more aircraft than Britain. While the US built 100,752 planes, in that year Germany built 39,807, Japan 28,180 and Britain 26,500.

2

BIRTH OF THE KAMIKAZE

Many Japanese officers understood the virtual impossibility of crushing the might of America's forces using conventional means. Captain Rikihei Inoguchi, who was the senior staff officer to Admiral Onishi, says simply that Japan's situation was 'beyond wisdom'. In such a case, he felt that the only chance for Japan – 'barring a miracle' – lay in the hands of Kamikaze youth. This meant the weapon of suicide. Supporting this idea were reports that conventional pilots were sustaining 50 per cent casualties again and again without beneficial results.

Admiral Takijiro Onishi, the aviation pioneer, inaugurated Kamikaze tactics when he arrived in the Philippines in mid-October 1944 and proposed the setting up of Special Attack units. Not a single officer opposed him. Author Ivan Morris notes succinctly that the decision to adopt Kamikaze tactics was approved in a matter of minutes but that the psychological foundations had been built up over many centuries.

Noted for his dynamism and daring, Onishi was probably the ideal organizer of Kamikaze strategy. He had flown all types of planes and knew as much about aviation as any person in Japan. He had been studying aircraft since the First World War when he had been a lowly officer on a seaplane tender. After he arrived in the Philippines to take up his post as Commander of the First Air Fleet, he often said that Japan's salvation depended on sacrificial Kamikaze attacks against the enemy.

Proposals for using crash-dive tactics (in which pilots would crash their bomb-laden planes onto the decks of enemy vessels, ending their lives by achieving a 'splendid death' in the eyes of the nation) started to float around Army and Navy corridors as early as the autumn of 1943. Two Navy captains, Eiichiro Jo and Motoharu Okamura, were particularly forceful in putting forward their views on the desirability of suicide attacks, especially in mid-1944. Jo, who had served as naval attaché in Washington as well as aide-de-camp to the Emperor, said that with ordinary tactics Japan no longer had a chance of stopping American forces, which were numerically superior to Japan's. Okamura, a well-known fighter pilot, met with Admiral Onishi in mid-1944 and discussed the use of 'human bullets' – that is, manned bombs called Ohka (meaning 'Cherry Blossom') – in suicide missions against American carriers. (Captain Jo went down with his ship at the Battle of Leyte on October 25. Captain Okamura became the commander of the Ohka unit and committed suicide on August 15, 1945.)

But it was not until October that the first 'Special Attack squad' would be officially inaugurated under the leadership of Naval Lieutenant Yukio Seki. Captain Jo wrote: 'We cannot knock out numerous enemy carriers by conventional methods. We should form Special Attack units which would smash bodily [into the enemy's carriers]. Allow me to lead the first such unit.' Jo at that time was commander of the converted aircraft carrier *Chiyoda*.

The use of suicide weapons was especially promoted when Japanese losses swiftly mounted after the Battle of the Philippine Sea in June and the fall of Saipan in July. On Saipan suicide took on a new meaning. There were mass suicides among the 32,000 defenders, including large numbers of women and children who hurled themselves off the tall cliffs. According to military discipline, suicide on Saipan ceased to be a right and became a duty. What happened on Saipan, historians said afterwards, was reminiscent of the mass suicide of Jews at Masada in AD 73. Some historians used the word holocaust to describe the full horror of what happened at Saipan.

In the same month US Marines landed on Guam and Tinian and, in the autumn, US warplanes hit Taiwan while Flying Fortresses (the B-29 heavy bombers) had begun their raids on Tokyo and other Japanese cities. In October, General MacArthur launched his invasion of the Philippines.

For Special Attack – or Kamikaze – missions even the most inexperienced pilots were eligible to take part if they were led to the target by a seasoned pilot. Actually, the basic requirements for Kamikaze pilots were modest: youth, alertness and zeal. Flight experience was of minimal importance and expertise in landing a luxury. What was important was getting the plane into the air, finding a target (that is, in most cases, being led to it by a more experienced pilot), and then plunging into it.

Green pilots had little chance of successfully attacking enemy ships by ordinary methods and returning to base, or surviving an encounter with enemy planes. For Kamikaze missions, all types of planes, even obsolete models, were mobilized while the newest models were saved for ordinary missions. In general, it was important to save the lives of seasoned pilots because they could be depended on to fly one combat mission after another. Only they were capable of surviving air battles. But circumstances in the Philippines required a change in thinking:

> In the case of the US invasion of the Philippines [says the veteran flyer Takeo Tagata] there were only a few planes guarding the islands against a powerful American naval armada. Veteran Japanese pilots were leading Kamikaze missions from the Philippines. This happened because for every mission, a fairly seasoned pilot was needed to fly the lead plane. Inexperienced pilots could not be depended on to reach their targets. Also, experienced pilots participating in a Special Attack mission were necessary for helping sustain the morale of the fledgling pilots. In the early period of Special Attack, or *tokko* operations, seasoned pilots went along in order to provide air cover for the Kamikaze planes. But as attrition progressed, it became difficult to provide escorts.

Why did so many students volunteer for a one-way mission against the enemy? (Captain Okamura said there were so many volunteers for suicide missions that he referred to them as a swarm of bees, explaining: 'Bees die after they have stung.') The fact is that innumerable soldiers, sailors and pilots were determined to die, to become *eirei*, that is 'guardian spirits' of the country. To die for the country was regarded as a great honour. Many Japanese felt that to be enshrined at Yasukuni was a special honour because the Emperor twice a year visited the shrine to pay homage. Yasukuni is the only shrine, deifying common men, which the Emperor would visit to pay his respects.

From the autumn of 1944 through the early summer of 1945 the focus of the nation was on the Special Attack units. An important reason for the flood of volunteers was the enthusiasm generated by the newspapers for Kamikaze operations. Well-known military men, veteran diplomats and columnists daily lent their voices to the recruiting campaign. Here are a few examples:

The spirit of the Special Attack Corps is the great spirit that runs in the blood of every Japanese. . . . The crashing action which simultaneously kills the enemy and oneself without fail is called the Special Attack. . . . Every Japanese is capable of becoming a member of the Special Attack Corps.

> From Lieutenant Sekio Nishina quoted in *Nippon Times*, October 1944

Youths with only primary school education can become members of the Special Attack Corps after a short period of training.

> From Rear Admiral Etsuzo Kurihara, Chief of Public Affairs of the Navy General Staff, in the journal *Jitsugyo no Nippon*, January 1945

Japan has weapons called aircraft. If a pilot is willing to crash a plane into the enemy, we need not fear the enemy's mobile units, and B-29 bombers will not be able to intrude into the mainland of Japan. [Admiral Onishi then cited the menace of American aircraft carriers.] If an enemy carrier came into sight we would be able to destroy it with a crash-dive attack, and if B-29s came into sight we would be able to use body-crash (*tai-atari*) tactics. Once we make the decision to use body-crash tactics, we are sure to win the war. Numerical inferiority will disappear before body-crash operations. Those who make body-crash attacks disregarding their lives merit the name of godlike soldiers.

> From a statement by Admiral Takijiro Onishi in October 1944

Once quite ordinary students of colleges and universities now realize the actual situation facing their homeland and are undergoing serious training for ramming attacks day and night. . . . Their training is actually harder and more fierce than the actual final ramming actions. Also, their training is based on a firm conviction of victory. . . . It is the noble spirit of the Special Attack Corps that will render the impossible possible.

> From Rear Admiral Etsuzo Kurihara

In articles and speeches Admiral Kurihara often mentioned the name of a 'Kamikaze' admiral, Masafumi Arima, who 'has been especially associated with the Special Attack Corps. I believe this is only too natural, for I have known him for a long time and he has long been devoted to mental cultivation and spiritual training ever since his Naval Academy days. That he became a powerful member of the Special Attack Corps is but natural.'

Japan had needed a big-name 'Kamikaze hero' – and it got one in the person of Admiral Arima, commander of the 26th Air Flotilla at Manila. This English public-school-educated officer, who was descended from a family of Confucian scholars, decided to boost his men's morale by making a suicide dive against an Allied task force in Philippine waters. Lithe, soft-spoken and always decked out in full uniform despite the blistering heat of the tropics, Arima's mild exterior rendered his last desperate act more of a surprise. In September 1944 American planes struck Manila for the first time and heavier raids were soon to come. When a month later an American task force was sighted east of Luzon in the Philippines, a decision was made to launch all available planes, both Army and Navy, against it. As the planes were about to take off from the 26th Air Flotilla, Arima suddenly announced that he himself would lead the attack. While staff officers tried to argue with him, he began removing all insignia of rank from his uniform and climbed into the lead plane of the second wave of fighters. Nobody dared to stop him. A radio message said that at 3.33 p.m. American warships were spotted 240 miles from Manila. Quickly, all planes were ordered to attack, with Arima leading the way.

Rear Admiral Masafumi Arima perished on October 15, 1944 reportedly crashing into an American aircraft carrier close to the Philippines. Arima had joined the list of 'suicide heroes' only days before Kamikaze tactics received an official stamp of approval.

Afterwards, a memorial service was held at the Arima family temple, the Daikoji in Ijuin, in Kagoshima Prefecture on Kyushu. Arima had earlier told a journalist that the only way to combat the Americans' material superiority was to conduct crash-dive actions. Before he boarded the commander's plane and took to the air, he remarked that although he was not young there was no reason why he should not participate in the coming action.

There is some dispute over whether Arima's plane crashed into a US aircraft carrier. An American report says that none of the 30-odd Japanese planes that flew with Arima got close enough to attack the task force, that almost two dozen were blasted out of the sky. It says Arima's plane missed the carrier *Franklin* and crashed into the sea.

At the end of May 1944, Major Katsushige Takada, the commander of the 5th Army Squadron participated in an unauthorized suicide attack, deliberately crashing his plane on an American ship during the Battle of Biak Island.

Crashing into American Flying Fortresses by fighter-interceptors was practised before Kamikaze tactics against naval forces were officially approved by the Air Defence Command. The first *tai-atari* (body-crashing) performance was carried out on August 20, 1944, against B-29s over Yawata, home of the giant Yawata Steel Mill, to the east of Nagasaki. (Yawata and Kokma cities merged after the war and became

Kita-kyushu city.) Eighty B-29s flew from Chengtu in China and reached Yawata around 5.30 p.m. The sky was clear without a single cloud. The Japanese intercepting fighters waited for the B-29s at an altitude of 7,500 metres and watched as the Flying Fortresses invaded the sky over Yawata at a lower altitude, 7,000 metres. Sergeant First Class Shigeo Nobe, flying a twin-seater fighter, with Corporal Denzo Takagi in the rear seat, swooped down on the leading B-29, firing his cannons. The B-29 evaded the fire and the cannons failed to hit the target. Then, Sergeant Nobe shouted into the radio: '*Nobe, tai-atari kekko!*' ('Nobe, executing bodily crash!') His fighter crashed into the B-29 and the two planes were engulfed in a huge crimson ball and fell towards the earth. At that moment, a large black object, an engine from the other plane, flew off from the explosion and hit the left wing of the following B-29. It ripped off a wing, sending the second B-29 plummeting to the ground. Nobe and Takagi became the first flyers to crash into a B-29.

These daylight raids by the Americans over Kyushu caused two major newspapers, *Asahi* and *Mainichi*, roundly to condemn US pilots and to demand that all captured airmen be beheaded. Meanwhile, the domestic media renewed efforts to summon young men to join in suicide missions. The newspapers tempted the youth, saying that those who had given their lives in body-crashing exploits had won their place at the Yasukuni Shrine dedicated to Japan's war dead. (The shine's ornament is the sixteen-petalled chrysanthemum which is the symbol of the Emperor.) They also declared that there were 'glorious opportunities' for crashing into naval forces and ramming bombers of the enemy. The newspapers reflected the statements of many political and military leaders which said that if self-sacrifice was the only way to save the sacred soil of Japan, then the whole population must be ready to die.

The second flyer who rammed a B-29 was Lieutenant Junior Grade Mikihiko Sakamoto over Omura in Nagasaki Prefecture on November 21, 1944. One hundred and five B-29s, flying from Chengtu, invaded the sky over Omura at a height of 7,000 metres at 9.45 a.m. There was a naval air base in Omura and it was also an industrial area. The movement of the American planes was closely followed as soon as they took off from Chengtu. Forty-three Zero fighters and 16 others intercepted the enemy bombers over Omura. Lieutenant Sakamoto crashed his Zero fighter into one B-29 and the two planes caught fire and plummeted to the ground. Sakamoto was a graduate of the Naval Academy. (One pilot, Takaji Inumaru, shot down three B-29s in 1945, flying a Suisei aircraft. He had a special cannon pointed upward outside the cockpit so that the Japanese pilot, flying beneath the

B-29, could get off deadly fire against an unsuspecting bomber carrying a crew of 11.)

At the end of February 1945 the Tokyo–Yokohama area came under attack by heavy bombers. It was the beginning of massive air raids on Tokyo and the surrounding industrial areas by B-29s based in the Mariana Islands. Some of the raids involved hundreds of planes and had the purpose of destroying the ability of the city of Tokyo to function.

Meanwhile, Kamikaze attacks were taking their toll on the invasion fleet, causing not only casualties, but also shock and exhaustion for the American forces. To ward off suicide attacks, all-out air support was called in. Admiral Nimitz, the Pacific Fleet Commander-in-Chief, ordered the Flying Fortresses based in the Mariana Islands to divert temporarily from their daily raids on the mainland of Japan to attack bases in Kyushu where many Kamikaze bases were scattered and from which the suicide missions were carried out against American vessels around Okinawa. The US raids continued, reducing a number of cities to rubble. It's estimated that 40 per cent of Tokyo was destroyed, 58 per cent of Yokohama, 35 per cent of Osaka, 56 per cent of Kobe, and 40 per cent of Nagoya.

Admiral Onishi continued to speak out, adhering to the belief that Kamikaze tactics were the only way to defend the Empire and lead the nation to victory. In one of his speeches he said: 'The gods will provide us with victory only when all Japanese are devoted to the spirit of special attacks. Death is not the objective, but each person must be resigned to death and try to destroy as many of the enemy as possible.'

When calls were made for volunteers for suicide missions, the large numbers of favourable responses especially from students at colleges and universities stunned the generals and admirals overseeing Kamikaze operations. The authorities soon realized that there were more than twice as many volunteers who wished to join the Kamikaze, or Special Attack Corps, as there were available planes. After the war, some commanders would express regret for allowing superfluous crews to accompany sorties, sometimes squeezing themselves aboard bombers and fighters so as to encourage the suicide pilots and, it seems, join in the exultation of sinking a large enemy vessel.

It is known that in the last year of the war many Special Attack pilots had been university students who majored in the humanities and law rather than in science, engineering or mathematics. Most of these pilots, whose studies had been interrupted by the war, were far from being the jingoistic zealots often pictured in the West. Some of them had literary works at their bedside during the last days before their final mission; not a few had studied foreign languages; some were devout Christians. From their last letters and poems we know that their ardour came mainly from love of family, country, the Japanese way of life, and devotion to the Emperor. Many felt that by their death they would be able to repay the 'past favours' they had received from parents, school and friends. So eager were many minimally trained pilots to take part in suicide missions that when their sorties were delayed or aborted, the pilots became deeply despondent. Many of those who were selected for a bodycrashing mission were described as being extraordinarily blissful immediately before their final sortie.

Flight instructor Takeo Tagata says he actually began training pilots for suicide missions on Taiwan before the first official Kamikaze sortie took off from Mabalacat, in the Philippines, in October 1944. In that month the newspapers and radio in Japan began making extensive use of the word Kamikaze. Another wartime pilot, Hichiro Naemura, thought even a year earlier that 'only the spirit of self-sacrifice' would obviate a lengthy war of attrition. It appears that an overwhelming number of pilots agreed that the only way to counter superior American forces in 1944 was by the resort to 'special tactics', the euphemism for suicide missions. Like many a pilot of those days Naemura was fond of quoting the defiant words of the legendary hero and military strategist Masashige Kusunoki (in 1336 he fought a last suicidal battle against an enemy overwhelmingly superior in numbers) who was known as the patron saint of the Kamikaze corps:[1] 'Would that I had seven lives to give to my country!'

The success of suicide tactics was an article of faith not only for Admiral Onishi but also for men like Admiral Matome Ugaki, who commanded the Fifth Air Fleet in the Philippines; for generals like Kyoji Tominaga, who was head of Army Air Forces in the Philippines until early 1945, and for other admirals like Kichisaburo Nomura, who had served as Ambassador in Washington before Pearl Harbor and took part in the doomed Japanese-American negotiations prior to the attack on December 7. After praising the 'exalted spirit' of his yet untried Kamikaze pilots, Ugaki made a bravado entry in his diary of October 20, 1944: 'Not even an enemy who is a million strong, or has a thousand aircraft carriers, [now] needs to be feared.' Ugaki, like Onishi, became one of the most fervent supporters of massed suicide attacks against the Allied fleets.

To maintain morale and perpetuate the Kamikaze spirit, the air force of the Army and Navy as well as the civilian population was occasionally fed a bizarre fairy tale. For example, a sensational report was distributed, saying that a Japanese pilot, out of ammunition, had dived on a British destroyer upside down and, aiming straight for the bridge, had drawn his samurai sword and decapitated the ship's captain as he flew by. During the war such daydreams or fairy tales appeared in a popular monthly magazine for children. Another report, perhaps mythical, said the elephants in Burma were 'full of joy' at being liberated from 'the bestial British'.

But another story was true. (It is recorded in official Japanese military history.) A pilot was said to have crashed his plane into a torpedo that was headed for a Japanese ship. The *Nippon Times* in April 1944 said that Kiyu Ishikawa had saved a large ship in a convoy by hurling his plane at the torpedo that was launched by a US submarine. The sergeant major had met his death heroically and had become a model for soldiers and pilots, said the report. The pilot's deed had also come to the attention of the Emperor who had granted the pilot posthumous promotion to second lieutenant. In death, like other fallen servicemen, he received deification at the Yasukuni Shrine.

Such exploits had their effect on the youth who increasingly volunteered for the Special Attack squadrons.

In August 1944 the Domei news agency reported that suicide pilots were undergoing training, the first time that this was mentioned in the press. The report underlined the virtues of patriotism and called on families to urge their sons and husbands not to think twice about sacrificing their lives if and when this became necessary.

Previously, suicide tactics had been used as a last resort, when a plane was damaged and the pilot could make up his mind either to ditch his plane and risk capture – or 'body-hit' an enemy ship or plane. These were individual, impromptu decisions by men who were mentally prepared to die according to the tradition of Bushido. From the middle of 1942 there were cases of both Japanese and American pilots deliberately crashing their disabled planes into opposing targets.

By the summer of 1942 when American pressure was being brought to bear on Japanese-held islands in the Pacific, and the Imperial Navy was suffering one blow after another, there was an escalation of suicidal attacks by Japanese ground forces. One general, Jun Ushiroku, is said to have been particularly interested in knocking out American armour on Okinawa, using human-bomb attacks on US tanks; that is, having foot soldiers, with satchel charges strapped to their backs, throw themselves beneath the approaching tanks. It is said that at that juncture Japan lacked the time and resources to manufacture sophisticated anti-tank weapons. Ushiroku was appointed Commander-in-Chief of the Third Field Army with its headquarters at Mukden, now called Shenyang, in Manchuria in August 1944 and was captured by the Russians when Japan surrendered. (Possibly the idea to use satchel charges against enemy tanks was borrowed from the Russians. But the Russians made use of dogs. In 1941, during fierce fighting against Nazi panzers, the Russians, themselves short of anti-tank weapons, attached anti-tank mines to the backs of dogs who were trained to eat only under tanks that had their engines running.)[2]

On rare occasions an officer who rejected the use of suicide weapons was able to get into print. Thus, in March 1945 the monthly magazine *Taiyo* (Ocean) carried a 21-page discussion of Kamikaze operations by ten seasoned Navy pilots. One of them, Lieutenant Commander Iwatani, was strongly critical, saying:

> In previous wars, with the Russo-Japanese War a good example, there have always been death-defying missions. Airplanes are, at all times, death-defying machines. But a method of attack with certain, unavoidable death was introduced this time for the first time. Previously, no permission was granted for such a method. The fact that the Navy is resorting to such tactics shows how grave the war situation is. But this is clearly outside the rules. I cannot predict the outcome of the air battles but you will be making a mistake if you should regard Special Attack operations as normal methods. The right way is to attack the enemy with skill and return to the base with good results. A plane should be utilized over and over again. That's the way to fight a war. The current thinking is skewed. Otherwise you cannot expect to improve air power. There will be no progress if flyers continue to die. I believe so in the light of available human resources.

Some of the participants in the discussion lamented the fact that there were not enough planes produced and that mechanical problems as a result of poor quality control were hindering operations.

To heighten morale the government gave unlimited publicity to real or imagined Kamikaze successes. Official propagandists, who made it appear that the Imperial Army and Navy had developed a radical means of countering powerful Anglo-American forces, often cooked their statistics to reinforce belief in the superiority of the Japanese spirit. In the case of the Okinawan campaign, figures announced in Tokyo for American losses from Kamikaze operations were sometimes magnified six times.

But there were also honest difficulties in reporting the results of suicide missions. No Kamikaze pilot could know whether his sacrifice had actually sunk a ship or put it out of service. As to the accompanying escort planes, their pilots often reported the sinking of aircraft carriers, battleships and cruisers when what they really saw were giant columns of water or huge pillars of smoke which from distant observation resembled shipboard explosions but actually came from exploding planes that crashed into the sea near the enemy warships. Unable to confirm the damage to enemy ships, the pilots who returned to their home base would invariably paint Kamikaze successes much bigger than they were in fact.

An example is the Battle of the Philippine Sea, waged between June 19 and 20. In that battle Tokyo claimed that a great victory was won over US naval forces, that more than 5 aircraft carriers were sunk or damaged, 1 battleship sunk, and over 100 planes destroyed. The reality: 2 battleships, 2 carriers and a cruiser were damaged. But it was true that over 100 US aircraft were downed. However, unannounced was the fact that 3 Japanese aircraft carriers were sunk and 426 of their planes lost. Thus, instead of it being an important victory, some high Japanese officials were gloomy at the turn of events. On the 21st of October 1944 the following headline appeared in the *Nippon Times*: 'Results of Taiwan Aerial Battle Greatest Since Pearl Harbor.' Imperial headquarters claimed that more than 57 warships had been sunk or damaged, including 19 aircraft carriers, 4 battleships and 7 cruisers. Admiral Shigeru Fukudome, Commander of the Second Air Fleet on Taiwan, exulted. But the truth was different. Special Attack forces had damaged 2 US cruisers but lost over 600 planes in three days of action, while the Americans lost 76 planes. Toshikazu Kase, a Foreign Office official (he had directed Japan's negotiations with the US prior to Pearl Harbor) says candidly: 'It was customary for GHQ [in Tokyo] to make false announcements of victory in utter disregard of facts, and for the elated and complacent public to believe in them.'[3]

On the subject of official Kamikaze documents, there were many secret documents issued by the General Staffs of the Army and the Navy that are still held by the Defence Research Institute in Tokyo. Excerpts from some of them are reproduced in this book. The first official Kamikaze attack was carried out on the orders of Admiral Onishi in the Philippines;

but there existed no basic directive issued by the Imperial High Command to inaugurate suicide attacks. Onishi secured verbal agreement from the Navy General Staff before he proceeded to assume his command in the Philippines.

THE FIRST UNOFFICIAL KAMIKAZE

Forgotten is the name of the first unofficial Kamikaze of the Pacific War – although the word Kamikaze had not then come into common use. The pilot was First Lieutenant Fusata Iida who led a group of Zero fighters launched from the flattop *Soryu* to protect bombers and torpedo planes in the second wave of attacks on Pearl Harbor on December 7, 1941. Iida's plane received a hit from anti-aircraft fire as he was strafing Kaneoe Air Field, and his fuel started to leak. Soaring to a higher altitude he led his 3rd Air Control Group in the direction of the mother aircraft carrier. In a short while, he waved at his men and turned his plane back to Kaneoe Air Field. He dived and crashed into one of the airplane hangars which collapsed in a tower of flames.

Before Iida took off from *Soryu*, he gave a pep talk to his men and told them that if his plane was hit by the enemy and he was not able to return to the carrier, he would crash into a 'worthy enemy target'. Today a monument at the Kaneoe Naval Base, at the site of Iida's crash, reads: 'JAPANESE AIRCRAFT IMPACT SITE. PILOT-LIEUTENANT IIDA, COMMANDER, THIRD AIR CONTROL GROUP, DEC. 7 1941.'

THE KAMIKAZES FROM TAIWAN

Taiwan was an impregnable fortress for Japan and its population was strongly pro-Japanese. During the war, 80,433 Taiwanese fought as soldiers and sailors in the Japanese Army and Navy. An additional 126,750 Taiwanese served as civilian employees and labourers for the military. Out of this total (207,183) approximately 30,300 died in battle or from illness. An all-Taiwanese 'Kamikaze attack' was launched by a 50-man unit on a US-held airfield on Leyte in late 1944. The unit was named *Koru Kuteitai* (Fragrant Airborne Unit). Japanese transport planes carrying the Taiwanese force landed on the airstrip and destroyed many parked American planes. But every Taiwanese trooper was killed.

NOTES

[1] Kusunoki was killed during his last battle by one of Lord Takaohari-no-kami's men. His head was severed and examined after the battle and confirmed to be Masashige's. There is a large statue of Masashige Kusunoki wearing a helmet and body armour on horseback in front of the Imperial Palace in Tokyo. The bronze statue, said to be the largest in Tokyo, was unveiled in 1897 as a guardian of the throne.

[2] A Russian general who took part in the fighting, Ivan Shavrov, told co-author Axell: 'A soldier in our trench held the dog and, when enemy panzers appeared, the dog was eager to race to the approaching tank and eat beneath it.' It is likely that Ushiroku knew of this Russian tactic. He was knowledgeable about Russian military affairs (he had served in Russia), and for ten years up to 1944 had held various positions with the Army General Staff, rising to Deputy Chief.

[3] Toshikazu Kase is the father of the co-author.

3

THE FIRST OFFICIAL
HUMAN BOMB

A historical marker at Mabalacat, a former Kamikaze base in the Philippines, reads: 'Lt Yukio Seki was the world's first official human bomb.' The marker gives the date for the first officially approved suicide mission of the war: October 25, 1944. It also lists the damage caused to the American fleet on that day in Philippine waters.

It is one of the ironies of the war that the first official Kamikaze pilot had not the slightest wish to commit suicide. Lieutenant Yukio Seki, a seasoned flyer, had every reason to believe that he was worth a good deal more to his country alive than dead. But fate dictated an early and violent end to the life of this bright, artistic, 23-year-old Naval Academy graduate when the eyes of his superiors fell upon the good-humoured, handsome officer as the best qualified pilot to lead the first officially approved suicide mission against the American fleet from Mabalacat, an air base about 80 kilometres north of Manila.

On paper it looked as if Seki volunteered for the mission but he had in fact been specifically chosen for it. But, unlike the exultation shown later by the younger Kamikaze pilots who couldn't wait for their crash-dive attacks against the enemy, for Yukio Seki his selection as leader of the one-way sortie drove him into despondency.

To be sure, as Kamikaze sorties greatly multiplied, there would be countless pilots added to the list of those who supposedly volunteered for them. In a dialogue between ex-Kamikaze pilots published in 1977 in the popular Japanese journal *Bungei Shunju*, one of them says there never was an appeal made in his air wing for men to volunteer for Kamikaze units; that the command headquarters simply assumed *everyone* wanted to do so. Therefore, the staff officers went ahead one-sidedly adding names to be included in the death squadrons. This practice so demoralized many of those awaiting their turn to be called up that they would often say to their superiors, 'Since you're going to kill us, please do it as soon as possible.'

The truth is, Yukio Seki agreed to become 'the first official human bomb' despite his inner voice which told him that a pilot with his experience and talent could serve the nation better by participating in many combat actions against the enemy, not just one. But he had no chance to back out after his superiors mentioned that not only was he the most favoured candidate to lead the first suicide mission, but that Admiral Takijiro Onishi himself (the 'Mr Aviation of Japan') who was in charge of all the Naval air forces in the Philippines was interested; that the admiral wanted a Naval Academy man for the task. Consequently when Seki was asked if he would accept, he could not say no. But if he appeared outwardly calm, beneath his cool exterior Seki was sick at heart.

Just before his fatal mission he made it known to a reporter that to send a skilled pilot like himself on a suicide mission was not only folly but a tragic error at a time when seasoned pilots were in very short supply. Since the nation badly needed experienced pilots, their lives should not be squandered. But this sober view was given privately, when it was too late to change his situation. Then, there was another, personal reason for Seki to wish to remain alive: he had recently married and, from what we know from his final letter to her, he was deeply in love with his bride.

This is how Yukio Seki 'volunteered':

On October 19 at the Mabalacat Airfield, in the Philippines, Seki was asked to report to the Deputy Air Wing Commander, Asaichi Tamai. When he presented himself, he saw that Captain Rikihei Inoguchi, the senior staff officer to Admiral Takijiro Onishi, was seated together with Tamai. (Onishi was Commander of the First Air Fleet.) Seki was offered a chair. When he sat down, Tamai placed his hand on Seki's shoulder and confided to him that the admiral was contemplating a suicide attack on a big American task force that was in the vicinity of the Philippines. Seki was being considered to lead the attack.

The atmosphere of the meeting was one of high tension and emotion. Another officer who was present reports that there were tears in Tamai's eyes as he spoke.

Tamai asked Seki if he would agree to lead a crash-dive mission of Zero fighters. The tall, young lieutenant was motionless. Five full seconds passed. Then, running his fingers through his long black hair, he responded positively in an unwavering voice that concealed his true feelings. After all he was a naval officer and an Academy graduate. He had to agree and there were no two ways about it.

'Yes, I will take on the job,' Seki heard himself say.

Tamai then asked a question:

'You're a bachelor, aren't you?'

'No. I have a wife, sir.'

Tamai had wanted an unmarried man to lead the first Special Attack mission but, surprisingly, the fact of Seki's recent marriage did not trouble Tamai as it should have. Indeed, Seki's background had made him an ideal choice; and the officers present would report this to the Air Fleet Commander, Admiral Onishi.

Seki had first tasted combat in the Solomon Sea, south of New Guinea, when the seaplane tender *Chitose* was attacked and received a hit from American dive bombers. During the attack, Seki was on the bridge. The ship was damaged near the engine room and was repaired at Truk Island. *Chitose* was carrying munitions to Guadalcanal Island after the Americans landed there.

Seki was born in 1921 in Iyo Saijo, a charming, quiet little town by the inland sea on Shikoku Island. When he was a small boy, his mother divorced his father, who later lived as an antique dealer in Osaka. Yukio, their only son, was brought up by his mother and both lived alone in a small house between a pharmacy and a stationery store, facing the town's main street.

In junior high school, Yukio played tennis and became captain of the tennis team. He was an outstanding player and one year his team won the championship in the Shikoku Junior High School Tennis Tournament. Although he wanted to attend high school, the family's financial condition did not allow him to do so. In 1938 he took an entrance examination for both the Army and Navy military academies. He was accepted by both and chose the latter. Graduating from the Naval Academy in 1941, he was assigned to the battleship *Fuso* and received his commission as an ensign in June of that year. He was soon transferred to the seaplane tender *Chitose* and was indirectly a participant in the historic Battle of Midway when the tender was part of the second echelon force that followed the main task force.

Seki's fellow officers noted his versatility, including his interest in art. One of his hobbies was drawing and in a sketchbook he kept on board ship he drew many pictures when he was off duty.

In November 1942, he returned to Japan and enrolled as a student at the Kasumigaura Naval Flying School in Ibaragi Prefecture. After completing basic training, Seki was transferred to Usa Naval Air Base in Oita Prefecture to be trained as a carrier-based dive-bomber pilot. In January 1944 he became a flight instructor at the Kasumigaura Naval Flying School. While he was at the school, Seki made friends with the Watanabes, a family living in Kamakura. Seki knew the family for two years and became fond of Mariko, one of their daughters. While he and his fellow instructors were drinking, one of them proposed that they should all get married by Navy Day, which fell on May 27. This was the anniversary of the nation's victory in the Battle of Tsushima Straits in the Russo-Japanese War. They all agreed.

That weekend, Seki went to Kamakura and visited the Watanabes. He proposed to Mariko in her mother's presence. Mariko consented and they were married at the Navy Officers Club in Tokyo on May 31, 1944. Seki's mother, Sekae, was the only family member from Seki's side who was present at the marriage rites and at the banquet that followed. She lived with the young couple for about a month before she left, saying that the newly-weds should be allowed a little time by themselves. The couple soon moved into a house near the flying school.

In September 1944, Seki was transferred to Tainan on the island of Taiwan as a flight instructor at that city's air base. Due to uncertainties at his post, he had to leave Mariko behind. But she came to Oppama, near Yokohama, to see her husband off. Seki boarded an amphibious plane at Yokosuka port. Three weeks after he arrived at Tainan Naval Air Base, Seki was again transferred, this time to the 201st Naval Air Wing at Nicholas Air Field on Luzon, the Philippines, as commander of the 301st Fighter Unit. When American raids intensified, the Air Wing moved to Mabalacat Air Field.

On the morning of October 20, the pilots of the 201st Air Group were ordered to assemble near their quarters in central Luzon, not far from the clear-flowing Bamban River, to hear an address by the renowned aviation pioneer, Admiral Takijiro Onishi. The placid scenery of the shallow river with the silvery plumes of marsh grass swaying in the autumn breeze caused some of the men to think of the Japanese homeland. The admiral, described as pallid and troubled, spoke slowly and haltingly:

Japan is in grave danger [he began]. The salvation of our country is now beyond the powers of the ministers of state, or the General Staff, and lowly commanders like myself. Therefore, on behalf of your hundred million countrymen, I ask of you this sacrifice and pray for your success. Regrettably, we will not be able to tell you the results. But I shall watch your efforts to the end and report your deeds to the Throne. You may all rest assured on this point.

He then added, soothingly: 'You are already gods, without earthly desires. You are going to enter on a long sleep.'

As he shook hands with all the pilots and wished them luck, he said: 'I ask you all to do your best.' Witnesses say the 53-year-old admiral had tears in his eyes when he finished his remarks.

After his interview with Tamai and Inoguchi, Seki went back to his quarters and wrote his last letters to his wife, Mariko, and to his mother and parents-in-law. The letters did not reveal his innermost feelings about his coming suicide mission. To his wife, Seki wrote:

My dear Mariko,

I am very sorry that I must 'scatter' [a euphemism for dying in battle; it refers to the scattering of cherry blossoms] before I could do much for you. I know that as the spouse of a military man, you were prepared to face such a situation. Take good care of your parents.

As I am departing, I recall innumerable memories that we share.

Good luck to mischievous Emi-chan [little Emi, Mariko's younger sister].

Yukio

Seki wrote a message in the form of a poem to the student pilots who had been under his command:

Fall, my pupils,
My cherry blossom petals,
Like I will fall
In serving our country.

To his parents, Seki wrote:

My dear father and my dear mother,

[After discussing a friend's difficulties and asking his parents for their help he said the following]

At this time the nation is at the crossroads of defeat, and the problem can only be resolved by each individual's repayment of the Imperial Benevolence.

In this connection, he who follows a military career has no choice to make.

[Here he mentions his wife's parents] whom I hold so very dear, to the bottom of my heart. I cannot write them about this shocking news. So please inform them yourselves.

Because Japan is an Imperial Domain, I shall carry out a body-crashing attack on an aircraft carrier to repay the Imperial Benevolence. I am resigned to do this.

To all of you, I am obedient to the end.

Yukio

Despite his apparent composure, Seki was unable to contain his frustration. He told a fellow officer, Lieutenant Naoshi Kanno, that he was deeply upset with the direction events were taking. He was also worried about his wife and parents. He knew, of course, that once he had agreed to lead a Special Attack mission there was no turning back. Just before taking off on his last sortie, Seki unburdened himself to a war correspondent, saying that he was not giving his life for abstract formulations like 'saving the Motherland' but for his beloved wife. The reporter was Masashi Onoda of the Domei News Agency.

A friend of Seki's, who met Kanno later, says that Kanno was himself out of sorts; that he had strong feelings about the formation of a suicide corps. 'If any commander orders me to take part in a Special Attack mission, and refuses to lead it himself, I swear I will cut him down,' he said.

Possessed of unquestioned flying skill, Kanno had only a few months earlier tangled with an American B-24 bomber and, after failing to shoot it down, decided to destroy it by ramming. Avoiding the bomber's deadly gunfire, on the third try he came in close and with his propeller gnawed into the plane's rudder with a thumping crash. The impact caused Kanno to black out momentarily but, regaining consciousness, he saw the disabled bomber crash into the Pacific. Like many pilots, Lieutenant Kanno lived in expectation of death. But what made him different was that on his pilot's kitbag he had written an inscription that read: 'Personal effects of *the late Lieutenant Commander* Naoshi Kanno.'

It was the custom for military men to receive posthumous promotions. In any case, Kanno had written off any chance of his own survival. In June 1945 during the Okinawan campaign he met his death when he was shot down south of Kyushu, leaving behind him a reputation for valour.

Tamai and Seki spent most of the night planning the first officially sanctioned suicide mission. The next morning Seki got up at dawn to breathe the early morning air for the last time. The first Kamikaze unit was soon in readiness for takeoff. After a quick breakfast, Seki asked a fellow pilot to take a picture of him for his wife. He also handed Tamai a lock of his hair. Some minutes before takeoff Seki pulled out a handful of folded bank-notes from his pocket and handed them to a friend who was staying behind, asking that the money be used to build new planes.

Later, Radio Tokyo gave an eyewitness account of the scene at Mabalacat Air Base, outside Manila, just before takeoff. After describing a ripple of excitement that swept through the ranks of this 'special death corps', the radio station said:

> In front of field headquarters the pilots donned flying togs and goggles and calmly received their instructions from the flight commander, who told them that their targets would be aircraft carriers; that when the men dived into them, they should aim for the weakest part of the ship. He also told the men they were not a bomber force but human bombs.

The radio station said none of the men wore parachutes.

At 7.25 a.m. on October 21, the Zero fighters (codenamed 'Zekes' by the Allies) were lined up on the tarmac at Mabalacat. Seki took his seat in the cockpit, adjusted his goggles and after waving farewell to the ground crew took off with his unit in the direction of a large group of American escort carriers. (In 1941 the US Navy had built more than a hundred of these baby aircraft carriers, also called 'jeep' carriers, by superimposing flight decks on merchant ship hulls.) But Seki's unit was unable to discover the US fleet and returned to base. His unit took off again on October 22, 23 and 24 but returned each time after failing to find targets. They were accompanied by four escort fighters. On October 25 after flying for 3 hours and 25 minutes they reached their targets 30 nautical miles off the coast of Samar and succeeded in attacking a US task force. It was their fifth attempt. They started their attack at 10.45 a.m. High above the American ships, Seki's nine planes arrived unchallenged although there was a small combat patrol in the air. Five minutes later when the Kamikaze pilots had picked their targets, Seki gave the signal to dive. Seki's plane was in the lead and he was the first to crash into a target. He peeled off, his plane trailing smoke, and performed a steep dive aimed at the flight deck of one of the carriers.

Seki had boasted to a military reporter that when he found a carrier he would drop a 500-pound bomb in the middle of its flight deck.

In the engagement on the 25th, the pilots hit two of Admiral Clifton Sprague's escort carriers, sinking one of them, *St Lo*, and damaging the other. At the same time the escort fighters were engaged in a fierce dogfight with American planes.

Did Seki sink *St Lo*? There is some uncertainty about this. These facts are known. A Zero fighter pulled out of a steep dive and headed for the carrier 100 feet above sea level. The carrier's guns opened up but missed. Reports say the pilot (probably Seki) was calm and deliberate and kept his plane dead on course. Less than a minute later the pilot dropped a bomb in the centre of the flight deck, then his plane crashed and exploded, the remains of the plane and pilot dropping over the bow. The bomb exploded and burning gasoline set off more violent explosions.

St Lo suffered a total of eight explosions before sinking with heavy loss of life. One plane had sunk the carrier. Or as an observer summed up: 'One pilot, one Zero, one bomb, one carrier.'

The skill of the pilot in accomplishing his deadly mission was a good indication that he was none other than Yukio Seki.

Petty Officer First Class Hiroyoshi Nishizawa, who led the escort unit, reported by radio the results of the first official Kamikaze attack in history. According to Nishizawa, an American carrier and cruiser were sunk while another carrier was severely damaged. The records show that no cruiser was sunk, only *St Lo*. Two American Grumman fighter planes were shot down while one escort fighter was lost. Nishizawa was killed the following day when his plane was shot down.

When Emperor Hirohito was informed of the results of the first suicide mission, he declared: 'Was it necessary to go to this extreme?' He added: 'But they have certainly done a good job.' The Emperor also told a senior admiral that the resort to suicide attacks had filled him with grief.

In late October 1944 the following item appeared in Tokyo newspapers:

'Five Kamikaze heroes have been promoted two ranks in death and awarded posthumously various grades of the Martial Order of the Golden Kite, the Order of the Rising Sun, and the Order of the Paulownia Leaves.'

A proclamation signed by Admiral Soemu Toyoda, Commander-in-Chief of the Combined Fleet, said the five men had carried out 'deliberate ramming attacks' and that 'the memory of these gallant officers and men who died heroic deaths for the cause of their country will forever live in the minds of the nation'. It added: 'Wherefore their meritorious services are hereby proclaimed to the entire Navy on October 28, 1944.' Seki's name was at the top of the list.

As a consequence of Seki's mission there was enthusiasm bordering on euphoria among Kamikaze strategists. Hundreds, even thousands, of volunteers came forward. Onishi persuaded Admiral Fukudome, the commander of the Second Air Fleet, to join his First Air Fleet in performing suicide tactics. Both men began preparing for continuous and expanded crash-dive operations against the enemy. Onishi told assembled pilots that all units would become Special Attack units. Some of the pilots were reportedly stunned to learn that they, like Lieutenant Seki, would have to sacrifice themselves in suicide missions whether they liked it or not. Onishi, it was clear, was not going to brook criticism of his Kamikaze policy.

Meanwhile, the idea was being widely circulated that because of the suicide weapon, the Americans and their allies would become demoralized.

Shortly after the death of Yukio Seki a lock of his hair was delivered to his mother by Captain Sakae Yamamoto, the commander of the 201st Air Wing, who returned to Japan after being injured during an air raid on the Philippines. (Many Kamikaze pilots left behind a personal memento because their remains could never be returned to their families. Some of these mementoes are on display at various museums throughout Japan.) The lock was placed in a small white box, the kind that usually contained cremated ashes. After the naval captain left, Seki's mother fell to the floor and wept. For a week after Seki's Kamikaze sortie, important officials visited his mother, informing her that her son had been posthumously promoted to a naval commander's rank at the age of 23. Meanwhile the chancellor of Tokyo's Waseda University called on everyone to pray for the souls of Seki and his fellow pilots. In his words: 'We are far superior in our spiritual strength to American and British devils. Now we must demonstrate this spirit in all-out effort.'

A reporter who wrote an article about Yukio Seki's mother after peace returned to Japan said that it seemed as if her pilot-son had been born just to die in the war.

After the war, Asaichi Tamai, the deputy wing commander who had recruited Yukio Seki to lead the first Kamikaze mission, became a Buddhist monk. Tamai told friends that he could not achieve nirvana – a state of pure bliss – without first 'comforting the souls' of all the pilots he had sent on a one-way mission in Pacific waters.

4

WOMEN'S STORIES

A PILOT'S WIFE

The riverside Tomiya Ryokan, a Japanese inn situated in the southern Kyushu town of Chiran, is part of a two-storied wooden house that stands today near the Futomigawa River in the heart of town, across the street from a noodle shop. Chiran was famous during the war for its Kamikaze base and, for hundreds of pilots awaiting the call-up for their final sortie, the inn became a popular meeting place. This was largely due to the personality of Tome Torihama, the 42-year-old proprietress, who befriended the pilots and became known as the 'Special Attack Force Mother'.

A newspaper reporter who lived in Chiran during the war remembers two unforgettable stories closely associated with the Tomiya Ryokan.

On May 8, 1945, a young woman, looking tired, appeared at the Tomiya Ryokan. She had come all the way from Tokyo to meet her husband, Second Lieutenant Wataru Kawasaki, sensing that he was shortly to leave on a suicide mission. She first went to Hofu Air Base, in the southernmost part of Kyushu, but was told that he had moved to Chiran. At Chiran she got off the train and went straight to the air base but was not able to locate her husband. Someone suggested that she should go to Tomiya and enquire.

Tome Torihama welcomed Tsuneko, the distressed wife, and sent one of her daughters to find Lieutenant Kawasaki who was rooming some distance away. Meanwhile, she took the wife upstairs to her own room and combed her hair and applied cosmetics to her face.

'You should look your best for the reunion,' she said.

The lieutenant arrived and said, 'Oh! It's you! It's you!'

Tsuneko was wearing a white blouse inside her reddish trousers. Her husband was overjoyed to see her but tried to hide his emotion as best he could.

Tome let Lieutenant Kawasaki and his wife stay at her inn. She offered them a room upstairs in the family quarters.

On May 11, at 4 p.m., the Special Attack planes lined up at Chiran's airfield. Stars glittered in the expansive sky. In the dark, white *hachimaki* – the tightly fitted headbands with the Rising Sun emblem worn by the pilots – were conspicuous. The pilots carried with them air sickness pills, anti-sleep tablets, a candy bar containing an iron supplement, and a small bottle of wine. Some of them wore a thousand-stitch waist band called a *senninbari* as a good luck charm to ward off evil. The idea was to get one thousand young girls to each add a stitch to the cloth. The reason for the waistband is expressed in an anonymous pilot's farewell poem:

> On my last attack
> I am not alone,
> For my *senninbari*
> Is tied to my waist.

The town's people, carrying small paper rising-sun flags thronged the runway to bid farewell to the *tokko* flyers. As they marched past the lines of people, the latter shouted encouraging words. Lieutenant Kawasaki stopped when he saw his wife. She was wearing the same pair of reddish trousers as on the day of her arrival. Tome was standing behind her. Lieutenant Kawasaki and his wife stood there like two inert stones for a few moments, saying nothing. Then he resumed marching. If he had looked back he would have seen his wife collapse into Tome's arms. She had fainted.

Lieutenant Kawasaki's plane began taxiing. By this time, Tsuneko had regained consciousness and she ran after her husband's plane, shouting '*Anata! Neh! Anata!*' (My dear! Oh! My dear!) The planes flew in a circle over the base. Tsuneko still shouted at the top of her voice, '*Anata! Neh! Anata!*' waving a white handkerchief frantically.

Soon there was no one left on the airfield except for some of the ground crew and Tsuneko. She remained there, peering into the southern sky, looking dumbfounded. It was now daylight and it started to rain hard. Tsuneko went back to the inn on foot, soaked by the downpour.

Around noon that day, an orderly came to the inn and told Tsuneko that her husband had returned to the base after his plane developed a mechanical difficulty. In the late afternoon, Lieutenant Kawasaki came to Tomiya looking forlorn. He obtained permission to lodge at Eikyu Ryokan, a Japanese-style inn in the town, with his wife, while waiting for his next sortie.

After almost two weeks, that day came. On May 24, Tsuneko went to the airfield, accompanied by Tome. The lieutenant's wife looked haggard.

'Don't show tears to your beloved husband. You should not pity him,' Tome said.

As they reached the base, Tome combed Tsuneko's hair and gave her face a touch-up.

After the planes were gone, Tsuneko and Tome returned to Tomiya restaurant. Tsuneko seemed to have dissipated all her energy. She looked absent-minded. From time to time she sobbed violently. But again that afternoon, Lieutenant Kawasaki showed up at Tomiya. His plane had again developed engine trouble and he returned to the base to await his next sortie.

Six days later, on May 30, Lieutenant Kawasaki died while testing a Type 1 fighter. It crashed, killing him instantly.[1]

Following a Shinto funeral, Kawasaki's widow, accompanied by Tome, went to the train station. Red-eyed and mentally depressed, she bid Tome farewell and sat in the train, leaving Chiran behind her. She made the long journey to Tokyo carrying a wooden box containing the ashes of her pilot-husband.

THE FIREFLY

Tome Torihama, the proprietress, and her two daughters, Miyako and Reiko, lived on the second floor of the restaurant. Miyako and Reiko worked during the day as volunteers at the Chiran Air Base, attending the needs of Kamikaze flyers, cleaning the triangle-shaped makeshift billets, laundering, mending uniforms and doing other miscellaneous jobs. Tome died at 89 years of age in 1992.

A total of 2,620 men perished, taking off from Kyushu bases as Kamikaze flyers after the Americans landed on Okinawa on April 1, 1945. Among them, 1,036 were Army pilots. The rest were Navy men. Their average age was 21.62 years. Out of this number, 439 men took off from Chiran. Very probably every one of them had visited Tome Torihama's restaurant.

Tome tried her best to play the role of mother to these young pilots and many of them found solace as well as some of the comforts of family life in the homely atmosphere she offered. The men drank beer or sipped sake. Often they sang. Some of them wrote their last letters at the restaurant. Reiko, then a third-grader at a local junior high school, was treated like a younger sister by the pilots.

When the rainy season starts in late May, fireflies make their appearance along the banks of the Futomigawa. When dusk comes, they begin to wander, flicking their lights as they enter a porch near a small garden of Tome's restaurant which, during the war years, was covered by wisteria.

In mid-May during the last year of the war, Technical Sergeant Saburo Miyagawa came to the restaurant for the first time. He was alone. The following month he was scheduled to go on a Kamikaze mission. Almost every day he came to the restaurant and got to know the Torihamas well. He chatted and joked with Tome and her two daughters.

Miyagawa visited the restaurant for the last time on June 5, accompanied by a fellow flyer. It was the day before he was to make his sortie. That day happened to be Miyagawa's 20th birthday. Reiko gave him as a birthday gift a Rising Sun *hachimaki* headband she had made. Miyagawa in turn gave the family his wristwatch and a fountain pen.

After Miyagawa had his supper, Tome, Rieko and Miyako sat with the pilots in the wisteria-covered porch. As dusk gathered, fireflies criss-crossed the porch. Miyagawa, watching them, suddenly said:

'Oh, the fireflies. Tomorrow, I will return here as a firefly.'

'You'd be most welcome,' Tome replied.

'Yes. Tomorrow night, around nine o'clock. Please leave your door ajar so that I can come into the house,' Miyagawa half jokingly said.

'I promise you I will do so,' said Tome.

'If you see me, please greet me by singing *"Doki no Sakura"*.'

This is a song about cherry blossoms used as a metaphor for classmates at a military school.

Tome and her daughters nodded.

The next day, Reiko and Miyako waved off Miyagawa as his plane took off from the airfield in the rain. Before evening set in, it stopped raining. Miyako, remembering the promise they made to Miyagawa, though not taking his words seriously, kept the door ajar. Tome and the two girls spent some time on the porch and, shortly before 9 p.m., Reiko, followed by her sister, went into the restaurant to listen to the nine o'clock news on the radio. As she opened the door, a firefly flickering its lights entered through the door. Reiko and Miyako exclaimed: 'Mother! It's Mr Miyagawa. He's come back!'

The firefly was close to the ceiling, flickering. There were men from the Chiran Air Base in the restaurant. With Tome leading the song, all broke into the tune, '*Doki no Sakura*'.

The song, which was sung during the war years, is still very popular among the Japanese people. It includes these words:

> You and I are cherry blossoms from the same class.
> We bloomed at the same flight school.
> Once in bloom, the petals are ready to scatter.
> Let's scatter beautifully for the Motherland.

SHOUKO MAEDA

This description of the inside of a suicide aircraft was made by school-girl Shouko Maeda early in 1945:

Cockpits of the *tokko* pilots are full of cherry blossoms. Sunburned high school girls who work at the base have adorned the cock-pits with cherry blossoms. [The girls got their suntan from working outdoors at the airfield.] When the planes take off, the girls wave cherry blossom branches frantically at the departing flyers. The Special Attack planes get into formation after they are airborne and then circle high above the airstrip, bidding farewell. The formation then flies over Mt Kaimondake, appearing as little dots in the sky. The mountain is 924 metres high and can be seen clearly from the air base. From the ground the scene is heart-wrenching. The girls and family members, as well as friends and townspeople, remain standing for some time after the planes disappear from sight, flying in a southerly direction. Then, from high in the sky, cherry blossom petals come falling down, one by one, like snowflakes at the beginning of a light snowfall. The petals have been blown out of the cockpits opened by the pilots who have just flown away.[2]

In the spring of 1945 a 15-year-old schoolgirl named Shouko Maeda, who attended Chiran Women's High School, located close to the Kamikaze base, was asked to help clean the billets of the Special Attack flyers. In those days students were mobilized to work in war-related factories or agricultural fields and, therefore, wore work clothes to school instead of the traditional uniform.

Each day, after finishing her work at the base, Shouko kept a diary. Here are excerpts:

March 27, 1945. Today, out of the blue, I was told by our teacher that I was to work as an attendant for the *tokko* pilots. Surprised, I rushed home and changed into my school uniform and walked to the air base. I saw for the first time the men's humble barracks. Everything was new to me. The whole day I spent learning how to clean billets and make beds. I was moved to tears to see how our men lived and slept in such a confined space. They sleep on straw-padded bedding with a single khaki blanket. I felt ashamed that I slept in a comfortable bed at home. The men spend their last night in these conditions and take off on their last mission never to return to their small barracks. I feel thankful to them. I returned home by 5.30 p.m.

March 28. Today I was assigned to the billet of airmen who were about to leave on a Special Attack mission. I did not know how to face them. I thought I would lack courage. But I did my best to regain my strength of will. I swear that from tomorrow I shall do my best to launder or mend their uniforms and serve them as well as I can.

March 30. I spent the morning laundering. After I had cleaned the billets, I engaged in conversation with the airmen. They belonged to the 30th Shinbu Squadron led by Lieutenant Ouki and were all very young. I thought the lieutenant was very dignified. Yet he spoke to us in a gentle manner. The men were very much devoted to their squadron leader. Later, we went outside with them and in a pine forest broke into songs that were familiar to us. It was so enjoyable!

[Note: Each Kamikaze squadron took its name from classical martial literature. Shinbu means 'mastering martial strength'.]

March 30. Lt Ouki and his squadron were to depart today. Therefore I went to the [Shinto] shrine early in the morning and plucked cherry blossom branches and presented them together with mascot dolls we had made as farewell gifts. The men were as pleased as a group of children. Next we boarded a truck and went up to their planes. We helped load the planes with food and drinks. They all boarded their planes shouting to us cheerfully: 'Live to a ripe age!' and 'Take good care of yourselves!' We could see our mascot dolls swaying in the cockpits. But all the men returned to the base later owing to poor weather over the target area. The men were cursing their bad luck.

April 2. Junior Lt Yokoi asked me to sew a button on his trousers. He was going to take off in a few hours. I felt a bit shy so I asked Miss Mori, a friend, to come to the billet with me. Lt Yokoi was shaving his moustache off. He said laughingly that this was going to be a special day for him and he had to look neat. At 3.30 p.m. the planes started to taxi for takeoff. We all waved Rising Sun flags frantically at them. One by one, they were airborne. But soon afterwards, Mr Miyazaki's plane turned around and came back, followed by Lt Ouki's. They returned after circling the airfield. Mr Miyazaki's engine was muttering, br-brr-grr-grr. It was awful. Lt Ouki's plane also developed trouble: he was not able to keep his wings in balance. Ditto Mr Fuke's plane. It was the second time Lt Ouki and his men had to turn back owing to mechanical troubles.

While repairs were being made, we joined in singing with Lt Ouki and his men in their barracks. We sang our school song and also 'The Sun Goes Down', a very popular song. Then, Junior Lt Miyazaki engaged in a conversation with me about philosophy. It was too difficult for me to comprehend the meaning of his words. But I tried my best to be a good listener.

One of the men asked me what I would do if the enemies landed. I replied that I would try to kill at least one of them and follow the example set by you flyers. I was told that I should not lightly waste my life as there were other duties women had to perform for society. I thought: these are men about to die. And yet they are telling me to safeguard my life. Deep in my heart, I bowed low to them.

April 3. This is the men's fourth attempt to engage the enemy. Lt Ouki led a squadron of ten planes, taking off at 4 p.m. But they left Chiran for good this time, heading towards the far-off southern skies. Only Corporal Kawasaki stayed, being ill in bed. Prior to takeoff, I offered to help remove the camouflage net covering Mr Yokoi's plane. He chided me, saying, 'Look, your hands will get dirty,' showing me his gloves. I pleaded with him to let me help, and I did. Mr Yokoi was so pleased. He told me: 'I can now depart feeling contented. But I regret we must leave Kawasaki behind, alone in bed.' I appreciated what he said. The two men were close friends. Mr Yokoi had a few more hours to live but his thoughts were with his ailing friend. I learned that Lt Ouki was taking with him the ashes of a friend who died in an accident. All of them, taking off, had treated us so kindly, like their own little sister. I was so touched that I almost forgot my sadness at their parting. Mr Iwai even wrote a note addressed to me, thanking me for my work. I was deeply moved by it. As we had been taught, we all prayed that the men of the 30th Shinbu Squadron would be successful in their mission . . .

After the war Miss Maeda married and became Mrs Shouko Nagasaki. Recalling her days among the Kamikaze pilots at Chiran Air Base where many of the girls also helped in the canteen, she recorded these memories for a local newspaper:

Before the men took off, we helped to load light snacks, usually balls of rice, into the cockpits. One day, I gave a branch of cherry blossoms to a pilot who was already seated in the cockpit. In appreciation he kept saying, 'Thank you! Thank you!' We all believed that cherry blossoms symbolized these young men: the blossoms bloom gorgeously and then scatter in haste after a short life, without complaint. From that day on, we adorned each cockpit with branches of fragrant cherry blossoms. In Chiran at that time, they were in full bloom.

On the morning of April 12, we made garlands of flowers for the departing men. We went down to the rice paddy fields and plucked milk vetches. As we were busily gathering the small flowers, Junior Lt Okayasu passed by. He stopped and, smiling, ripped off his insignia of rank from his lapels and threw them at the girls who caught them. Then he walked on.

We stood in silence, awe-struck. It was for us an expression of his determination to be a human being when he flew off later that day, freed from the strictures of military hierarchy, of all restraint.

Okayasu took off shortly after 4 p.m. and did not return.

Mrs Nagasaki described the ritual of departure, the solemnity mixed on occasion with the singing of songs to lift the men's spirits:

As the time of departure approaches, the men of the squadron line up in formation in front of the command post. A short speech is given by the base commander or by a senior staff officer. Then they all face east in the direction of the Imperial Palace [in Tokyo]. Small, white ritual sake cups are passed to the men. Sake is poured. They all make a toast. Then they disperse and wait for takeoff. The men spend the remaining time sitting on the ground, sometimes singing martial songs or enjoying smoking, or exchanging banter. Then it is time to take off. They head for their planes which are kept in concrete shelters, patting each other on the back.

Two unusual incidents stuck in her mind. The first concerned a father and his son:

> One day I saw an elderly man run, panting, to one of the planes. The pilot was already in the cockpit with the engine roaring. The elderly man reached the plane and the pilot jumped down to greet him. I saw them speaking to each other. Then the elderly man took a string off his *haori* and handed it to him. [The front of the *haori*, or kimono jacket, is tied together using two strings instead of buttons.] They shook hands tightly. Although each showed 'a stiff upper lip' I realized they were father and son. I choked. Soon, the son climbed back into the cockpit and the plane started to move. The father stood like a piece of stone for a long time after the plane disappeared into the sky. I could not stop crying. The father had given his son the kimono string as a symbol of their bond.

The second incident involved an elderly couple:

> On May 25 more than 50 planes took off from Chiran Air Base. As enemy raids became more frequent, the planes were dispersed outside the airfield. They would taxi to the airfield as time for a sortie approached. Many people would come to see the flyers off. On that day I noticed an elderly couple watching intently as each plane taxied onto the airfield.
>
> As the couple stood by, the wife bowed deeply to each plane as, one by one, they passed in front of the crowd.
>
> Suddenly, the canopy of one of the planes opened and I saw the pilot throw out a long red paper ribbon. The woman opened her umbrella and, holding it high, waved it. The plane flying the red paper ribbon from the canopy reached the airstrip and climbed into the sky, the woman continuing to wave her umbrella. Later I learned that the pilot was Junior Lt Yoshio Nambu of the 49th Shinbu Squadron and that he had promised his mother that he would throw down a red paper ribbon so that she and his father could identify him. The elderly couple had travelled more than 24 hours to Chiran, coming all the way from Tokyo, despite incessant air attacks on the railroad lines, to see their son off on his final mission.

Mrs Nagasaki also remembered an incident involving a young boy, probably a fourth or fifth grader in the local primary school, who was walking near one of the billets one morning when the commanding officer, taking notice of the boy, jokingly asked:

'Do you want to become a Kamikaze pilot when you grow up?'

The boy shook his head, saying innocently:

'No! I want to live to an old age!'

The officer and several Special Attack pilots with him broke into hearty laughter at the boy's answer.

'LUCKY YOU WERE BORN A GIRL!'

Kimiko Kabu, the wife of a Kamikaze pilot, kept a diary from the day she became engaged to Toshio Kuramoto in the autumn of 1944, at which time Toshio gave his fiancée a diary. She was 18 and he was ten years older. When Kimiko graduated from a women's high school in Kyushu in the spring of 1941, Toshio was working for the Mitsui Mining Company and he had an apartment near Kimiko's home. Later, Toshio Kuramoto was conscripted by the Army and fought in China as an infantryman. Afterwards, a corporal in the reserves, Toshio was recalled to active service in 1943 and volunteered as a cadet in the Army Air Force.

In January of 1944, Kimiko was allowed to visit her fiancée at Chiran Air Base. She took a train that crossed Kyushu and Toshio greeted her in his cadet's uniform. At the base, she was invited to observe his flight training from the command post situated under a tent. Everyone treated Kimiko kindly, knowing that she was engaged to a cadet. In April, Toshio was transferred to Tachiarai Flying School which was closer to her home and meant she could now meet with Toshio more often.

On October 29, 1944, Kimiko made an entry in her diary upon learning from newspaper reports that a Kamikaze attack (obviously Lieutenant Yukio Seki's) had been launched against the American invasion fleet in Philippine waters. The entry reveals the depth of Kimiko's feelings:

So divine! A group of young eagles led by a 24-year-old. I am utterly speechless by their action. But however worthy the sacrifice they made, they were not orphans. They must have parents, wives, children, brothers and sisters. When they took off, did they see the faces of their wives or lovers? Their sweet faces? . . . . The newspaper reports broke my heart. I was so deeply moved.

Kimiko did not then imagine that Toshio and she would face the very same trial in just a short period of time.

Kimiko and Toshio were married on February 15, 1945 when Toshio was a second lieutenant assigned to Kameyama Air Base, near Osaka. Because he was not able to take a long leave, they were united at a Shinto shrine near the base with Kimiko's mother in attendance. Kimiko wore a pair of blue trousers made from the kimono she had on when she visited Chiran for the first time. She remembered that Toshio had told her it was his favourite colour. In those days women were encouraged to wear trousers rather than skirts as this was more in accordance with wartime conditions when Japan was beginning to feel the austerity accompanying the punishing effect of air raids.

Toshio told his bride that he was going through the most strict training, learning 'how to fly extremely low so that enemy vessels will be hit without fail'. She did not realize then what this meant – that her husband and the other pilots were undergoing training for a suicide mission.

Lieutenant Kuramoto had joined a Kamikaze squadron at Akeno Air Base in Mie Prefecture on March 27. Then he and his men were transferred to Kumanosho Air Base on Kyushu so they took a train to that southern main island. On the way to the base, Toshio got off the train at Moji in northern Kyushu and visited Kimiko at her parents' house. Although they had dinner together, Toshio did not confide to Kimiko that he had joined the Special Attack Forces. He was able to spend only two hours with her and then hurried to the railway station.

In April, Kimiko received a telegram from Toshio to come and visit him. She was excited that she was now able to live with her husband. Toshio was lodged at Wataya Ryokan, a Japanese-style inn in Kumamoto City. Kumamoto City, the prefecture capital, is known for the majestic Kumamoto Castle that stands in the heart of the city. When Kimiko arrived at the inn, the maid who met her at the entrance told her that Lieutenant Kuramoto left for the air base this morning in haste as they were shortly taking off on a mission. The maid paused for a moment and said gravely:

'Please, dear madam, this is the moment to master one's courage.'

Kimiko now sensed for the first time that her husband was going on a suicide mission. She was jolted and unable to speak. In a state of panic, Kimiko was led to her husband's room by the maid who was surprised at the wife's unpreparedness. The maid apologized, saying: 'Sorry, madam, I shouldn't have told you.'

At this moment she introduced Second Lieutenant Osamu Shibata, who belonged to her husband's unit. Shibata wore a head bandage from an accident that occurred during a training flight and had, therefore, been left behind. Shibata said the unit was not taking off that day and that he would escort her to the base the next morning. The base was not very far from the inn.

Kimiko, alone in the room, had a frightful night. In the morning, Kimiko and Shibata started out for the base as a heavy rain kept pouring down. They took a train from Kumamoto and got off at Namazu, which was the third stop from Kumamoto, taking only ten minutes. A bus from the base met them at the station, re-entered the base and stopped before a triangle-shaped billet. (One of these oddly shaped billets is on display at the Chiran Peace Museum.) In the makeshift billet a few flyers were idling. While one of them went out to find her husband, she was told that because of the rain all flights had been cancelled.

Soon, however, Toshio arrived. He told her that thanks to the rain they were able to meet. Using an umbrella they went on foot to a nearby farmhouse where he was lodging, Toshio carrying his wife's travel bag. They walked on a footpath through a field of rapeseed. Yellow rapeseed flowers were in bloom and glistened in the rain. The peaceful scenery suddenly aroused in Kimiko an earnest hope that peace would soon return to the world.

She folded up the umbrella so that her action would hide the tears running down her cheeks.

Kimiko was pleasantly surprised to see that Toshio was living at a well-to-do farmhouse. On the way to his room she saw purple hydrangeas in the garden outside the window. Once they were settled in, she timidly hesitated for a moment, then asked her husband:

'Did you volunteer as a Kamikaze flyer?'

'Where did you get that idea,' Toshio responded.

'From the maid at Wataya.'

Toshio looked jovial and lied to his wife.

'No. Never! That's wrong!'

But Kimiko felt that he was not telling the truth. She thought that he was probably too tormented to speak frankly.

The rain continued and Toshio went to the base every morning and returned every evening for dinner. Kimiko would often stand under the eaves of the farmhouse, watching the rainfall.

Rain, rain, rain. The gentle sound of spring rain. She found it delightful. After all, it was the rain that ensured her husband's life – and hers, too. She had many chances to think about life, and the thought that dominated her thinking was that without him there was no life for her. During these rainy days she would tuck in her sleeves and stretch her arms in the rain, thinking meantime that Toshio would never admit to her that he had joined a suicide unit.

The rain continued for a week.

Then Toshio's unit received orders to transfer to another air base called Miyakonojo, also on Kyushu. The unit returned to Kumamoto for one night before proceeding to the newly assigned air base where the couple lodged at the Wataya Inn.

That night everyone in the unit was invited to a gala farewell dinner. Kimiko was not invited but she heard the men singing loudly together. Listening to the songs and the conversation of the men, she could sense the wistful mood of the gathering.

At last, Toshio returned, inebriated, to their room. Soon, she felt deep in her heart, they would be parting from each other for good.

The next morning, she went to Kumamoto Station to see Toshio off. It was raining again. The front of the station was slippery with dirt as workmen were constructing an underground air raid shelter. She tried not to show her tears. But she cried profusely the moment after the train pulled out from the platform. She went back to her uncle's house in Hakata to wait for her husband's call. It was at Hakata that a Mongol fleet landed on Japanese soil in foiled invasion attempts in the thirteenth century.

That evening, Toshio telephoned from Miyakonojo, saying he would be there for a week and asking her to join him there. She was instantly overjoyed and went immediately to her parents' home where she told her mother that she was convinced that Toshio had volunteered as a Kamikaze flyer. Hearing this, her mother began sobbing.

At Miyakonojo, Kimiko and Toshio stayed at the Fijinoi Inn. As before, rain continued to fall. In the morning, Toshio went to the base, leaving Kimiko crying alone in their room, writing something in her diary, then Toshio suddenly returned.

'Lucky you to have been born a girl!' he said laughingly. 'You can shed tears while we boys are not allowed such a luxury.'

That evening the rain stopped and the pair went for a walk. Dusk was gathering and the town appeared immensely beautiful, Kimiko was thinking, with its lush trees and flowers, and its shiny wet pavements. Everything was so eerily peaceful. Toshio had yet to tell her the truth but Kimiko had gathered herself together and was filled with happiness as she strolled with him. It was a halcyon night, she thought.

On April 22, she wrote in her diary:

'Let's not think of tomorrow. Live today to the full. What happy days I am having! I have such a kind husband. He loves me deeply. Even if we were to be parted for good, he will always live in my heart.'

On May 3, a dinner for the unit was held at a restaurant that stood next to the inn. She heard, by accident, a corporal, Tadashi Mukai, say to the proprietress of the inn, after letting out an ironic laugh: 'This is going to be our last big feast!'

Late that night, Toshio came back to the room. He had, like the others, been drinking. Kimiko pretended to be nonchalant.

'Do you sally tomorrow?'

'No,' he lied. 'It is just going to be another training flight.'

In the morning, a military vehicle pulled up in front of the inn. Everyone from the inn and from the restaurant lined up on both sides of the street to see the men off. Toshio stopped in front of them and said: 'Thank you very much for taking good care of us.' And he gave a smart salute. Just before he boarded the vehicle, he turned around and looked intently at Kimiko. He then executed a salute in her direction.

But Toshio returned to the inn later that day. His plane had a minor collision with another plane as they were taking off.

At dawn on May 11th, Toshio left, this time for good. Kimiko assisted him in getting dressed. She helped him put on his underwear. This was the last time she touched the skin of his body. Toshio took off for the Okinawan waters never to return.

Kimiko was then pregnant. On January 27, 1946, five months after peace had returned to Japan, she gave birth to a girl, naming her Ryoko, a name that had been chosen by her late husband.

NOTES

[1] All Japanese Army and Navy planes were given the name Type xx (followed by a number) according to the Imperial calendar: 1940 was year 2600. The Navy adopted the Zero fighter in that year (zero). Type 1 was adopted in the year 2601. Similarly, the Army adopted the Hien plane (Type 4) in 2604 – or 1944 in the Christian calendar. Incidentally, the Imperial chronology can be found on a monument in Jakarta, the country's independence monument, situated in the heart of the city. The Indonesians proclaimed their independence in 1945 after Japan surrendered to the Allies.

[2] Samurai warriors in feudal days often inserted cherry blossom branches in the back body armour as they headed for the field of blood. It is a 1,000-year-old tradition.

5

SEX, MARRIAGE AND MORALE

During the frenzied Kamikaze phase of the Pacific War a special branch of the Army Air Force codenamed *Tsubame Butai Honbu* (Central Office of the Swallow Unit) was set up to offer counselling services for pilots and also to provide information to pilots who were married and wished to know, for example, what support their families could receive after their demise. The services also included helping love-sick flyers but the office was mainly set up to address the physical as well as mental well-being of the men. Not surprisingly, pilots' morale was given high priority, especially as there were quite a few Kamikaze pilots who changed their minds – that is, their original enthusiasm for self-sacrifice had waned. A fair number of pilots did not fulfil their missions but came back to their base with pretexts or had ditched their planes on the way to the targets. It was discovered that Kamikaze pilots stationed at bases near towns with large female populations and cultural attractions were much more likely to have a change of mind than pilots at more remote bases.[1]

Regarding the libido of young Kamikaze flyers, there seemed to be a wide difference of opinion within the military establishment. While the immediate superiors of the flyers would encourage the boys to couple with women near the base, especially on the night before the final sortie, those who wrote the official documents were more apt to place a taboo on all sexual activity, regarding it as blunting, even compromising, patriotic ardour.

From a document circulated among Special Attack units and issued by the Chief of the Education Department of the Office of the Army Air Force on June 25, 1945:

> In case there is a long waiting period between the formation of a Kamikaze unit and the final sortie, mental pressure increases and in many instances results in a change of determination about being a Kamikaze pilot. [This 'change of determination' was sometimes the result of visits to neighbourhood flesh-pots. The document, which implicitly holds up chastity as an ideal for young pilots, adds] Although there are some who seek to conclude their lives in pure and clean ways, there is a tendency among many Kamikaze pilots to seek earthly pleasures. This condition [the long waiting periods] allows innocent men to try such pleasures, resulting in increased tenacity for life.

At that juncture, showing tenacity for life went against the flood of patriotic speeches and articles. The gist of their message was summed up by a popular slogan: 'To die for the nation is to live'. These words were contained in a speech made in July 1945 to a communications training centre by Rear Admiral Etsuzo Kurihara, Chief of Public Affairs of the Navy General Staff. Meanwhile, the man known as the 'father' of Kamikaze strategy, Admiral Onishi, was fond of telling members of his Special Attack units about to depart for their one-way missions that they were 'already gods without earthly desires'. One commander of a Special Attack unit, addressing his Kamikaze pilots before their final sortie, was less polite. 'Exert all your energy for this is an opportunity that comes once in a thousand years,' he said, adding: 'All of you come back dead!'

Many Special Attack pilots were comforted by a paradox: 'In death there is life.' In fact, these words were written in a notebook by a general officer before he was killed in a final 'Banzai charge' on Saipan. His bones, he wrote, would remain behind as a bulwark in the Pacific. For him, being taken alive was the ultimate disgrace. (At the International Military Tribunal for the Far East, General Tojo, who had been prime minister and was on trial as a war criminal, said that 'from ancient times the Japanese have deemed it degrading to be taken prisoner, and all combatants have been instructed to choose death rather than be captured as a prisoner of war'. Tojo himself attempted suicide shortly after Japan's surrender, shooting himself with a revolver, but he survived, but not before being given several blood transfusions by the

Americans. As Churchill said in his narrative of the war, the Japanese 'were steeled for sacrifice'.)

But if priggish officials were advocating chastity for suicide pilots, there were other officials who showed tolerance and understanding towards wartime excesses, at least those displayed by romantically inclined Kamikaze flyers. There was a case where a pilot had received orders to transfer to a new air base but had fallen in love with a girl and intentionally damaged his fighter plane so he would not have to depart from his beloved. When officials reviewed the case they concluded: 'We cannot call the pilot's behaviour abnormal. We might consider such an act as being committed by someone who, faced with certain death, could easily resort to so outrageous an act.'

Of course, many of the cases dealing with Kamikaze flyers had to do with family matters. The following advice, given in question and answer form, was distributed to all Air Armies by the Army General Staff Office, and entitled 'Marital Problems of a Sergeant Major from the 325th Squadron':

Question: I intended to marry and submitted an application for marriage to my superiors but was told to wait because I was living in the barracks. After I was accepted as a member of a Kamikaze unit, I asked the lady to cancel our engagement, but she strongly wished to be wedded to a To-Go flyer ['To-Go' was a codename widely used by the Army and Navy, signifying *tokko*, or Special Attack Corps.] Thereupon I re-submitted my application for permission. In the meantime, the parents of the two families conducted shukugen [a marriage rite] in my absence. After that the lady I was engaged to began living at my parents' home, and was looking after them. As much as I desired to officially register her as my spouse, it has been impossible to do so without the permission for marriage from the Army. I would like to obtain official permission before I depart on my final mission. Therefore, I'm asking if I can entrust someone with a letter of attorney in the event that I must depart suddenly, so that permission for our marriage can be granted. I have studied the issue and according to the Law Governing Registration of One's Marriage by a Trustee or by Mail, if the applicant dies at the time of receipt the registration will be nullified.

Answer: Should the Master-Sergeant receive an order to sortie the next day and did not find the time to write a letter of attorney, he can verbally authorize an appropriate person to do so.

[But in this particular case, the Master-Sergeant was allowed to file a registration of marriage by telegraph.]

One problem was decided astonishingly quickly, without any 'red tape'. It was written up in a document distributed by the Army General Staff Office and entitled 'The Problem of a Bereaved Family of a Corporal from the 225th Squadron'. It also was in question and answer form:

Question: The Corporal's father, a carpenter, was called up for military duty. The father's whereabouts are unknown. [Presumably he is missing in action.] Meanwhile, the Corporal's family, in addition to the missing father, comprises the father's second wife, 42 years of age, and seven brothers and sisters. The family does not own any property and had relied on the earnings of the carpenter-father. After the father was conscripted, the 17-year-old brother supported the family as a tenant farmer. But now the Corporal is anxious about his family and asks how they can survive after his demise.

Answer: It is possible to obtain a loan for livelihood assistance or for educational expenses, or free medical treatment from the Military Personnel Assistance Society under the Military Protection Institute. We have contacted the municipal office of the Corporal's township in order to help the family.

Close attention was paid to the physical well-being of Special Attack pilots, in the first place to their obtaining comfortable off-base quarters and providing the men with a balanced diet. The following document was also distributed by the Army General Staff Office and is entitled 'Personal Circumstances, Provisions and Health of To-Go Personnel':

On billeting pilots, the commanders of Kamikaze units are to engage first-class ryokan [Japanese inns] as lodging for the flyers, with emphasis on those with good views, attractive baths, decent kitchens, toilets and beds. Regrettably, private homes may not provide the physical comforts of ryokan, although the former excel in offering warm family atmosphere full of sympathy and sincerity.

There is a short section in the document dealing with physical training: 'Training should range from 30 minutes to 40 minues daily. The focus should be placed on night-time training. Experience teaches that the men show no sign of fatigue from daily training.'

On food and beverages. The document says that in order to:

maintain the highest possible physical and moral condition of the Kamikaze pilots so they can best exert their skills, the Central Office has secured the enthusiastic support of the Army Air Force as a whole, working closely with various related organizations. The subordinate Air Divisions are exerting aggressive supervision and leadership to materialize the best possible conditions so that the units responsible for providing provisions will meet all of the requirements.

For To-Go pilots, the following are provided beyond the special allowances that are made for ordinary flyers: wheat flour, food oil, meat, fish, canned products, sweets, fruits, soft drinks, sake, whisky and cigarettes. Additional amounts of these products are made available to the Division Headquarters.

The document adds that, although the condition of food and beverage supplies for 'To-Go' units vary with each location because of differences in local procurement, on average these are the daily provisions made available:

Staple food	Rice	786 grams (2600 calories)
Side dishes	Animal or fish meat	200 grams
	Vegetables	600 grams
	Others	100 grams
	Noodles	90 grams
	Eggs	120 grams
	Food oil	10 grams
	Milk	$\frac{1}{5}$ litre
	Sake	$\frac{1}{3}$ litre
Total		About 4,000 calories

Note: In late July 1945 when these food provisions appeared in the aforementioned document and were available for Kamikaze pilots, a pervading food shortage in Japan caused the government to announce that research was being carried out on the use of acorns as a food product. The government said there were *30 existing factories that could make acorn flour*.

Officials were aware that the thought of the possibility of dying in vain tormented many Special Attack pilots. Not only did the enthusiasm of some of these pilots drop off, but they also became extremely sensitive to various conditions, such as the equipment, weather, and obtaining

intelligence about the enemy, often resulting in many cases in their returning to base. It takes very strong willpower to sortie again after turning back once. Under such conditions, the morale of some men drops
because they are under great stress. Research offered likely reasons for
this development: (1) The individual is uneasy, thinking that he would
be able to save his life if he can come up with a convincing excuse for
not wanting to sortie. (2) The pilot has a deep inner feeling of isolation.

In the documents there is the case of a pilot breaking up his plane
by violently shaking it, while in other incidents some pilots were
suspected of intentionally ditching their planes after turning back from
the target area.

Another document distributed by the Army General Staff Office and
dated July 20, 1945, which deals with the character and training of
Kamikaze pilots, also mentions how the suicide pilots can become gods
while they are still on earth. (By training and discipline.) The document hints that there is another ingredient necessary: that the men be
'burning with an ardent desire'. It is appropriately entitled 'A Manual
for Handling Members of Divine Hawk Units'. *Kamiwashi* (or Divine
Hawk) was another name that was sometimes used for Kamikaze flyers.
The opening sentences of the document reflect obligatory war-time
twaddle:

> Divine Hawks strike at arrogant enemies and destroy them by
> sacrificing their lives, driven by a strong urge for justice which is
> as heavy as the mountains, and who regard their lives as light as
> feathers. This is the spirit of the Divine Hawks, one that demon-
> strates their aspirations for ensuring the perpetuity of our Imperial
> nation and invincibility of the Divine Islands. [The name 'Divine
> Islands' or 'Islands Blessed by Gods' – in Japanese, *Shinshu* – was
> often used throughout history as another name for Japan.]

The manual also contains practical advice concerning the mental state
of suicide pilots and injects a religious note:

> Divine Hawk volunteers can become gods by proper training.
> If this is not done they can develop a mentally dangerous con-
> dition. . . . Divine Hawk members should not be treated as
> extraordinary men. They should neither be spoilt nor given an
> excessive amount of freedom. . . . Needless to say the Divine
> Hawk unit members are also members of the Imperial Armed
> Forces and they must observe discipline worthy of Imperial Armed
> Forces soldiers. . . . We should pay added attention so that these

heroes burning with an ardent desire to serve the nation do not besmear their honour by displaying inappropriate behaviour.

Since leadership within the Kamikaze units was of vital importance and not only for lifting morale, some of the qualities that make for good leadership were enumerated. Officials said that proper attention must be paid in selecting the unit leader, that he must possess superb character, knowledge, skill and the ability to be a leader of men. The following points were listed as essential in selecting members of a Kamikaze unit: skill, capability and character. Because a pilot would likely lose interest or become melancholy if given a duty or an aircraft to fly that was below his capabilities, officials made this recommendation: 'We must consider the experience the volunteer has in flying certain types of aircraft so that he is able to exert his utmost capabilities. In case there is no aircraft suited to his skill, a request should be submitted to the Army Commander for his transfer to a unit with suitable aircraft.'

Finally there was attention paid to the subject of morale. First there was this poetic description:

The morale of Divine Hawk unit members is like a sharp blade, an awesome weapon, as it is at the highest tension and therefore vulnerable. Unless it is ground constantly it could turn into a blunt sword. Consequently in order to maintain high morale, the members must lead a highly disciplined military life. They must be encouraged to improve themselves through studies and practice until the moment of the sortie.

The document said that unexpected failures or bureaucratic red tape while a pilot waits for the sortie can have a harmful effect on his morale; that because the bases are located in the homeland, there is a general slackening of spirit of hostility towards the enemy. The morale of the Kamikaze pilots is at the highest when they sortie after an enemy air raid [has taken its toll] against the civilian population of Japan.

In the last year of the war, impassioned speeches and articles appeared almost without end in Japan, designed to keep revulsion of the enemy at a high level. Indirectly, the publicity appearing on the radio and in the press and on public platforms helped to keep Kamikaze morale high. Quite naturally, the more these pilots hated the enemy the more they would feel right about killing themselves. Many speeches and articles painted Anglo-Americans as little more than savages whose military establishments routinely committed bestial acts. Needless to

say, none of the belligerents was exempt from this type of coarse
propaganda.

What follows are three examples of the kind of propaganda designed
to stir up intense hostility towards the enemy. The Evil Empire for the
Japanese were the United States and Great Britain combined:

■ A Japanese Domei news agency report alleged early in July 1945
that the 'aim of the British-American administration of occupied
Germany is to exterminate the German race'. (The inference was
that Japan's turn would be next.) The report added: 'The German
race has now become a second "Jewish race", their right of existence not being recognized.'

■ Historian-journalist Soho Tokutomi, in a speech at Hibiya Public
Hall in Tokyo on October 7, 1944 (afterwards printed in major
newspapers), said 'the United States is a country made up of the
pirate spirit of the Anglo-Saxons and the Colonial bandit spirit.'
The speaker mentioned American anti-Japanese prejudice in the first
quarter of the twentieth century when Japanese children 'could not
enter American schools and study together with American children
because it was claimed that Japanese are of an inferior race'. He
cited an anti-Japanese Immigration Law that was enacted by the US.

■ In late October 1944 a blustery article appeared in the mass-
circulation *Asahi* newspaper, written by Admiral Kichisaburo
Nomura, who had been Ambassador to Washington and was
involved in the critical Japanese-American talks before the attack
on Pearl Harbor. Hailing the 'brilliant exploits of the Kamikaze
corps', Nomura wrote: 'The Americans have called the Japanese
"monkeys" and cried aloud that we should be wiped off the face
of the earth.' He added: 'In the face of enemy attacks the Japanese
Special Kamikaze Attack Corps [Nomura also called them 'Death
Squadrons' in the article] inspired by sublime patriotism will self-
blast themselves against the enemy.'

NOTE

[1] The Army Air Force documents mentioned in this chapter were provided
by the Defence Agency's – the equivalent of Japan's Ministry of Defence –
research institute. Although the cases cited deal with the Army Air Force,
the Navy undoubtedly had similar cases involving its Special Attack pilots.
All of the Army documents were marked classified and have not been
published previously.

6

THE SUICIDE MANUAL

Early in 1945 an 88-page manual that minutely prepared Kamikaze pilots for their suicide mission was compiled by the Shimoshizu Air Unit in Chiba Pefecture, near Tokyo. The manual, dated May 1945, bears the name of the unit commander, Major Hayashino. It gives precise information on how to cause maximum damage to an enemy ship, what to do and think as the target looms closer with only seconds remaining before impact, even telling the pilot – no doubt enhancing the probability – that he will see his mother's face ('neither smiling nor crying') during the final milliseconds of consciousness. The manual tells the pilots – who have heard it said many times that after the crash they will become gods (*kami*) – that they will meet their friends and joke with them in their god-like state.[1]

Is there anything a pilot can do if he is nervous before a mission or approaching a target? Yes, says the manual in one word: piss. At the moment of impact the pilot is advised to shout at the top of his lungs to increase his self-confidence. If a pilot can't find a target, he should return to base and not waste his life lightly. If it comes to this, says the manual, the pilot should be 'jovial' and 'without remorse'.

Written in concise, vivid language, the manual is officially entitled 'Basic Instructions for To-Go Flyers' (To-Go is a codename for Special Attack Corps) and was given to pilots to take along in the cockpit for consultation. Some of the information appearing in the manual has a mystic quality. For instance, to lift up his spirits, the pilot is told that at the termination of a successful mission (the impact with the target), there will occur at that precise moment at the Shinto grand military shrine in Tokyo – Yasukuni Jinja – a spontaneous outpouring of joy. It is, the pilot is told, a personal recognition of the pilot's success. Some of the pages reopen memories of the September 11, 2001 terror.

The following are highlights from the manual:

PAGE 3:

The Mission of To-Go Units

Transcend life and death. When you eliminate all thoughts about life and death, you will be able to totally disregard your earthly life. This will also enable you to concentrate your attention on eradicating the enemy with unwavering determination, meanwhile reinforcing your excellence in flight skills.

Exert the best in yourself.

Strike an enemy vessel that is either moored or at sea.

Sink the enemy and thus pave the road for our people's victory.

PAGE 12:

Take a Walk Around the Airfield

When you take this walk, be aware of your surroundings. This airstrip is the key to the success or failure of your mission. Devote all your attention to it.

Look at the terrain. What are the characteristics of the ground?

What are the length and width of the airstrip?

In case you are taking off from a road or a field, what is the correct direction of your flight? At what point do you consider taking off?

In case you will take off at dusk, or early morning, or after sundown, what are the obstacles to be remembered: an electric pole, a tree, a house, a hill?

PAGE 13:

How to Pilot a Fully Dressed Up [heavily equipped] Aircraft That You Dearly Love

Before taking off. [After taxiing the plane from the camouflaged emplacement to the airstrip.] You can envision your target firmly in your mind as you bring your plane to a standstill.

Breathe deeply three times. Say in your mind: '*Yah*' [field], '*Kyu*' [ball], '*Joh*' [all right] as you breathe deeply.

Proceed straight ahead on the airstrip. Otherwise you may damage the landing gear.

Circle above the airstrip right after takeoff. Do so at the minimum height of 200 metres. Circle at an angle within 5 degrees and keep your nose pointed downwards.

PAGE 15:

Principles You Should Know
Keep your health in the very best condition.

If you are not in top physical condition, you will not be able to achieve an ideal hit by *tai-atari* [body-crashing].

Just as you cannot fight well on an empty stomach, you cannot deftly manipulate the control stick if you are suffering from diarrhoea, and cannot exert calm judgement if you are tormented by fever.

Be always pure-hearted and cheerful.

A loyal fighting man is a pure-hearted and filial son.

Attain a high level of spiritual training.

In order that you can exert the highest possible capability, you must prepare well your inner self. Some people say that spirit must come first before skill, but they are wrong. Spirit and skill are one. The two elements must be mastered together. Spirit supports skill and skill supports spirit.

PAGE 21:

Aborting Your Mission and Returning to Base
In the event of poor weather conditions when you cannot locate the target, or under other adverse circumstances, you may decide to return to base. Don't be discouraged. Do not waste your life lightly. You should not be possessed by petty emotions. Think how you can best defend the motherland. Remember what the Wing Commander has told you. You should return to the base jovially and without remorse.

PAGE 22:

When Turning Back and Landing at the Base
Discard the bomb at the area designated by the commanding officer.

Fly in circles over the airfield.
Observe conditions of the airstrip carefully.
If you feel nervous, piss.
Next, ascertain the direction of the wind and wind speed.
Do you see any holes in the runway?
Take three deep breaths.

PAGE 23:

The Attack
Single-plane attack. Upon sighting a target, remove the [bomb's] safety pin.
Go full speed ahead towards the target. Dive!
Surprise the enemy.
Don't let the enemy take time to counter your attack. Charge!
Remember: the enemy may change course but be prepared for the enemy's evasive action.
Be alert and avoid enemy fighters and flak fire.

PAGE 33:

Dive Attack
This varies depending on the type of the aircraft.
If you are approaching the enemy from a height of 6,000 metres, adjust your speed twice; or from a lower height of 4,000 metres, adjust speed once.
When you begin your dive, you must harmonize the height at which you commence the final attack with your speed.
Beware of over-speeding and a too-steep angle of dive that will make the controls harder to respond to your touch.
But an angle of dive that is too small will result in reduced speed and not enough impact on crashing.

PAGE 37:

Where to Crash (the Enemy's Fatal Spots)
Where should you aim?
When diving and crashing onto a ship, aim for a point between the bridge tower and the smoke stack(s).
Entering the stack is also effective.
Avoid hitting the bridge tower or a gun turret.
In the case of an aircraft carrier, aim at the elevators.
Or if that is difficult, hit the flight deck at the ship's stern.

For a low altitude horizontal attack, aim at the middle of the vessel, slightly higher than the waterline.

If that is difficult, in the case of an aircraft carrier, aim at the entrance to the airplane hanger, or the bottom of the stack.

For other vessels, aim close to the aft engine room.

PAGE 38:

Just Before the Crash

Your speed is at the maximum.

The plane tends to lift. But you can prevent this by pushing the elevator control forward sufficiently to allow for the increase in speed.

Do your best. Push forward with all your might.

You have lived for 20 years or more. You must exert your full might for the last time in your life. Exert supernatural strength.

At the very moment of impact:

Do your best. Every deity and the spirits of your dead comrades are watching you intently.

Just before the collision it is essential that you do not shut your eyes for a moment so as not to miss the target.

Many have crashed into the targets with wide-open eyes.

They will tell you what fun they had.

PAGE 39:

You Are Now 30 Metres From the Target

You will sense that your speed has suddenly and abruptly increased. You feel that the speed has increased by a few thousand-fold. It is like a long shot in a movie suddenly turning into a close-up and the scene expands in your face.

The Moment of the Crash

You are two or three metres from the target. You can see clearly the muzzles of the enemy's guns.

You feel that you are suddenly floating in the air. At that moment, you see your mother's face. She is not smiling or crying. It is her usual face.

PAGE 40:

All the Happy Memories

You won't precisely remember them but they are like a dream or a fantasy. You are relaxed and a smile creases your face. The sweet atmosphere of your boyhood days returns.

You view all that you experienced in your 20-odd years of life in rapid succession. But these things are not very clear.

In any event, only delightful memories come back to you.

You cannot see your own face at that moment. But because of a succession of pleasant memories flashing through your mind, you feel that you smiled at the last moment.

You may nod then, or wonder what happened. You may even hear a final sound like the breaking of crystal.

Then you are no more. [Emphasis added]

PAGE 43:

Points to Remember When Making Your Last Dive

Crashing bodily into a target is not easy. It causes the enemy great damage. Therefore the enemy will exert every means to avoid a hit.

Suddenly you may become confused. You are liable to make an error. But hold onto the unshakeable conviction to the last moment that you will sink the enemy ship.

Remember when diving into the enemy to shout at the top of your lungs: '*Hissatsu!*' ['Sink without fail!']

At that moment, all the cherry blossoms at Yasukuni Shrine in Tokyo will smile brightly at you.

PAGE 44:

How to Carry Out Your Last Sortie

The last assault should be carried out in the following manner: in commencing it, observe carefully the positions of the other friendly planes and the movement of the targets. Don't let the enemy ships outwit you.

Your target may evade you. But always remain calm. Try again. Don't give up trying.

When attacking enemy vessels that are moored, observe their positions and the terrain around them well.

Mind the enemy's smokescreens.

Observe anti-aircraft positions.

PAGE 48:

Types of US Planes and Performances

[The manual gives maximum speed and range for each type, their bomb loads, armament, and maximum height each plane is able to climb. There is no mention about which types excel in manoeuvring or are inferior.]

PAGE 78:

Diagram: Sunshine and Moonshine
[The diagram deals with times for sunrise/moonrise and sunset/moonset.]

PAGE 87:

How to Fly Through the Enemy's Radar Screen
When you lower your altitude to within the 'dead angle' of the enemy's radar, you must confuse the enemy detection system. It is possible to conceal your approach. [Charts are provided on recommended altitude changes.]

Here are the main entries in the *Table of Contents*:

The Mission of a To-Go Unit
How to Decide on the Method of the Last Dive
Principles Everyone Should Know
Commencing the Attack
Ultra-Low Altitude Attack
The Best Place to Crash Into a Ship
Types of American Planes (Identification)
. . . and Their Performances
Taking Advantage of Clouds
Sunshine and Moonshine
How to Fly Through the Enemy's Radar Screen

NOTE

[1] The extraordinary manual in its entirety has not been published in the West and has received little or no mention in the literature on the Pacific War.

7

A GENERAL WHO LOVED BRAHMS

In November 1944 during sporadic pauses in the Philippine fighting, Lieutenant General Kyoji Tominaga, commander of the Fifth Air Army, was fond of a turn at the piano in the Lassalle University auditorium, playing the melodies of Brahms, Chopin and Tchaikovsky. Brahms was his favourite composer. A Kamikaze pilot, who was a graduate of a Tokyo music school, sometimes accompanied the general in a piano duet. The young man was awaiting his orders for a final sortie. The general had begun to play the piano when he was admitted to the Army Military Preparatory School in Kumamoto, on Kyushu, at the age of 13. At that time his classmates nicknamed him 'Monsieur' because he impressed them as being richly cultured. Before the general quit the Philippines in January, he had waved off more than 700 suicide pilots who hoped, vainly it turned out, they could do enough harm to a powerful American invasion fleet to cause it to abort its mission. At that time the headquarters of the Fifth Air Army was located on the Lassalle University campus in Manila.

General Tominaga, the son of a medical doctor, who was also head of all Army Air Forces in the Philippines, had had no experience in aviation before being appointed to his Philippine post, his first front-line duty in his long career. But in this position he often inspired the men of his Special Attack units, adding to his words just the right dash to encourage them. Before his flyers took off for the last time, he would

address them in a filial manner, often saying, 'I will not let you go alone!'
And: 'I shall board the last plane and shall [also] smash into an enemy
ship!' But he used these rousing words to boost morale. Looking back
more than half a century, pilot Hichiro Naemura holds the opinion
that Tominaga was a person who was 'inordinately vain' and was flam-
boyant at times. He says that when Kamikaze pilots were sallying forth
from the Philippines, the general would unsheathe his samurai sword
and brandish it as the planes took off, while the others waved their
hands. Such a gesture as the waving of a sword would have been considered in poor taste by many. In any case, many top-ranking officers,
including generals and admirals, seeing Kamikaze pilots off on their one-
way missions, were often seized by involuntary emotion, often finding
its expression in bombast and vigorous gestures.

Tominaga survived the war, although his luck turned sour when in
his last weeks in the Philippines he contracted a wasting, febrile disease;
and, seven months later, when he had a new assignment to command
a division in Manchuria, he was taken prisoner by the Russians. (After
his capture, the Russians accused him of being a spy and gave him a
harsh 75-year sentence. Many years earlier Tominaga had been an intelligence officer in China and was fluent in the Russian language. He
had served as a military attaché at the Japanese Embassy in Moscow.
He was released ten years after the war, two years after Stalin's death.)

Tominaga had risen to Vice War Minister in March 1943 and in
late 1944 was appointed Commander-in-Chief of the Fourth Air Army
in the Philippines in preparation for what was to be 'the decisive
battle' in that country against an American-led invasion force. While
serving in the Philippines, a total of 62 suicide operations were conducted under his command in which more than 400 planes were hurled
against American naval vessels.

The following incident reveals the general's style.

It is 5 a.m. on November 12, 1944 and a large group of Kamikaze
flyers and support personnel have assembled on a Philippine airfield to
hear a final message from General Tominaga, who heads the Army Air
Forces in that country. All the men are standing respectfully at attention. The order for the pilots, members of the Banda Unit of the Special
Attack Corps, to engage an American task force has come. Dozens of
planes stand in the centre of the field. The grass is still wet with dew
and countless stars continue to flicker in the early morning Philippine
sky. The pilots are out to avenge the death of their Army and Navy
comrades who have recently perished in fierce encounters with the
Americans. At the air base, ground crews have worked all night on the
planes to ready them for this day's action.

Everything is now ready for the start of the mission. The pilots are full of macho talk: they wish 'to smash the enemy vessels' by suicide-dives onto their decks. Tominaga begins to address the men:

You are soldiers of His Majesty the Emperor, unequalled in loyalty and bravery. You are members of the Banda Unit, about to display the spirit of Japan, the Land of gods, and the righteousness of Japan, and thereby become cherry flowers in full bloom after which your unit was named.

You are about to lay down your lives for His Majesty the Emperor.

A man's life is lighter than a feather, and the mission with which you are charged – of destroying the enemy vessels – is heavier than Mount Fuji.

Sometime ago you lost your superior officer whom you loved and respected. Do not suffer yourselves to be discouraged but endeavour to do also his share, who is no more, so that you may be completely successful in your task. I wish you success from the bottom of my heart.

Then the general, his speech finished, takes a brush in hand and, on pieces of white silk cloth, writes a poem, dedicating it to the boyish flyers who are soon to take off on their 'body-crashing' mission. Tominaga entitles the poem 'To the god Troops of the Banda Unit'. Each pilot is presented with a copy of the poem. Here is the poem, in free translation:

> The spirit of the Land of Gods
> Is seen in the cherry blossoms in full bloom.
> Glorious are the figures of our officers and men.
> A man's life is light,
> And a great mission is heavy.
> But our men are not afraid of death.
> They do not die in vain.

After this is done, cups of sake are handed out and the general and his men drain the libations of rice wine that are offered to the success of the pilots.

Now the engines roar and the wings of the planes vibrate. Final instructions are given by a staff officer to the squadron leader and his aides. In their arms the pilots carry the urns containing the relics of a certain Captain Iwamoto and four other pilots who perished in earlier engagements.

The staff officer informs the men:

'Your objective is the aircraft carriers and battleships of the enemy lying within Leyte Gulf. Do not aim at small-sized vessels with the idea that you must do something now that you have gone into action.'

The officer explains why some other planes are going along on the mission.

'A certain number of fighters will accompany you, partly to protect you and partly to know for certain your war results. I wish you every success.'

Now the men proceed to a corner of the airfield where others await them to give them a final rousing send-off. Sake cups are once again passed around. Then Sergeant-Major Itsuo Tanaka turns to his men with the instruction: 'Remember to avenge the death of our unit commander.'

With the urns carefully carried in one arm, the men climb into their planes. The sergeant-major is already settled in his plane when a fellow pilot runs up to him and hands him a photo of their late commander.

'Be sure to come immediately behind me,' he shouts as he accepts the photo. The sergeant-major was previously wounded in the head as a result of an explosion and the appearance of his face under white bandages touches all of the men.

Presently, the planes begin to take off. Tanaka is first to go. He is immediately followed by three other planes. The members of the ground crew, with various emotions, wave their caps to the four pilots as they fly off on their last mission across the morning sky.

On November 14th the Japanese Imperial Headquarters announced that the Banda Air Unit, sighting an enemy convoy entering the Gulf of Leyte, sank one battleship and one transport on November 12th, in 'death-defying ramming actions'. The US 'scorecard' is at variance with the Japanese. It says that two repair ships were damaged.

In a meeting with the press a few days before the sortie, Tominaga declared that the entire Air Corps of the Imperial Japanese Forces are *hisshitai* ('certain-to-die squadrons') and that when they sally forth to meet the enemy none of the men expect to return alive. But the general denied that he ever ordered the pilots to participate in Kamikaze attacks. All the pilots had volunteered, he insisted. 'I have never given commands for self-ramming against the enemy to the Army air units. But the men are prepared in their hearts to self-ram without my orders and are carrying out this action.'

The general concluded by saying, 'The authorities at home are well aware of the vital significance of decisive aerial battles in the

Philippines and have sent us aircraft constructed by almost super-human efforts. For this I am deeply moved and grateful.' But Japanese losses steadily mounted in December and January as the Americans poured in more men and equipment.

Tominaga remained in Manila until the third week of January 1945. At that time Japan's Army and Navy air forces in the Philippines were practically depleted and Kamikaze strikes had ceased. It was at this juncture, with the American-led invasion force steadily advancing in the Philippines, that Tominaga suddenly quit the Philippines, flying out to Taiwan. His departure remains to this day a maze of controversy. There are even diabolical rumours that the general 'deserted' his post. (Incidentally, Admiral Onishi, who commanded the First Air Fleet in the Philippines, was also accused by many of abandoning his men in the Philippines when he moved to Taiwan at the order of the High Command. But the difference is that Tominaga left for Taiwan without explicit orders.)

Ten years after the war, Tominaga wrote a 20-page statement entitled 'To My Beloved Son, Shigeru: The Truth About My Retreat From the Philippines'. The statement is dated August 13, 1955. The general wrote it at his residence in Tamagawa Kaminoge in Tokyo. What follows are pertinent excerpts:

> I arrived in the Philippines in September 1944 as the Commander-in-Chief of the Fourth Air Army after serving as Vice War Minister. I apologize to you for bringing about public criticism and shame upon the family over my conduct when I retreated from the Philippines in January 1945. Immediately after my return from harsh imprisonment [in Siberia] to Japan in April 1955, I heard of the denunciations made against me and I thought I should make public the truth. However, I thought such an action would have been misinterpreted as a dishonourable attempt at exculpation so, at the same time, I recoiled from mentioning the names of others who could be hurt. I decided to remain silent and bear the infamy . . .
>
> Let me describe the developments in those critical days in the early part of December 1944:
>
> (1) The 14th Field Army in the Philippines abandoned its initial strategy of fighting a decisive battle against the enemy and adopted a 'perseverance and self-sustenance' strategy as it was then called.

(2) Despite the Imperial High Command's order to conduct decisive air battles over the Philippines, the Southern Army Group Saigon instructed me to begin preparations to extract the Second Air Division, which formed the mainstay of the Fourth Air Army, to be moved out of the Philippines.

(3) The Southern Army Group continued to interfere in small details of my command which were so irritating and troubling to my mind. The presence and departures of heroic Special Attack flyers was mentally gruelling and deprived me of sleep. Consequently, I contracted a febrile disease. I submitted my resignation to Field Marshal [Count Hisaichi] Terauchi, C-in-C of the Southern Army Group on account of failure to exert energetic command because of illness at the most critical moment. However, the Southern Army Group Headquarters dispatched an air staff officer to my bedside and pleaded with me not to resign. I had no choice but to continue at my position.

Lying in bed I began planning how to defend Manila to the last man, but later the plan was altered. At that time I began to feel that I should not let my staff officers die in vain, but that at an appropriate moment evacuate them to a safe location and utilize their abilities for coming battles. I was evacuated from Manila on January 7 and arrived at Echague [250 kilometres north of Manila] on January 10. I was still bedridden. I continued to nurse the thought about evacuation of my staff officers. There was a statement in the operational order issued by the Southern Army Group that the Fourth Air Army could make use of the bases in the southern part of Taiwan for its operations. As the strength of the Fourth Air Army had dwindled, I knew that there was a prevailing mood at my headquarters that it should be moved to Taiwan. However, as the Commander I had not taken any position on the matter. I felt that the attrition of our strength alone did not justify retreating to Taiwan. There obviously was a question of morale in taking such a course. I do not clearly remember the exact date now, but it was either a day before I left the Philippines or on January 20, two days before my departure when I was taking a bath in a makeshift drum can – I was feeling better that day – when my Chief of Staff, Major-General Masami Kumabe, came to my side looking somewhat flurried.

General Kumabe said to me: 'We just received an urgent communication from Tokyo. The Fourth Air Army is now placed under the command of the Taiwan Army. The Taiwan Army will be directing air operations from the estuary of the Yangtze to the

Philippines through Taiwan. Taking into consideration your state of health, I urge you to proceed to Taipei immediately for operational consultations.'

In short, the general conveyed to me (1) a cable pertaining to an important change in my responsibility, and (2) advancing his opinion as Chief of Staff in regard to an action to be taken by the Commander. Here was the birth of an error. I did not realize at that time that the basic change in my Air Army's operational responsibilities as told to me [in the cable] by General Kumabe was, alas, false. On January 22, I landed at Taipei on a reconnaissance plane piloted by Warrant Officer Mitsuo Naito, who had nursed me and looked after me at the headquarters after I became bedridden, and immediately went to meet with General Ando, commander of the Taiwan Army. General Ando looked surprised at how wizened I looked. It did not take long to sense that General Ando was not anticipating my arrival for operational consultations. Usually a meeting like this would start by General Ando offering a greeting like, 'It was good of you to have come so quickly. Thank you,' but he appeared baffled. I became anxious and asked, 'Did you receive a cable from the High Command about the change in my operational responsibilities?' He responded, 'What are you talking about! There is no such cable in existence.' I was stunned.

Tominaga's hand-written statement continues:

I recalled that when I departed from the Echague airfield, General Kumabe said to me, in a formal tone of voice, 'I shall wait for an order from you when I should leave the Philippines' and felt a strange sensation as if I was presented with a riddle. But I had not even dreamed of what actually took place. Later, I confronted General Kumabe and he said, 'The truth was I had read in such haste a cable sent by Field Army Commander General Yamashita to the High Command recommending in what manner the Fourth Air Army should be utilized that I mistook it as an order coming from the High Command. What I reported to you was based on an error.'

Often the C-in-C of the Field Army would cable copies of their communications with the High Command to the C-in-C of the Fourth Air Army under his command. But I doubt very much that the Chief of Staff of an Army could make such a flagrant error, mistaking a copy of a message sent to Tokyo as an order coming from there. But before criticizing General Kumabe or castigating his duplicity, I must reproach myself for my rashness. I was the one who failed. I myself should have read such an important cable carefully despite the state of my health, and formally rendered my signature.

General Kumabe in November 1944 replaced General Seiichi Terada as my Chief of Staff. I knew General Kumabe as he had once served with me in the same regiment. But General Kumabe showed no enthusiasm in preparing the defence of Manila. He would simply come to my bedside to report in a deceptive manner that 'all preparations are progressing as planned' to his Commander who was anxious to see their progress . . .

It was my grievous error, helped by my illness, to have believed such an untrustworthy man, taking his verbal report about such an important message. It was the gravest mistake I made during my career with the Army. Needless to say I must assume the blame but I cannot conceal my indignation towards the Chief of Staff . . .

I acted following the recommendation put forward by the Chief of Staff, but I did not blindly succumb to the Chief of Staff's opinion. Although I was at that moment suffering from an extreme case of nervous prostration, I carefully deliberated alone on the question and came to my decision.

The question arises: Were Kamikaze generals (and admirals), who constantly waved off pilots to certain death, under greater emotional stress than other officers in combat situations? In any case, Tominaga also had a physical ailment at the time. In an earlier chapter (Sex, Marriage and Morale), there is mention of counselling services for Kamikaze pilots. Apparently, there were many cases of junior officers who suffered nervous breakdowns, and many suicide pilots were subjected to counselling.
Tominaga adds:

The atmosphere at our [Philippine] headquarters was grim. We almost dissipated our air strength while airfield battalions and other ground units were transferred to the 14th Field Army. Consequently there was very little significance for the Fourth Air Army headquarters to remain in the Philippines. There arose voices that headquarters should be moved to southern Taiwan and begin rebuilding our strength. . . . There was some talk that the Commander-in-Chief should not lead a retreat from a dangerous front, while at the same time I had to consider the anxieties tormenting the staff officers. I came to the conclusion that in order to save my men I must take a bold decision to lead them out of their quandary. I took the decision alone, without asking anyone's opinion but after difficult deliberation, and at the risk of public criticism.

One could say it was either a compassionate act or a pathetic decision. . . . Now that I am in good health, reflecting on my deed calmly, although cowardice played no part at all in my leaving the Philippines, it is clear that I made an inappropriate decision. Assuming that the operational responsibilities were changed, I should have let the staff officers go first to Taiwan, even though they insisted that I should leave first. I should have followed them later.

A war correspondent for the *Mainichi Shimbun*, Takashi Muramatsu, was at the airfield in northern Luzon when General Tominaga took off in a two-seater reconnaissance plane for Taiwan. The airfield was located in a jungle about six kilometres from the small town of Echague. Muramatsu, who was waiting for a plane that would take him back to Tokyo, later recalled:

I saw several cars appear through the early morning fog. As I watched intently, General Tominaga, his Chief of Staff and other staff officers alighted. The general recognized our group of war correspondents and came over to us. He said he had orders to leave for Taiwan. He mumbled something about his leaving before us but hoped he would meet up with us again. The general looked wizened with bandages around his neck. A Shinshitei, the newest and fastest reconnaissance plane at the time, was being readied for the general. He tried to climb into the cockpit but was too weak to do so. One of the staff officers pushed him up into the cockpit. The plane began taxiing but the airstrip was too soft from the rain that had fallen earlier and so was not able to take off.

Thereupon, staff officers found a Guntei, an old and slow-flying reconnaissance plane with fixed landing gear, and dragged it out of the jungle. They carried the general into the cockpit. All this took time and we were worried that enemy planes might appear at any time. I questioned myself as to why they had to evacuate the general, taking so much risk. The answer to the questions surrounding General Tominaga, I believe, could be found in the suspicion I felt towards the staff officers then. I sensed that they had to send the general off by all means even at the risk of having him shot down, flying in a slow plane, by the enemy. Otherwise, the staff officers could not themselves be evacuated to safety. If there had been a formal order from the High Command, the evacuation of the commanding general would have been conducted in a more orderly manner. In that case, staff officers would have accompanied the general. But there was no need to send off the general like a fugitive.

Six months after Tominaga left the Philippines for Taiwan, he received a new appointment, as commander of the 139th Division, headquartered near the Manchu-Soviet border. The division was hastily formed in July 1945 out of older men recruited from Japanese residents in the area. In August, after Russia entered the war, Tominaga was taken prisoner, accused of spying, and held for ten years.

General Kumabe, who is mentioned as a contributor to Tominaga's difficulties, committed suicide after the war.

8

TWO SURVIVORS

THE MORTALITY OF PILOTS

Takeo Tagata, an Army warrant officer, was stationed at Taiwan's Taichung air base when General Tominaga landed there from the Philippines. Tagata, an experienced pilot and Kamikaze instructor, says that he remembers hearing rumours that a high-ranking officer had recently arrived in Taiwan, having allegedly 'deserted his men'. Tagata also heard from the rumour mill that the base commander at Taichung refused to meet the surprise visitor on the grounds that he had 'disgraced the Army'. But the fact is, Tominaga received no official censure, although he was removed from the active list, temporarily as it turned out. As in many such controversial cases, speculation is rife. In Tominaga's case there was speculation that the reason no judicial action was taken against him was that it might adversely affect troop morale.

Takeo Tagata was among those seasoned pilots who, after crash-dive tactics were adopted as a 'tragic necessity' in the latter part of the war, were selected to be Kamikaze instructors. Before his selection (his first duty as instructor was on Taiwan) he had acquired fighting experience in Burma and China, logging a total of 200 combat missions in China.

Although he often had a brush with death, Tagata survived the war and, in the year 2001 (he was then a spry 85 years old), during a homecoming visit to his birthplace on Kyushu accompanied by the authors of this book, he had this to say about his life as a pilot: 'Flying was full of hazards even without a war. As fighter pilot trainees, the men performed difficult manoeuvres and because of this the rate of fatal accidents was high. But due to the hazards inherent in flying, especially in those war years, the pilots had less fear of death than other service people.' Tagata said that before the war there was, like clockwork, a pilot's funeral almost every month at every air base to which he was assigned.

The future instructor of Kamikaze pilots had his first taste of aerial warfare on September 20, 1937, over Baoding, some 150 kilometres south-east of Beijing. For this mission, Tagata flew in a formation of three Type 95 fighters, each carrying two 250-kilogram bombs. The pilots took off from an airfield in the southern outskirts of Beijing and reached the battle site in 30 minutes when they saw a convoy of about 30 trucks carrying Chinese troops. One of the three Japanese aircraft remained at 3,000 metres in order to give air cover, while Tagata and the other plane swooped down. Tagata descended to 100 metres above ground and then released his bombs in quick succession. The first bomb missed its target and exploded on an agricultural field but the second bomb hit a truck which exploded. No enemy planes were sighted throughout the mission.

'Afterwards,' says Tagata, 'I realized I was terribly nervous from beginning to end.'

At this time Tagata was a lithe, 21-year-old, spit-and-polish bachelor sergeant in the Army Air Force who was already regarded as an excellent pilot. Tagata's first experience in a dogfight occurred exactly a month later, also in China, on October 20, 1937:

With Captain Nishikawa in command, I took off in a formation of three fighters escorting six light bombers on a mission to bomb an enemy air base in Taiyuan. We flew a distance of about 200 kilometres. As we reached the enemy airfield, flak from more than 30 anti-aircraft guns greeted us. Our bombers attacked the airfield and the Taiyuan railroad station. Suddenly three Russian-built Ilyushin-15 fighters rose and challenged us. We fighter planes headed straight for the enemy. At the sight of the approaching enemy planes, I became very nervous. I felt as if all the strength was leaving my body. I was probably shaking. I tried to breathe deeply, repeating the exercise three times. This made me feel better. I opened fire at an enemy fighter but did not score a hit. So did my two fellow fighters. The enemy planes turned back, swooping down to evade us. Captain Nishikawa ordered us not to pursue them as our primary mission was to protect our bombers.

This was my first experience in firing at an enemy plane and in being fired at from the ground.

Tagata had mixed impressions of China. He was taken aback by widespread corruption and ennui. Coming from Japan, where loyalty to the flag was taken for granted, he found disconcerting the absence of strong patriotic feeling among local people. Nevertheless, he sized up the Chinese people as hard-working and good-tempered, who in the main hated fighting and brawling. As for politics in China, the image he formed of Chiang Kai-shek, the head of the Nationalist (or Kuomintang) Party, was that of a leader removed from his people and open to foreign bribes. As to Chiang's adversary, the peripatetic Communists, led by Mao Zedong, they were in his view under the thumb of Moscow. Tagata couldn't help noting to his surprise that the masses of China seemed to fear more the excesses of their own soldiers and officers than that of the foreign armies bivouacked on Chinese soil.

For Tagata, China was an endless bog – a mass of muddy roads which resembled thick swamps. He searched for an answer to a question that had often puzzled him: why was China so different from Japan? And he came up with this answer: 'The Chinese thinking is: "Why do you need an automobile when a bicycle or rickshaw will do?"' China had adopted a culture that was very different from Japan's; the Chinese placed their family or clan above the public interest, whereas the Japanese were taught to put the public interest over the private, including that of the family. Tagata concluded that the Chinese attitude was a result of imbibing Confucianism unalloyed. On the other hand, Confucianism, which had come to Japan many centuries earlier through Korea, had been kneaded and amended to fit Japanese needs.

Five years passed before Tagata scored his first 'kill' – against British planes. This occurred on March 28, 1942 over Burma. Previously, he had flown many such missions over Burma and China, engaging enemy planes including Spitfires, Hawker Hurricanes and Tomahawks. On that day he took off in a small formation of newer, Type 97 fighters, led by Second Lieutenant Nagoshi from Maubi Air Base. Tagata had by this time been promoted to Warrant Officer. Their mission was to fly at an altitude of 3,500 metres to protect Maubi and Migaradon Air Bases. On that day clouds covered the sky at 4,000 metres.

Tagata, with the 'eyes of an eagle' (he tested 2.5 or the highest on the Japanese scale), spotted enemy planes approaching at a distance of some 20 kilometres:

I immediately informed Lieutenant Nagoshi and Master Sergeant Akamatsu who had not yet seen the enemy formation. I increased my speed and headed in the direction of the foe, followed by my pilots.

Soon nine British Blenheim bombers were clearly recognized. They were also flying at an altitude of 3,500 metres. Due to the thick clouds around us, the Japanese planes were unable to climb immediately. But they did manage to climb a little bit and headed for the enemy bombers. Now they saw clearly the red and blue circles on the approaching British planes.

At Lieutenant Nagoshi's order, we started firing our cannon at a distance of about 200 metres at the second bomber flying at the edge of the formation. The rotating turrets of the British planes were shooting at us. All 18 guns. I kept on firing until I saw the faces of the enemy crews, at about a dozen metres, who were diving at a steep angle at maximum speed. (About 480 kilometres per hour.)

I knew I had scored some hits.

He now made a sharp turn and climbed back up once again to engage the enemy. From the wing of one Blenheim there gushed a white stream of gasoline. The aircraft, which was quickly losing altitude, fled in the direction of India.

'Meanwhile, I saw Lieutenant Nagoshi's plane dive steeply towards our base, violently banking his wings,' Tagata says.

'I'm hit,' Tagata heard him say over the radio.

Hearing this, he took command of the formation. Sergeant Akamatsu was right behind him. Tagata raised his fist to express fighting spirit. Now over the radio he heard a voice say: 'Warrant Officer Tagata has scored a kill!' They could see an enemy bomber aflame, plummeting downward. Tagata continues:

Looking around I saw three additional Type 97 fighters climb through the thick anti-aircraft fire thrown up by our bases. At this moment I scored another hit on a Blenheim which instantly burst into flames. The remaining seven Blenheims dropped their bombs over our Mingaradon Air Base. Columns of fire rose from the airfield. I could see a number of our planes explode on the ground. Some fuel tanks burned fiercely.

Actually, our Type 97 fighters were slower than the Blenheims and so, while flying at full throttle, I prayed that we would receive deliveries of the new and faster Hayabusa (Peregrine Falcon) fighters as soon as possible. With our three additional fighters in the air, led by my classmate from the Tachiarai Flying School – he was named Takada – we chased after the enemy formation for five minutes and caught up with them. We were then flying some 500 metres above the formation.

I began my dive followed by Akamatsu. Within seconds we scored another hit: a Blenheim went down belching a column of black smoke.

About ten minutes had passed since I first spotted our foes. We were now about 20 kilometres from our base. We still wanted to engage the remaining Blenheims but we gave up and returned to base, leaving the rest of the enemy bombers to my classmate's unit.

After Tagata landed, he learned that Lieutenant Nagoshi had crash-landed his plane at the base. In attempting to land his damaged plane it had rolled over. Nagoshi had taken many bullet wounds and died shortly after being pulled from the wreckage.

On June 16, 1943 Prime Minister Hideki Tojo told the Japanese Diet, or Parliament, that the war situation had reached a critical stage. Shortly afterwards, Tagata took up his new duties as fighter pilot at Taichung Air Base in central Taiwan. Previously he had been stationed at various bases on Japan's home islands. During the year that Tagata served on Taiwan he often flew night missions to intercept American planes (mainly P-38s) which attacked Kaohsiung, Pingtung and Tainan. On the days he wasn't involved in night missions, Tagata, as one of his unit's most experienced pilots, gave flying lessons to 'green' Kamikaze pilots. But as an instructor on Taiwan in late 1944, he did not train his students to attack enemy vessels:[1]

I had no experience in attacking ships [he says candidly]. The beginner flyers, including those fresh from college, had only about 100 flying hours each. They were given a basic six-month course in flying at the Army's aviation schools before being sent to me for my four-month training course. Also, these new pilots only had experience flying training planes. I had to teach them how to fly fighters; in this case, Type 97 fighters. It took time to teach the pilots the basic techniques in handling these planes.

Tagata described the instructions he gave to his pilots:

I taught three categories of aerial combat. First, fighting enemy fighters. Second, fighting enemy bombers. This was vital because *tokko* [or 'special attack'] included ramming enemy bombers – mainly B-29s. Third, was strafing ground targets.

You had to sweep down low to attack an ocean-going target. I taught pilots how to dive steeply. Students were given instructions in attacking ships, or crashing into ships, after joining combat units upon finishing my course. For four months, a student would fly on average 40 minutes a day. First I would demonstrate to the students each technique, flying in their presence as they watched from the ground. When I was face to face with the students I could tell that they were in awe at some of the difficult manoeuvres I performed.

Most importantly, I taught them to remain calm under all circumstances, taking utmost care so as never to lose their nerve when in the air. A pilot must be agile and flexible in manoeuvring a plane. I spent a considerable time pumping into them a fierce fighting spirit and a sense of mission or duty. At the same time it was also part of my job to ingrain pride and patriotism into each pilot.

My students were already convinced that the outcome of the war was to be decided by air forces; they understood that victory or defeat rested on their shoulders. Their morale was high; much higher, I would say, than when I was training at the Army Flying School in Tachiarai before the China Incident. This change reflected the perilous situation in which the nation found itself. Naturally, I admired these students. Their eyes were always glittering like acolytes at the simple joy of living during their nation's decisive hour in history. They felt they were going to play an important role in the war.

So, the training was hard and the students stood it uncomplainingly. They need a full eight hours of sleep to recover from the fatigue of the day's training. Many of the students had excellent aptitudes as pilots and I lamented the fact that they would be thrown into battle before they could acquire higher skills, or were ready to engage the enemy.

But this was war. Anyhow, I exerted my best to prepare them for combat. Their lives must not be wasted lightly.

Tagata said his Kamikaze students used a simulated aircraft in their training. Then a number of biplanes were flown in for the use of his students. There were 50 students and Tagata was the head teacher. (Tagata recalls that there was a marked contrast between Kamikaze flyers and the pilots of escort fighters on the night before a final sortie. The Special Attack [suicide] flyers appeared to have attained peace of mind while many of the escort fighter pilots were nervous and irritable and behaved rambunctiously.)

As Tagata was standing one morning beneath a tent for flyers at the Taichung Air Base (it was early morning of October 12, 1944), a stream of ominous reports kept arriving at the tent from radar stations in the south. Shortly before the Kamikaze flights were inaugurated, Taiwan was being exposed to repeated air raids by US carrier-based planes. Taichung was yet to be hit by the raids. But now about 40 American fighters were reported coming up from the south over the waters at 4,000 metres altitude. Tagata had a hunch that they were headed towards Chiai and Taichung, the former on the island's west coast.

Tagata then belonged to the Army's Eighth Air Division that was responsible for the air defence of Taiwan. At that time the Eighth Air Division had 110 combat planes and about 300 training planes. Out of the combat planes, there were 95 fighters, but 20 of them were obsolete planes. Seventy-five were state-of-the-art. The division had over 500 pilots but only 30 of them had more than five years of experience as pilots. Tagata had been flying for nine years and had logged more than 4,000 hours as a pilot. Tagata now shouted an order:

'Sergeant Matobara! Tell the orderly to bring us lunch. My guts tell me we will have to take off shortly. And when the next radar report comes we'll have to get our asses moving!'

Sergeant First Class Matobara was only 22 but he already had four years of flight time, logging 1,500 hours. I had known him for a year and a half. I knew he was a capable fighter pilot but he was yet to score a kill.

'Let's ask the orderly to bring us a quick lunch,' Tagata said.

'Yes, sir!' Matobara gave a broad smile. 'That's an excellent idea!'

There were only two Type 3 Hien fighter planes at our base. The rest of the fighters had previously gone into combat. The Hien, incidentally, was codenamed 'Tony' by the Americans. Ten minutes later another radar report was delivered. It said: 'The enemy formation is flying past Peitung and is continuing to head north.'

So my intuition was right. They would reach Kiai in 15 minutes, and Taichung in 25 minutes.

'It's going to be two against forty. So it'll be a long battle. Eat well. But don't stuff yourself!' I told Matobara.

'Mr Tagata,' he replied, smiling. 'Don't worry! We'll enjoy a feast of forty enemy planes!'

Each of us ate five rice balls and a dessert of bananas. As we were smoking a last cigarette, I was ordered to report to the command post. I hurried there. At the post, General Hoshi, the C-in-C of our Air Corps, and Major Kobayashi, our Wing Commander, both looked tense.

'Warrant Officer Tagata, reporting, sir!' I barked.

'Warrant Officer Tagata, you will lead an accompanying fighter to intercept forty enemy planes which are proceeding northward,' the major ordered.

I shouted my compliance with the order.

'Exert your best . . . And take care!' said Kobayashi.

'I shall do my utmost, sir!'

We still had ten minutes to go before takeoff when I returned to our tent.

'I received our flight orders,' I told Matobara. 'Are you well prepared? Let's give them hell!'

Matobara laughed heartily.

'We'll scare the Yanks, sir! Poor boys! They'll all shit in their pants!'

This was going to be the first dogfight for Matobara. Tagata told him to fly just as in a combat exercise.

'Although we are two against forty, don't be cowed,' Tagata continued with his advice. 'Do your best not to be shot down. My first order is to protect yourself. Shooting at the enemy comes second. Don't break formation. Stick with me every moment. Try to break up the enemy formation. Let's divide them. If I am shot down, disengage and flee.'

Tagata also told Matobara that upon sighting the enemy to fasten his seat belt and take three deep breaths. 'That will calm you down.'

'I went to the toilet and pissed. I then drank a glass of cold water. Water always tastes best before entering into a battle.'

Now Tagata and Matobara test-fired the cannons and gave the planes a final check. At 9.25 a.m. the propellers started spinning. General Hoshi and the ground crews lined up to send them off. Tagata took off followed by Matobara. When they reached 200 metres in height, they again tested their cannons. Each of their planes was equipped with two 20-millimetre cannons and two 12-millimetre machine-guns. The two pilots circled the base and bid farewell.

Tagata decided to ambush the enemy who were flying between Taichung, Kaiai and Pukang at an altitude of 4,000 metres. Light clouds were hanging at 6,000 metres above ground. Ten minutes after take-off they were cruising at 300 kilometres an hour along the coastline.

'Watch for the enemy sharply! Battle formation!' I yelled into the radio.

It was thirteen minutes after takeoff. Battle formation required the following plane to fly 30 metres behind the lead plane:

Now I saw a speck in the sky between Kuan Shan Mountain (height: 3,715 metres) and Kaiai. It was the enemy! I made a 15-degree turn and headed north-east. Ten seconds later I saw five specks. I consulted my watch. It was 9.40 a.m. 'Enemy sighted!' I screamed into the radio.

I banked the aircraft and opened the lid of the sighting tele-scope, meanwhile wiping the front windshield with my gloved hand. I also checked various gauges. Fastening my seat belt I took three deep breaths. Now I saw the enemies clearly – they were a bunch of Grummans, 36 of them flying at 4,500 metres north-west of Mount Kuan Shan, the highest peak on Taiwan. The enemy was now 15 kilometres from us. I jotted down the numbers: 9.41 – 36 planes.

I glanced at the rear-view mirror to see my face. I looked calm and managed a confidence-building smile.

Now I started to climb at 400 kilometres an hour while clos-ing on the enemies. They had not yet sighted us. Was it because we Japanese had better eyesight? Anyway, we were told that in general Americans had poor eyesight and many wore spectacles. They were now flying in formation, coming towards us at 250 kilometres an hour.

'Enemies sighted!' Matobara's excited voice came over the radio. 'Whew! So many of them! We'll have some fun, Mr Tagata!' He shouted and I could see him raise his fist in defiance.

Tagata had already had a good deal of experience as a fighter pilot, more than seven years. He continues:

The enemy spotted us when it was at a distance of about ten kilo-metres. The lead plane banked and I quickly noticed that the enemy formation was thrown into confusion. Probably they did not know that we were only two planes. Some of them swooped down while others rose steeply. Meanwhile, many it seemed tried to discover if there were more of us in the sky. But a moment later they resumed a tight-knit formation, then broke up in order to try and encircle us. The enemy's lead plane, followed by a group of eight Grummans, banked its wings violently in order to commence battle.

I decided to challenge the formation.

Fearlessly, three Grummans swooped down below us, to act as decoys and try to fool us, while the nine leading planes climbed and turned to the right. The second group of nine planes also climbed, making a left turn. The rest of the Grummans now climbed, making a right turn. The enemy was now close, less than two kilometres.

I decided to confuse them instead of trying to score the first kill. I felt I could have shot down the lead plane, but that would have placed both of us in danger. Rather, I opened full throttle, lowered the nose of my plane slightly, and increased speed from 500 kilometres an hour to 640 kilometres an hour, the Hien's maximum speed. I flew straight through the enemy formation and took them by surprise.

The distance to the Americans was now 800 metres. As they tried to readjust their positions, I attacked the second group of nine Grummans with my cannons from about 500 metres above them. Seconds later, Matobara attacked a plane from another group that was climbing from below and was about 30 metres from him. A salvo from his cannons sent a Grumman spinning towards the ground in flames. It was his first kill.

But Tagata was furious. He says: 'Instead of praising him for his first kill, I cursed him. He had neglected the other 35 planes. It was the most dangerous move in the battle against the enemy formation. The second formation of six Grummans rose from the left, firing at Matobara. I immediately came to the rescue.'

Tagata fired a series of salvos against the six Grummans:

Together with Matobara, we rose 1,000 metres higher than the Americans. I then lowered the nose of my Hien fighter. The Grummans, now climbing steeply after us, were caught in a panic. They scattered and descended in an effort to force us out of position. I went after the Americans' lead plane. It was making about 550 kilometres an hour. A second enemy plane bravely rose to protect the lead plane. I dodged him and kept climbing.

Tagata says the skill of the American pilots he was engaging would have been regarded as 'medium-class' in the Japanese Air Force. 'I felt,' he says, 'as if I was teaching air combat skills to the enemy.'

Now, nine more Grummans were rising, firing at Tagata and Matobara at a distance of about 300 metres:

> I executed a somersault and fired at the enemy's second plane from about 100 metres. Matobara sent a salvo into the third plane. The Grumman I shot at caught fire and fell, spinning, towards the ground. As the eight remaining Grummans scattered, we again climbed steeply. Now I found a prey in the last Grumman flying in a formation of six. I dived at 600 kilometres an hour and fired from about 80 metres distant. Shells hit the enemy's engine and petrol tank. My speed caused me almost to skim the burning US plane. It shot downwards like a comet.

Now Tagata took in the entire situation. There were 33 Grummans left:

> Out of them, 13 were not in a position to threaten us [he says]. The remaining 20 were coming at us from left and right, concentrating their fire on us. I headed for a formation of eight Grummans as they were closing on us, rattling their cannons. They were about 300 metres below us towards the right. I turned my nose right at them. They broke their formation and fled left and right. I thought it was almost a scene out of a training exercise for dogfights.

Now, another formation that was in front of the two Japanese pilots headed towards them from the left at a distance of about 600 metres:

> I dodged and started climbing so that I could attack from above. I increased my speed to 600 kilometres an hour. The Hien was 40 kilometres an hour faster than the Grummans and I used this advantage to the full. I flew at more than 620 kilometres an hour from time to time. I now made a sharp turn. Matobara was following me at a distance of 50 metres. Good chap! I raised my arm in a gesture of praise. He banked his wings to thank me.
> I caught the lead plane of the enemy formation at a distance of about 80 metres. There was a gush of gasoline from its left wing. It dived, trailing a white mist, then flew eastward. I had no time to ascertain what happened to that plane. Meantime, the Grummans changed their formations. They regrouped in seven formations of three, a formation of five, and another of six planes. They were trying to encircle us.

After 15 minutes from the commencement of the air battle, Tagata and Matobara had shot down 8 Grummans. In the next ten minutes Tagata scored two more kills. Altogether, the enemy lost 11 planes.

But Tagata's plane had received six hits including a direct hit on his fuel tank in the right wing. The tank had exploded, ripping the wing cover. Luckily the fuel tank was almost empty.

After being hit, Tagata plunged straight into an enemy formation, his cannons blazing. While his opponents quickly avoided him, he veered sharply to the right, turned off the fuel switch and glided towards the ground. He ditched in a rice paddy.

Miraculously the plane did not turn over but Tagata hit his head on the front panel and lost consciousness for a short while. He had received light injuries. Regaining his senses, he heard bullets whizzing past him, hitting the ground. He jumped from the cockpit and started running for cover. More than 20 Grummans swooped down on him, firing their cannons. He reached a stone wall and, panting violently, took his pistol from its holster and shot at the pursuing planes. The Grummans flew off.

Tagata then collapsed on the spot and slept for at least an hour. He was bleeding from the forehead. In his uneasy sleep he dreamt of his son, who was smiling at him. When he awoke he walked on a narrow footpath for about 15 minutes.

As he was walking he saw a water buffalo in the paddy. The buffalo lowed peacefully at him. Tagata mused: perhaps the animals were wiser than man; they do not slaughter or decimate each other. A few days later he saw another water buffalo and it occurred to him for the first time that the ancient custom of animal-worship made much sense. As an animist faith, the Shinto religion of Japan worships foxes and other indigenous animals. These animals are regarded as emissaries of the gods. In this vein, Tagata thought that man had something to learn even from mere animals; that animals could be 'mentors' to the human family.

Soon he reached a farmhouse and a Taiwanese family greeted him warmly. They treated his wound and put bandages on his head. Later he learned that Matobara had returned to the base unscathed.

While he was stationed on Taiwan, Tagata made up his mind to get married. As a pilot he had always prepared himself for death in the skies but he had also disciplined himself to avoid all thoughts of mortality. Choosing, therefore, to 'get on' with a normal life while being stationed on Taiwan, Tagata wrote a letter to his elder sister Shizue (she was four years his senior), stating his basic requirements for a bride. It was she who would find him a wife. Tagata's desires in a woman were straight-forward: he wanted a helpmate who should, however, as the wife of a serviceman, be mentally prepared for his sudden demise. He also wanted someone who would look after his parents well on his behalf. He made a special point of seeking a partner who combined kindness and congeniality. Such arranged marriages were common then.

A short time later, Tagata was ordered to fly to Tachiarai, on the Japanese island of Kyushu, to lead a group of ten pilots receiving Type 97 fighter planes to be used for training purposes on Taiwan. After spending a night at Tachiarai, which became a Kamikaze training base, Tagata boarded a train for Kuroki, his hometown not far from the centre of Kyushu. The journey lasted an hour and a half and it was then that he met his future wife, Teruyo, for the first time. He took an immediate liking to her.

Tagata married Teruyo, who was five years younger than he, in July 1943. He gave his betrothed a gold ring with a tiny diamond, which his mother had bought at her son's request. A wedding banquet was held at a Japanese restaurant, attended by some 50 members of the two families, in Kawasaki village, which borders Kuroki. Teruyo was from the nearby village of Hirokawa. For the wedding, Tagata wore his Army tunic while Teruyo was clad in a kimono. Teruyo's elder brother, an army sergeant who later died in the fighting on New Guinea, was present at the wedding. As there was no time for a marriage rite at a Shinto shrine, they skipped it. After the marriage banquet, the groom and bride took a taxi to Tagata's farmhouse where they spent their first night. The very next morning he had to return to his base.

Teruyo joined her husband on Taiwan the following month. She took a Japan Airlines flight and landed in Taipei (then known as Taihoku), where Tagata met her. Teruyo was clad in a traditional kimono. The Tagatas lived in a spacious five-room house provided by the Army and the pair spent many happy days together. Often he entertained his men at his home. He discovered that Teruyo was not exactly a talented cook but, anyhow, food was plentiful on Taiwan (unlike mainland Japan where there was a scarcity of food and drink) and the men enjoyed the local beer. Afterwards, when Tagata entertained his fellow pilots at their new home in Taiwan, Teruyo would drink beer with the guests but not Tagata, who was a teetotaller. Teruyo's hobby was knitting. At 27, Tagata was glad that he had finally married.

Teruyo spent ten months with her husband on Taiwan. In June 1944, after she became pregnant, Tagata sent her back to Kuroki on a transport ship. At first she strongly resisted Tagata's plea that she should return to Japan, but he told her frankly: 'You may have to go home carrying my ashes if you remain here much longer. You would certainly not enjoy such a trip. So please go.' In the event, there was danger for Teruyo on her voyage home as American submarines now lurked in the sea between Taiwan and Kyushu, taking their toll of Japanese shipping.

In the last months of war Tagata had various assignments in different parts of the home islands, flying reconnaissance planes and fighter aircraft. When the war ended and flying was not permitted under the American occupation of Japan, Tagata took up a new career as an organic farmer. He says the new toil was both creative and satisfying.

At a reunion in Tokyo during the first year of the new millennium, two of Tagata's former Special Attack students, Masao Iijima and Minoru Masuyama, recalled that it was 'a good day when Tagata would fly with them'. Both men were 18 years old when the war ended in 1945; Tagata was more than ten years older. They remembered Tagata's curt reactions ('Good!' and, sometimes, 'Excellent!') to their performance during flight lessons. After the war both Iijima and Masayama were captured by Chinese troops who arrived on Taiwan from mainland China. Since they were given no food as prisoners, the pair immediately set to work growing their own vegetables. On being repatriated to Japan, Iijima became an accountant and Masuyama an art teacher. Iijima recalled sadly that at war's end some of his fellow pilots committed suicide by putting a pistol inside their mouths. He had no inkling that one of his closest friends, a quiet 19-year-old, would do this on the day of Japan's surrender, a tragedy he still remembered. After the suicide, a high-ranking officer showed up at the barracks and confiscated all hand guns from those who knew about or had witnessed the shooting.

A PILOT WHO BECAME AN ENTREPRENEUR

While attending the prestigious Kansai University College in Osaka, Hichiro Naemura developed a love for gliders and became president of his flying club. In pre-war Japan many high school and university students joined flying clubs that would periodically arrange competitive races up and down the countryside. In those years, Japan had set out to become second to none in the world in air and naval power and, consequently, when these student flyers left school they were warmly welcomed by the armed forces, especially after the country went to war with the ABCD powers.[1]

All or nearly all of the students were imbued with patriotic fervour and, later, when Japan was obviously losing the war, they didn't hesitate to offer their lives in an effort to stave off defeat. They were sustained by the knowledge of posthumous glory, that after death those who took part in Kamikaze missions would be treated as 'godlike heroes' who gave their all for the benefit of the country. They would even be honoured with promotions, the fallen pilot jumping two ranks. But in addition to the honour, this was a consideration for the bereaved family, allowing it to draw an added pension payment. Another honour was deification at Tokyo's grand Yasukuni Shrine. When Kamikaze pilots before their last sortie said 'Let's meet at Yasukuni', it was more an expression of solidarity or comradeship rather than a firm belief. Very few Japanese actually believed they would meet at Yasukuni Shrine once they became gods.

As a student, Hichiro Naemura was fond of reading and travel in addition to flying. He was also interested in learning English and had enrolled in an English course. Ambitious and intellectually curious, he had as a student pilot travelled all over Japan, at first flying a First World War vintage biplane, but mostly a modern trainer aircraft provided by the *Asahi* newspaper. (Later, his university flying club acquired a modern trainer aircraft.) Politically aware, he had generally regarded America highly before the war broke out, preferring not to dwell on reports that Japanese immigrants faced discrimination in America. True, racial and religious prejudice was a blight, he felt, but he knew this was common to many countries. Two years before the war, Naemura had contributed a provocative essay to his college journal in which he said his great desire was to invite Australia to join the Asian family of nations since, geographically, Australia was a part of the Orient. He wanted, he said, to own a ranch there because of the wide open spaces of Australia. But there was another attraction connected to his love of flying. If he lived there, he daydreamed, in his spare time he would use a horse to pull a glider and in this way fly across the Australian desert. In 1998 Naemura visited Australia and flew a glider, executing somersaults and loop the loops to the applause of the crowd. He was then 77 years old. A video cassette shows the veteran flyer performing these aerobatics. 'My adolescent dream was fulfilled,' he said. Three years earlier Naemura flew to California to participate in an air show in Long Beach and told local reporters: 'Today my wife, Kazuko, who is with me, and I will share prayers and grieve for the *tokko* pilots. My former [Kamikaze] students who died in the war could have enjoyed flying for fun and sport if they had been living in peacetime.' He added, 'Today I will be flying with them.'

Not only was Naemura a devotee of flying but, like a number of his compatriots, he viewed air power as essential to a country's security. When in 1943 he graduated from his university Naemura was already an accomplished pilot and therefore he enrolled as a junior officer in the Army Air Force. When Japan's fortunes in the war began to ebb and Naemura heard about 'suicide tactics' and the formation of Army and Navy suicide squadrons, he was full of admiration for these selfless flyers. 'I envied them for their commitment to the people and the nation,' Naemura, who became a bomber pilot and was later an instructor of Kamikaze pilots, commented in the second year of the new millennium when he had reached the age of 81.

When war erupted with America, Naemura took the news calmly. 'I was then giving my full attention to flying and I believed that Japan would win the war,' he says. 'I did not expect the war to be a long, drawn-out, total kind of war.' In the two years preceding hostilities, goods were plentiful in Japan and Naemura spent much of his time flying gliders.

In April 1941 all of Japan was shocked when US General James Doolittle attacked Tokyo and other cities with a fleet of bombers that had taken off from an aircraft carrier a few hundred miles off the Japanese coast, the first American retaliatory strike after Pearl Harbor. Naemura says that in 1942 he had actually applauded the daring of Doolittle and his raiders when they made that first token bombing of the Japanese main island of Honshu. (Fourteen of the 16 crews survived the low-altitude bomb run, crash-landing in China and Russia.) Naemura recalls that he actually clapped his hands upon hearing the news, thinking it was 'quite a feat of airmanship'. But he adds: 'I also made a silent pledge to turn the tables and some day perform an equally bold mission against the California coast.' He was then a 22-year-old student flyer, and he admits that he regarded war as just a sporting game.[2]

But his respect for America fell, he said, when as an Army pilot he was sent to the Philippines and he saw American planes hit civilian targets, including his hospital. He had been ill with typhoid fever and spent two weeks in a local hospital. For the first time in the war he became bitter towards America.

Hichiro Naemura was born in 1920 as the last child of seven sons and one daughter. His father was a successful textile trader, his company being called the Naemura Knit Fabrics Inc. As a child he often climbed the hills of Ikoma and Rokko, looking down on the port city of Kobe and the sea. He would look up into the sky and envy the high-flying birds. Often, his father took him to the Army airfield in Joto, near Osaka, or to the Kizukawa civilian airfield. With awe the young Naemura saw airplanes taking off and landing. He remembers seeing, when he was eight years old, the German Zeppelin airship flying over Osaka. When he was in college, his father bought him a German Contax camera which was a real luxury item in those days and he loved taking snapshots of gliders and airplanes. The Naemuras then lived in the heart of Osaka and had two live-in maids.

As a college student, Naemura was an avid fan of Hollywood films. He remembers almost all of the Hollywood stars of that period. But he was also fond of American popular songs and he frequented a night club, the Akadama, in Dotonbori, a neon-light district in Osaka where American music was played. He loved dogs and owned two of them: an Akita named *Kuma* (Bear) and a pointer named *Hachi* (Eight).

But above everything else he enjoyed flying and he avidly read American aviation magazines from cover to cover. In college he became a national celebrity as a student flyer, covering 4,000 kilometres around Japan, piloting an Army Type 95 trainer. Accompanying him was an Osaka City College student who sat in the rear seat. The trainer, a small 450 horse power biplane, was a gift from the *Asahi* to the College Flying Club Association. In those days *Asahi* was linked to the Army, while the *Mainichi* newspaper was considered a 'Navy paper'.

Upon graduation Naemura entered the Army Air Force and had a short tour of duty in the Philippines before being reassigned to the Japanese mainland, to Shimoshizu Air Base that was housed in a bomber air wing. Here he taught Kamikaze pilots basic navigation techniques, especially how to fly over the ocean. He also taught the suicide volunteers dive-bombing skills. Suicide attacks, Naemura says were 'much similar to and really an extension of the art of dive-bombing or launching torpedoes at enemy ships'. He describes one aspect of his teaching technique:

A large cross made of two strips of white cloth was laid on the airfield and my students would use the cross as a target. A student would fly towards the cross at a sharp angle, dropping a mock bomb which contained lime. The pilot had to keep his wings balanced, so the plane would not list to right or left because otherwise the bomb would not fall straight down. We asked the student to descend to an altitude of 300 metres. But in pulling up the plane to that height, the plane would sink to about 150 metres above the ground before gaining altitude. If on a real mission you had a ship in your sights, your plane would sometimes almost brush its masts or funnel. In normal [that is, non-suicide] missions we taught the student that once the bomb was released, he should fly straight ahead while gently pulling his plane up. If he climbed too fast the plane would expose its belly and wings to enemy anti-aircraft fire and thus present a bigger target.

In December, 1944, when Naemura was back in Japan, he recalls that despite the misfortunes of war there were days when life seemed completely normal in Osaka despite occasional enemy bomber runs preceded by the wailing of air raid sirens. Naemura fondly remembers taking his mother to a wartime performance at the Osaka Kabuki Theatre. (He still keeps a souvenir programme dated December 10, 1944.) On that day, he recalls, his mother wore her favourite, most expensive silk kimono. Having a few days' leave, Naemura also enjoyed (without his mother's attendance) watching a dancing troupe of half-naked girls performing at the Osaka Grand Theatre.

Naemura was at Tachiarai Air Base in Kyushu on August 15, the day the war ended, his unit being billeted at farmhouses near the air base. All the members of his unit gathered outside one of the farmhouses to listen to the Emperor's broadcast on Japan's capitulation. A public address system had been set up.

'My reaction was, "Shit! We should not give up but fight on!" I thought we could still deliver severe punishment to the enemy in our defence of the homeland, even forcing America to negotiate for peace. I really thought we could cost America a million lives.'

Naemura witnessed for the first time the launch of a suicide unit at Choshi Air Base in Chiba Prefecture, near Tokyo, in November 1944. The pilots departed for the Philippines via Taiwan. A few months later he watched a Kamikaze unit as it sallied directly for the Okinawan seas from Bansei Air Base in Kyushu. Bansei was a small airfield close by a beach near Chiran, in the southern part of the island:

The airfield was still pitch dark except for the red and blue landing lights dotting the sides of the 1,000-metre air strip [Naemura said]. Eleven Special Attack planes, all Type 99 dive-bombers and three escort fighters were being readied. We lined the airstrip as the men strode towards the planes. There were cries of 'Good luck!' and 'All power to you!' as the flyers walked past us, saluting, before they climbed into the cockpits. They looked light-hearted, as though they were taking off on an excursion tour. They had already listened to a briefing and a 'pep talk' from the wing commander. I saw no sorrow among the men about to depart for ever.

Naemura continues:

Because it was well past midnight, there were no schoolgirls or townspeople to wave off the pilots. But among the crowd were the mayor and deputy mayor of the town. The outlines of scattered clouds could now be faintly seen in the sky. The stars were glittering but it was a moonless night. After the pilots had tested their engines, the planes started taxiing one by one and were soon airborne, the pilots arranging themselves into formations of four planes each and circling over the base twice. We saw their deep green wing lights and also the white lights of their underbellies. We stood around until the lights were no longer visible. Probably because of the general light-hearted atmosphere, I did not experience a strong emotion.

But emotion was not long in coming. Naemura went to the command post and listened to radio communications from the just-departed unit:

I knew one of the pilots, Imada, closely from my university days. He and I were students at the Sendai Army Flying School and we also both served in the Philippines. Then we were both at Shimoshizu Air Base. In fact, we volunteered together to join a Special Attack unit on January 2, 1945. The day before, on New Year's Day, we spent visiting the Kashima and Katori Shinto shrines in Chiba Prefecture. Imada used to tease me, saying that I was his elder brother. Now, we heard a radio message that Imada was making his final assault. It was a profoundly moving moment.

As Naemura walked alone in silence back to his billet, he ripped off a branch of blossoms from a cherry tree and shouted: '*Imada! Imada! Imada!*' at the top of his lungs. There was no one around him as he watched the petals from the cherry blossoms scatter gently in the wind:

In the morning [says Naemura], I walked along the same path back to the command post. I heard my own footsteps clearly. Lieutenant Colonel Kenkichi Fujii, the wing commander, was present. I tersely told him that I was volunteering once more to join a Kamikaze unit. He said 'Lieutenant, your wish is granted' and nothing more.

Naemura was never himself assigned to a Kamikaze unit nor did he take part in escort missions. He flew Type 99 dive-bombers, carrying a load of tin foil strips which he scattered in the air to obstruct enemy radar. From the month of June, the Air Wing began receiving new fighters, equipped with air-to-ground rockets, which were to replace the dive-bombers. As America's landing on Japan's home islands was expected, the main mission of the Air Wing was changed to attacking the larger landing craft with rockets. Landing craft were not considered as worthy Kamikaze targets. Naemura was assigned to fly one of the new fighters.

Naemura said it was not a 'matter of shame' for Kamikaze pilots to turn back to the base if the weather deteriorated or they were unable to locate targets. Therefore, he said, there were instructions for the pilots, telling them how to return to the base on aborted missions. Naemura said he refused to believe that, except in very isolated cases, the *tokko* planes were only given fuel for a one-way flight.

'You don't lightly waste pilots and airplanes,' he said.

Nevertheless, one can imagine the desperate moments towards the end of the war when air bases were being bombed and strafed and aviation fuel was not always in plentiful supply. Naemura explained how one joined a suicide, or *tokko* unit:

> One did not become a Special Attack (*tokko*) flyer by volunteering. One became a *tokko* flyer only after he was assigned to a *tokko* unit. A *tokko* flyer is selected from those who volunteered. Naemura volunteered twice as a Kamikaze flyer because it was up to every air wing to form such units out of volunteers and once you were transferred to a different unit, you had to volunteer anew – that is, if you were prepared to go on a Special Attack mission. But there was no registration system for suicide pilots at the centre.

Naemura said *tokko* planes' fuel tanks were nearly always filled up because otherwise the effect of the crash on the target would be diminished: 'Every Kamikaze pilot wanted to cause the greatest possible damage to an enemy vessel. He knew that petrol would spread with an incendiary effect. I can't imagine any pilot agreeing to fly with half-empty tanks. Ground crew members also knew that fuel was as important as bombs. Often the flyers themselves made sure their tanks were full.'

Out of his experience, Naemura reached the conclusion that 'not everyone died' from the ranks of Special Attack flyers. He said that the Army had formed 510 suicide units up until August 15, 1945, and out of them only 141 units sallied. On average there were ten flyers to a unit. He said even among those flyers who took off on one-way missions, not every one died. Some pilots survived because of mechanical problems, poor weather conditions, or for other reasons:

Only those who were determined, died as Kamikaze flyers [Naemura said]. As long as you held the control stick in your hands, you were able to choose your fate. Those who had a change of heart, either turned back to base or ditched on the way to the final destination. But I am not saying that all those who turned back or ditched on the way were those who changed their mind.

As part of the preparation for an invasion of the Philippines, the island of Taiwan was subjected, from October 10 to 16, to an intensive aerial bombardment which did tremendous damage to military objectives and resulted in the destruction of over 900 Japanese aircraft and the sinking or damaging of very large numbers of ships and small craft. While the attacks were at their height the Japanese fleet came out to oppose them, but it retired on seeing that the American fleet's fighting strength was unimpaired. Japanese airfields on Luzon were also bombed at the same time. The lack of success of the Japanese fleet in the Pacific was matched by that of the Japanese Army in Burma, where the whole northern region of the country was cleared by a combined British and Chinese assault. On the other hand, Japan attained the limited objectives of her campaign in China proper, notably the recovery of certain air bases from which American aircraft had previously, in June 1944, begun to bomb the Japanese mainland. But this did not give Japan complete immunity, as the US Flying Fortresses found other bases within reach of Japan.

At this time, ace pilot Hichiro Naemura was in the midst of transferring from the Philippines to mainland Japan and he missed the news of the first pilot, Lieutenant Yukio Seki, who led a Kamikaze mission from a Filipino base. Naemura recalls: 'We were retreating and there was confusion everywhere you looked. But we were very much aware of the general atmosphere prevailing in the Army many months before the suicide attacks were initiated; short of employing "body-smashing" tactics we felt we could not hope to reverse the tide of war.'

When Naemura reached Japan he learned about the crash-dive feat of Lieutenant Seki and his men from newspaper reports:

When we learned of the first Army 'Special Attack' on the US fleet from the Philippines, our morale was high. More than that, it was tremendously boosted. It was for us the sublimest expression of love for one's loved ones and for one's country. Therefore, I volunteered for a Kamikaze mission immediately after the first Army Special Attack flight took off.

Naemura was then conducting a series of tests for a 'skip-hop-hop' bombing technique against ships, taking into consideration the enemy's heavy and concentrated flak fire. Experiments in skip bombing began in March 1943 by the Army Aviation Technology Institute and were completed in May 1944.

Naemura explained why pilots like himself saw a Kamikaze attack as having an advantage over a conventional one:

> We were convinced that it was difficult to return alive after delivering a bomb to its target. At the same time, we realized that, unless you got in real close, it was difficult to score a lethal hit on the enemy. The chance of getting away was very slim. In any case you were almost certain to die. So, your smashing into an enemy vessel assured you success and you were able to die with 'rewards' instead of wasting your precious life.

Naemura added:

> Friends in the West have asked me if I thought this was 'the Japanese way'. Did our new resolve invoke the image of the historical samurai for us? My answer is the Japanese way for us was being ready to die for our loved ones and for the country. It came spontaneously. As the months passed, I did not believe that we could win the war against the overwhelmingly powerful enemy, no matter how well we fought, but we also believed we were fighting a desperate war of self-preservation of our nation from the very outset of the war against the US. Our special Kamikaze tactics could delay the enemy's advance towards our homeland and inflict severe damage upon him. By delaying his encroachment we hoped that the enemy would agree to negotiate a truce.

As to invoking the image of the samurai of old, Naemura asked wryly if, in the same vein, the fighting American soldiers in the Second World War thought about the colonial Indian fighters in pre-revolutionary America.

'Of course, the historical samurai was very much in everyone's blood. I suppose it is like the automatic reflex action of Pavlov's dog.' But Naemura offered a cautionary word of advice to Westerners: they should not view the samurai legacy as something exotic. And he wondered how many Americans took at face value the Hollywood film,

The Teahouse of the August Moon. (The 1956 melodrama, taken from a Broadway play, is about American troops on Okinawa in 1944 who succumb to the Oriental way of life.) The film, said Naemura, was too exotic.

Naemura returned to the theme of victory in the war:

The war was a David against Goliath from the beginning. What we hoped for was to obtain an honourable peace after we had bled the enemy enough. No one who was realistic thought that Japan could actually win the war no matter what we were able to do. But we knew, objectively, that Kamikaze attacks were much more effective as compared to conventional attacks.

But the main problem was that to be really effective, the Kamikaze sorties needed experienced pilots to guide them. They were required to lead green pilots to the target area. Unless experienced pilots led the suicide attacks, the Special Attack Force would have been composed entirely of green pilots and, said Naemura, 'This would have had a negative effect on the morale of the men.'

Naemura said he never had second thoughts after he volunteered for the Special Attack Forces. All of the Kamikaze pilots believed they were fighting a 'defensive war for the life or death of our nation'. The issue was clear, he says. The Americans were bombing and strafing Japan's cities, causing many casualties. (Not surprisingly, as the war increased in ferocity, the root causes of the conflict became blurred.) To the Japanese, the US air raids were seen as a sheer act of barbarism. Hence, says Naemura, suicide tactics became one of Japan's responses. But these tactics, he says, were not actually imposed from above but were brought about by an ardent desire that was also shared by ordinary flyers.

In this connection the veteran flyer posed the subject of the Vietnam War and the reason why US troops were willing to fight and die so far from home. Naemura asked rhetorically: 'Were the American soldiers who fought in Vietnam "brain-washed"?' His answer: 'Perhaps – except for those youngsters who fled to England, Canada or Sweden by way of Russia.'

When the war ended, Naemura returned home and went into business for himself. But he didn't forget his love of flying. Thus in 1995 Naemura travelled to Long Beach, California, where at the age of 75 he performed acrobatic flights for an approving American audience. In the new millennium he was the proud owner of a successful chain of restaurants in the Osaka area. The business was being managed by his son.

NOTES

[1] America, Britain, China and the Dutch.

[2] Akira Yoshimura, a noted writer on military history, recalls seeing Doolittle's plane swooping over him on April 18, 1942. Yoshimura was then 15 years old and was flying a kite from the balcony of his house in Tokyo. He saw the pilot and co-pilot wearing bright yellow neckerchiefs and goggles. People nearby took down the number painted on the plane: 40–2344. (After the war, he learned it was Gen. Doolittle's plane.) Bombs dropped by the Doolittle raiders, who were skimming the roof tops, hit a number of civilian targets. (Yoshimura's recollections are from his May, 2002 article in the magazine, *Bungei Shunju.*)

9

CHRIST, ALLAH AND KAMIKAZE

As a flight instructor, Takeo Tagata discovered that a small number of his Kamikaze students were practising Christians. Christians made up less than 2 per cent of Japanese citizens and, sometimes, as often happens during a war, the loyalty of those who practise a religion different from the vast majority was suspect. But no suspicion was attached to a Christian if he was a Kamikaze pilot, whether he happened to be Protestant or Roman Catholic. (In John Hersey's classic work, *Hiroshima*, the author says that in wartime the pastor of the Hiroshima Methodist Church, the Reverend Tanimoto, was questioned by the police several times because at least one leading person in the community spoke ill of the pastor, saying he was not to be trusted. But, then, the Reverend Tanimoto had in his youth studied theology at Emery University in Atlanta, Georgia and spoke excellent English, two facts certain to interest the wartime police.) Tagata is categorical:

> In the Army there was no prejudice against any faith. We Japanese are polytheists and, therefore, tolerant towards different religious beliefs. My Christian students would go to a Christian church near the base. Sometimes I saw them praying, kneeling down in the evening, making the sign of the cross on their breasts. Mainly the Christians I knew were university graduates.[1]

He continues:

> In the evenings at the base canteen I would often talk with the young flyers over cups of coffee or munching cakes. Serious topics were avoided. We all tried to keep spirits high. So the subjects were light-hearted, such as childhood, hometowns, food, friends. Sometimes they would ask questions about flying techniques, but not about philosophical or religious or personal matters. I am sure they dealt with such topics among themselves. But I never heard a complaint or lament from them.
>
> Later I met one of the college-educated pilots, a Christian, whom I had trained as a pilot on Taiwan and who had joined the ranks of Kamikaze pilots after I had been transferred back to Japan. He laughed when he said that Kamikaze flyers all become *kami* [i.e., Shinto gods] upon death. He said he was a Catholic and that Christ had suffered on behalf of the people. He said that some of the town people regarded each of us as an *ikigami* [a living god] after we joined the Special Attack squadron. The Catholic pilot believed that Jesus Christ, being a *kami*, had suffered vicariously for man. 'That's the role of the *kami*.' [In actuality, a *kami* – or Shinto god – is unlike the Judeo-Christian idea of God. Perhaps 'holy spirit' or 'divinity' is a more appropriate name.]

While Kamikaze pilots talked about their spirits reuniting at Tokyo's grand military shrine, Yasukuni, the September Eleventh suicide-hijackers had absolute faith that they would enter paradise after death. (All Kamikaze pilots – whatever their faith or lack of it – were posthumously deified at the Tokyo shrine; this included Christians, who were also deified there.)

For the Al-Qaeda fighters, paradise meant accession to the happy life, even eternal life. (Similar to the Kamikaze pilots' enthusiasm for self-destruction there was, from 2002, what was called the 'grand aspiration' of thousands of youthful Palestinians for suicide bombings against the perceived enemy: Jewish targets in Israel.) They were secure in the faith that in paradise they would be reunited with family members and enjoy the full measure of celestial pleasures. In the words of one of the hijack leaders: 'You have to be convinced that those few hours that are left you in your life are few. From there you will begin to live the happy life, the infinite paradise. Be optimistic. The prophet was always optimistic.' Also: 'Keep a very open mind, keep a very open heart of what you are to face. You will be entering paradise. You will be entering the happiest life, everlasting life,' Also: 'When the time of truth comes and zero hour arrives, then straighten out your clothes, open your chest and welcome death for the sake of Allah.'[2]

During the war American intelligence analysts said that the Western abhorrence of suicide (which included the view that suicide was not the act of a sane person) was missing among the Japanese. But the analysts also reported that self-sacrifice in Japan was seen as an act of courage, not of cowardice, that it was regarded as a patriotic act. The Kamikaze pilots who were Christians similarly viewed suicide as an act of patriotism, not something sinful. Therefore, they had no reservations about taking their own lives.

It appears that at least some (if not all) Kamikaze-Christians looked upon a crash-dive suicide as just another form of death, not something forbidden by their faith.

Ensign Tsukuru Hayashiichi was baptized in a Protestant church in Japan and his mother, Matsue, had brought up her son to be a devout Christian. He graduated from Kyoto Imperial University and lost his life as a Kamikaze pilot on April 12, 1945, in the fighting around Okinawa. He had taken off from Kanoya Base in Kyushu in a Zero fighter which carried a 250-kilogram bomb. In his first letter to his mother, he wrote:

Everything is in the hands of our Lord. Life and death are determined by Him. I am going to crash into the enemy vessel singing a hymn. . . . I will be waiting for you at Heaven's gate. But will I myself be allowed to enter there? Mum, pray for me. I will not be able to fare well if I cannot be with you. Goodbye, Mum!

After her son's death, Matsue composed a poem:

You perished on the fighting front
To save your 100 million compatriots,
Bearing separation from your beloved mother.

Kamikaze pilot Takamasa Suzuki's father was a devout Catholic and he himself had gone to a Sunday school at a neighbourhood church since he was two years old. He survived the war and worked many years for the *Yomiuri Shimbun*, one of Japan's giant newspapers. Suzuki:

When the Second World War began, I was accepted by the Army as an air force cadet while I was studying at St Paul's University in Tokyo and I was sent to an officers' flying school in Maebashi, in Gumma Prefecture. On May 3, 1945, we were asked by our company commander who would volunteer for Special Attack, or suicide, missions. I spent whole nights asking myself whether I should volunteer or not. When you think you will be meeting certain death, you just can't go to sleep. Trivial things like playing soldiers in the bamboo thicket when you were a little child would cross my mind. I experienced only a modicum of rational thinking. I knew that Japan was doomed to lose the war but I thought I had to sacrifice myself for the good of the nation. I decided to volunteer and so I joined the *tokko-tai* [the Special Attack Force]. Three days later, on May 6, the entire company was assembled again. The company commander raged, losing his temper and calling us scum. There were only five or six men who volunteered out of 210 men in our company. When we graduated from the school on June 5, all of us cadets were assigned to field units.

Suzuki had chosen St Paul's University in Tokyo, run by American missionaries, because of his love for the English language. His hope was to promote English-language education in Japan to foster international understanding. After the war, in 1946, Suzuki returned to study at St Paul's and put forward the idea of a nationwide English-language speech contest for young students. When he joined the *Yomiuri Shimbun*, he initiated a National Annual Junior High School English-language Speech Contest. Suzuki was 22 years old in 1946. (The speech contest is still being conducted in the new millennium.)

Speaking of 'the Kamikaze phenomenon' in a post-war radio interview, Suzuki said:

Some people think that those men who exhibited abundant patriotism always volunteered for suicide missions. On the contrary, they did not always do so, as was evident from the men in my company. I thought I saw the true faces of men at war. When I volunteered, I prayed to the Lord. I swore that if I ever somehow survived the war, I would continue with my work to help spread English-language education.

Kamikaze pilot Kyoji Fukuya's family had been *Kakure Krishitan* (secret Christians) for more than 300 years. There were thousands of these so-called secret Christians in Kumamoto and Nagasaki prefectures who practised their religion clandestinely through the generations.

After the Shogunate prohibition on Christianity was lifted by the Meiji government in the second half of the nineteenth century, Fukuya's grandfather converted to Catholicism. Christianity had been banned in Japan by Hideyoshi (1536–98), who believed that the Christian missionaries were the agents of European invaders. Before Hideyoshi died, 26 Japanese Christians were executed in Nagasaki in 1597. In 1862, Pope Pio IX canonized the 26 Japanese martyrs.

On the 'secret Christians': because they practised the faith in secret for so long without priests, the original religion had deviated somewhat from the Roman faith. On August 15, the day the war ended, Master Sergeant Kyoji Fukuya was on his way from an Army hospital to Tachiarai Air Base when he was injured during a training flight and hospitalized. When Japan attacked Pearl Harbor in December 1941 it occurred to Fukuya that the day was 'Mother Mary's Immaculate Conception'. Mother Mary was chosen by the papacy in the sixteenth century as Japan's patron saint. Fukuya interpreted it to mean that 'it was Mother Mary's intention to use Japan as a divine tool to free enslaved people'. As it turned out, the war liberated many colonial possessions in Asia. Fukuya learned, while he was lying on a hospital bed, that the Americans had completely wiped out the city of Nagasaki with a 'special bomb'. The bomb earlier had struck down Hiroshima. In his mind, such acts were 'the work of an anti-Christ'.

Ironically, Nagasaki was the stronghold of Christianity in Japan and the city was known for its majestic Oura Cathedral, the oldest Catholic church in Japan. It was built in 1863 when the Shogunate ban on the faith was still in effect. It was in Nagasaki that Christianity had gone underground in Japan in the seventeenth century. For two centuries a rather large Catholic community held its own there and came into the open again after the Meiji Restoration (in 1868). The Dutch jurist B.V.A. Rolling, who was a member of the Tokyo International Tribunal for the Far East, has said, in alluding to the atomic bombing, that some people were left with the feeling that the Buddhas in Kyoto had protected that city better than the God of the Christians protected the city of Nagasaki. Kyoto, whose ancient temples attract countless tourists (Japanese and foreign), was one of the cities under consideration to be atomic-bombed because it was intact in the summer of 1945, unlike most other large Japanese cities. But Kyoto was struck off the 'hit list' when wise heads in Washington, knowing of the city's ancient treasures, prevailed.

When, on August 15, the Japanese government decided to terminate the war, Fukuya remembered that that was the day of Mother Mary's Assumption. He believed that this was a 'revelation' of Mother Mary's intent to 'save Japan' after it had 'accomplished its mission of freeing Asia's colonies'. Nevertheless, the Oura Cathedral was completely destroyed by the second atomic bomb. So was the statue of Mother Mary which had stood in front of the cathedral since 1867.

Naval Ensign Ichizo Hayashi, a Christian who was born in 1922, had graduated from Kyoto Imperial University. Joining a Special Attack corps, he wrote a last letter to his mother in which he spoke about the hours before what he called 'the final plunge'. He said that on his last sortie he would be given a package of bean curds and rice. This was, he wrote, very good luncheon fare. He would also, he said, take along a lucky charm: the dried bonito that had been given him by a friend. The bonito, he explained to his mother, would enable him to rise up from the ocean and swim back to her.

Expanding on his Christian faith, the naval pilot apparently remembered a passage from the Bible about a 'time to live and a time to die'. He wrote: 'We live in the spirit of Jesus Christ, and we die in that spirit. This thought stays with me. It is gratifying to live in this world, but living has a spirit of futility about it now. It is time to die.'

But he did not, he said, seek reasons for dying. His only desire was to seek out an 'enemy target to dive into'. In a final sentence, he asked his mother to pray for his admission to heaven.

But Hayashi's sortie was delayed a day so he added a postscript. He said newsreel cameramen had arrived at the base and had singled him out for a series of pictures. He hoped, he wrote, that he was photogenic. He added that the Commander-in-Chief of the Combined Fleet had visited their base and told him personally that 'Japan's fate rests on your shoulders'. He said the anniversary of his death would now be April 10, when he would crash-dive against the enemy. He did.

Although Captain Ryoji Uehara was a non-Christian, this commander of a Kamikaze squadron of Hayabusa fighters wrote a letter to his father and mother in which he mentioned his idea of heaven. Wrote Uehara: 'My belief is that death is a passage leading to reunion with my loved ones in heaven.' He had no fear of death, he said, adding: 'Death is nothing to be afraid of when you look at it as just a stage in the process of ascending to heaven.'

Nevertheless, he ended his letter with the words 'Goodbye for ever.'

Pilot Second Lieutenant Koshiro Ishizuka's mother was a devout Christian, and Koshiro had been baptized in his youth and was a graduate of Tokyo's Aoyama Gakuin College, which was founded and managed by Protestant missionaries. His father was the nationally famous physician, Sagen Izhizuka. On May 11, 1945, he took off on his last flight, a suicide mission from Chiran. Before he took off, Toshiro wrote, at the request of a newspaper editor, the following lines:

> We shall bring victory to Japan through our sacrifice. I am now filled with bliss and I firmly believe that we are dedicating our lives for the glory of the nation. The days I shared with my comrades in arms since our Special Attack squadron was formed have been the most fulfilling experience of my life. I became aware of the meaning of life. I doubt if I would experience such blissful moments even if I could lead an ordinary life for 50 years or more. I am ending my life after 25 years since I was given birth. However, to my mind my life has been worth much more than 75 years of ordinary living.

Each year on March 21, the surviving members of the 'Thunder Gods Corps' gather at Tokyo's Yasukuni Shrine. It was on that day in 1945 that the first *Ohka* ('human bomb') attack was carried out. (It ended in failure.) Not all of the survivors believe in the Shinto religion. Some are Buddhists, others are Christians, still others atheists. But, says a survivor, 'The last thing our dead comrades said to us was, "I will be waiting for all of you at Yasukuni Shrine."'

NOTES

[1] Co-author Hideaki Kase's mother was a Catholic who during the war attended a small church administered by a German priest who, not surprisingly, would lead the congregation in praying for a Japanese victory.

[2] John le Carré, the author of many acclaimed spy novels, saw fit to rebuke the West for its political blindness in first arming and exploiting Islamic zealots to fight Soviet troops in Afghanistan, and then turning its back on them, with the result that it is now seeking to find and punish legions of these warrior-fanatics (*The Sunday Times*, December 10, 2000).

10

'YOU ARE ALREADY GODS'

Vice Admiral Takijiro Onishi, the man most responsible for Kamikaze strategy, did not initially champion the desperate tactics that would cost many thousands of lives on both sides of the Pacific conflict. When plans for inaugurating Kamikaze units were drawn up, Onishi at first regretted the idea and was tormented at the thought of squandering young lives. But after being informed of the war situation (and the presence of a powerful American fleet in the western Pacific) he soon joined the front ranks of those supporting Special Attack Forces.

Onishi was physically bigger than average, with round, puffy features. Outwardly he appeared soft and flabby but he was a highly disciplined, indefatigable man of action, who sometimes invited criticism on account of his blunt, outspoken nature, not to mention his hard drinking, his visits to geisha houses, and zest for gambling (he had frequent success at bridge, poker and mah jong and it is said that he once won a national mah jong tournament under an alias). But as an expert in the field of aviation he had few peers. He had not only flown every type of aircraft, but also navigable balloons and was one of the first men in Japan to practise the art of parachuting. He believed in innovation, that the changing technologies demanded a change in tactics. Prior to the war, along with pilot Minoru Genda he formed a private working group called the Society for the Study of Aerial Might. Later it was revealed that the group had done the difficult research on which the attack on Pearl Harbor was based. (Genda was a staff officer to Admiral Nagumo when Nagumo's task force hit Hawaii in December 1941. Genda became Chief of Staff of the Air Self-Defence Force in 1959. Visiting Washington, DC in that capacity, he was asked by an American reporter whether he would attack Pearl Harbor again. General Genda replied: 'I am a soldier. I would gladly do it again if ordered by my government.')

Rikihei Inoguchi, one of the admiral's top aides, who sees suicide tactics as 'the ultimate extremity', once asked his chief when they were at Mabalacat in the Philippines if he would consent to a Kamikaze attack on an Allied task force that was fast moving out of range. After a long pause, Onishi replied: 'Suicide tactics are so final. I would advise using them only if there is a full chance that the goal may be achieved.'

But Onishi seems to have given his clearest view of suicide tactics shortly after they were given official approval. Again, Captain Inoguchi was alongside the admiral and recorded his comment: 'The fact that we have to resort to them shows how poor our strategy has been since the beginning.'

A biography of Onishi written by Taizo Kusayanagi says that early in October 1944 – only weeks before suicide strategy was officially put to the test – Onishi was unenthusiastic when appointed as the new head of the First Air Fleet in the Philippines with specific instructions to begin suicide operations. Before he departed from Tokyo to take up his new post he told his wife, Toshie, of his reluctance 'to kill young men like this'. His wife challenged her famous husband.

'That's what you say, but this is war,' she said. 'And young men are offering to give up their lives.'

'No, they must not be killed in this way,' protested Onishi.

But Onishi already knew that a Naval Special Attack Division had been established and that a call was out for volunteers from each air arm. Moreover an order had gone out to train *Ohka* (Cherry Blossom) pilots to man the piloted bomb that would be dropped from a heavy bomber.

On October 9, 1944, a small farewell for Onishi was held at the Munitions Ministry in Tokyo. Onishi extended his hand to Lieutenant General Saburo Endo, who was the director of the Aerial Weapons Administration Office of the Ministry. Onishi was his deputy.

'I have put in a lot of work here. But I cannot go on building planes. I am going to the front line,' Onishi said.

'I see you're going but I wish you would stay here,' Endo responded.

As Onishi was leaving the rather frugal party, he stopped and spoke to a Navy captain who was in charge of technology and development. 'From now on we do not need sophisticated planes. Build simple ones,' Onishi told the captain.

That night, after Onishi returned home he asked Toshie's mother: 'This may be my last request to you, but can you sing a cradle song for me?' The mother-in-law began singing but she started to shed tears and choked. 'Let me sing for you dear,' Toshie volunteered. Onishi scoffed and uttered: 'How can someone who is younger sing a cradle song for a boy? I'll sing it myself.' He flopped down on the bedding laid out on the tatami and began singing: 'Where did the baby's nurse-maid go?' It was a very old song and he repeated it two or three times off tune. He had no musical sense.

After he finished, he began singing 'Bara no uta' ('The Song of Roses'), a popular song.

> A rose in a small pot
> Received the dews of your affection
> Upon tender pink petals
> And smiled for the first time.

Onishi finished the song and told himself, as if talking to a child: 'Now it's bedtime. You should not stay up so late.' He changed into a nightgown and stretched his body on the bedding. In a few seconds he began to snore loudly.[1]

During the next few weeks Onishi was entirely won over to the idea of how vital it was to organize the Special Attack Forces. One of those who apparently impressed Onishi with his arguments for 'crash-dive' attacks on enemy vessels was Captain Eiichiro Jo. Jo had submitted a paper to his superiors which contained this sentence: 'No longer can we hope to sink the numerically superior enemy aircraft carriers through ordinary attack methods.' On his way to Manila Onishi flew into Taiwan where he held talks with Admiral Soemu Toyoda, the Commander-in-Chief of the Imperial Navy's Combined Fleet, who had become a firm supporter of Special Attack strategy. In Taiwan Onishi learned first-hand of the dangers posed by powerful American forces, especially aircraft carriers. In the Philippines, which had earlier been designated a 'decisive theatre of battle' by the Imperial High Command, Onishi told his staff officer Inoguchi: 'I met with Captain Jo while I was in Japan and heard his proposal to initiate Special Attack methods and I thought such tactics were too cruel for the men. I was still doubtful. But after I arrived here, I had no choice but to decide on adopting them. We were being mauled by our enemies one-sidedly.'

No doubt another major factor in fully converting Onishi was the explanation given by his subordinates of how much damage a suicide plane carrying a bomb could do to a target. Dropping a 250-kilogram bomb squarely on a carrier in the conventional way would naturally cause great damage; but a plane with the same bomb plunging into a carrier would destroy a carrier's deck and put the ship out of action for some days. Most importantly, an aircraft that was steered to a target would have a much better chance of accuracy and destructiveness.

After launching the first Kamikaze attack, Onishi was asked by Yukio Togawa, a *Mainichi Shimbun* correspondent, if he thought Japan could win with suicide tactics. Onishi replied: 'It is not a question of whether we can win. The answer will be, we shall not be defeated. We will not win but neither will we lose this war. That's the only way to save Japan from total capitulation. To do this, Kamikaze tactics are absolutely necessary.'

Some observers believe that Onishi had intended to restrict the use of Kamikaze tactics to a limited number of sorties, perhaps only during the battle for the Philippines. But, not only did the admiral say that crash-dive tactics were the best way to disable US carriers, but in the critical days before Japan's surrender, he urged continuation of the struggle, hopeless though it was, believing that masses of suicide pilots taking off from bases on the Japanese home islands could still make a difference or, at any rate, demonstrate the heroic Japanese spirit. On taking the lives of young pilots, Onishi was straightforward:

> These young men with their limited training, outdated equipment, and numerical inferiority are doomed even by conventional fighting methods. It is important to a commander, as it is to his men, that death be not in vain. I believe therefore that a broad perspective indicates the wisdom of crash-dive tactics. To think otherwise would be taking a narrow view of the situation.

Onishi was being entirely candid about the mortality of suicide pilots. Large numbers of the pilots were poorly trained in the last year of war and many of their planes were flimsy and outdated. (But due to the numerical superiority of the Americans, even conventional pilots who survived said they had not expected to outlive the end of the war.) At the time of Pearl Harbor in 1941, the Japanese Navy pilot had an average of 700 hours' flying experience, the number for the Army being about 500. When Kamikaze attacks started in 1944 the average for the Navy had dipped to 300 hours and for the Army to less than 200. Lieutenant Commander Tom Blackburn, a seasoned US Navy pilot, was categorical on the number of hours he considered the minimum required for a combat pilot: 500. In his view, to put someone in action with less than that was criminal. It appears, however, that many of the Kamikaze pilots in the last months of the war had only 40 or 50 hours of solo time before they were given a plane and orders for a final sortie.

In the last months of the war many Kamikaze pilots had received only the most basic training; and, in the end, new pilots had only enough flying hours needed to reach an available target and plunge to their death. Little instruction was given the pilots in the luxury of landing a plane. Advanced training was curtailed.

Meanwhile, to keep up morale it was necessary to provide the men with planes that could compete with Allied fighters, or even be superior to them in performance. Upon his arrival in the Philippines, Onishi had less than 100 planes belonging to the First Air Fleet, including approximately 35 Zeros and a dozen Tenzan torpedo bombers and Gingas medium bombers. (Respectively, these planes were codenamed by the Allies: Zeke, Jill and Frances.) But this number was soon heavily augmented by planes flown in from Admiral Shigeru Fukudome's squadrons on Taiwan. Within a short time, Onishi was promised an additional 100 Suisei dive-bombers (codenamed Judy) which could be used for reconnaissance but mainly for suicide attacks.

Onishi's death by his own hand at war's end meant the dauntless admiral did not have to confront the storm of protest that had been building up, when many civilians, the parents and families of the fallen Kamikaze pilots, would be raising questions about the wisdom of using suicide as a chief weapon of war. There would be a heated argument over the protracted use of such tactics – almost a year of crash-dive operations (from October 1944 to August 1945) that took thousands of lives.

Onishi, a true son of his nation, had a deep sense of tradition. Once during the last months of the war, when a *Mainichi* correspondent asked him why, if there were strong doubts about Japan winning the war, he continued with the suicide operations, Onishi mentioned the conflict that accompanied the Meiji Restoration – the transformation of Japan from a feudal state to a modern nation that began in 1867. He applauded the group of young warriors who had carried on the struggle to the very end. Onishi's explanation included this rousing statement: 'As long as history remembers how Japanese youth fought, sacrificing themselves in the country's darkest hour, Japan and the Japanese will survive.'

However, Onishi appears to have underestimated American resolve. Speaking of an endless war of attrition and the possibility of Japan losing millions of lives, Onishi told a group of his Kamikaze pilots on Taiwan in March 1945: 'America is a country that cannot spiritually bear the loss of lives in the numbers that would be involved if every Japanese continued to fight to the death.'

Onishi's last thoughts before his suicide were addressed to the fallen Kamikaze pilots. The admiral wrote:

> I call upon the departed spirits of the members of the Special Attack squadrons. You fought superbly well for which I extend my deepest gratitude. You perished, turning your flesh into cannon balls, with faith in final victory. However, your aspirations were not materialized. I express my thanks to the departed men and their beleaguered families by taking my life.

Remembering the throngs of youthful zealots who volunteered for his Kamikaze squadrons, Onishi repeated what he had often told Kamikaze pilots: 'You are already gods, without earthly desires.' Then, with skilful brush, Onishi composed a stylized poem, a haiku:

> The air is clear
> In the immediate aftermath of a storm
> And the moon looks so serene

The man who guided Kamikaze operations and had been Japan's leading naval aviation pioneer, who wanted – if he could – to turn the Imperial Japanese Navy into an air force, had nerves of steel. When he launched the first suicide squadrons during the battle of the Philippines in late 1944, in which Naval Academy graduate Lieutenant Yukio Seki led a small group of other pilots on a one-way mission – history's first officially approved suicide flight – Onishi was pleased to learn that Seki had jumped at the opportunity of being leader of the suicide unit. The admiral apparently hadn't learned or didn't want to hear that far from jumping at the opportunity offered him, Seki had had no other choice; that in fact he had gone to his death feeling the service had blundered in wasting his piloting skills that could have been used again and again.

Resourceful, imaginative, blunt in his espousal of the importance of air power, often the nonconformist, Onishi was highly respected in aviation circles if he was sometimes bitterly opposed by the more conservative forces in the Navy. As the Deputy Naval Chief of Staff,

Onishi had helped draw up the plan to attack the US fleet at Pearl Harbor in 1941. In fact, Onishi together with Admiral Isoroku Yamamoto and Vice Admiral Matome Ugaki are considered the masterminds of the Hawaiian disaster. He had been the Commander-in-Chief of the First Air Fleet in the Philippines in 1944 and three years earlier Onishi had been Chief of Staff of the Eleventh Air Fleet on Taiwan in 1941. It was this Air Fleet that wiped out an entire squadron of General MacArthur's heavy bombers sitting at US air bases in the Philippines hours after the attack on Pearl Harbor. As to the attack on Pearl Harbor, Onishi is said to have first opposed the idea, telling Yamamoto that the harbour was too shallow and would allow damaged US ships to be easily repaired. It was better, he argued, to engage the US fleet on the high seas in order to hunt down and destroy the American aircraft carriers. But seeing the excellence of the preparations, the countless drills that had been carried out, and the allowances made for dive-bombing in shallow waters, he quickly relented and helped with the planning.[2]

In 1944, Onishi gave a public lecture at Asahi Shimbun Hall in Tokyo. He was then Deputy Director of the Aerial Weapons Administration Office of the Munitions Ministry. He said there was little record of 'gallant actions' by the Ashikagas and Hojos, who defeated Kusunoki's forces. He contrasted the lack of tales of gallant actions on the part of Ashikaga-Hojo forces with the many tales of 'tragic gallantries' of Kusunoki. (Masashige Kusunoki, a fourteenth-century warrior and one of Japan's great heroes, is considered the epitome of loyalty and devotion to the Imperial dynasty. He became the inspiration for the Kamikaze pilots of the Pacific War.)

Onishi cautioned his audience, saying, 'We should not rejoice at the many reports of extraordinary bravery appearing in the newspapers,' because the cold reality of the war situation proved that when things were actually progressing in Japan's favour, there were much fewer reports of bravery in the press than vice versa. Onishi concluded with his customary frankness: 'The current situation shows that the war is not developing in our favour. The reason why such a situation has come about owes to the fact that our Air Force is regrettably vastly outnumbered by the enemy and air supremacy in most cases is lost to our opponents.'

Onishi often expressed himself frankly, even bluntly, about the 'end of the era' for the big battleships and urged, instead, the need for a massive air force. Unceremoniously, he dismissed those responsible for building *Yamato* (the biggest battleship in the Second World War) and *Musashi* as fools. He once said that building the super battleships was like making horse-drawn carriages in the age of automobiles.

Convinced that only an unorthodox strategy could change the war situation, when he arrived in the Philippines in mid-October 1944, Onishi visited a front-line Navy air base at Mabalacat, north of Manila, and addressed a group of key officers at their headquarters located in a cream-painted building with green trim. He began by saying he had come to discuss 'something of great importance'. The war situation was indeed grave as the appearance of strong American naval forces in Leyte Gulf had been confirmed.

To hear about the gravity of the war situation was not a surprise to the assembled officers. But what came next was.

'In my opinion,' he said, 'there is only one way of assuring that our meagre strength will be effective to a maximum degree. That is to organize suicide attack units composed of Zero fighters armed with a 250-kilogram bomb with each plane to crash-dive into an enemy carrier. . . . What do you think?'

Officers of the 201st Air Group at Mabalacat gave the admiral their fullest support.

At this moment in time, other top-ranking Japanese military leaders were coming round to the same conclusion about suicide tactics. Vice Admiral Kimpei Teraoka, former commander of the First Air Fleet, made this diary entry in October 1944: 'We conclude that the enemy can be stopped and our country saved only by crash-dive attacks on their ships.'

Inoguchi, who listened to Onishi's Mabalacat speech, later explained why the officers – and many pilots in other combat units – had been urging for some time that crash-dive tactics be used against American carriers. He said it was understandable if one kept in mind that, considering the heavy odds Japanese flyers faced in 1944, their chance of survival from any action against American carriers was extremely slim, whatever the method of attack. Then Inoguchi asked: 'If one is bound to die, what is more natural than the desire to do so effectively, at maximum cost to your opponent?'

When the historic meeting with Onishi was over, Inoguchi couldn't help noticing that the sense of relief that could be seen on Onishi's face was tempered by a shadow of regret.

NOTES

[1] The dialogue between Onishi and his family is taken from post-war interviews the biographer Taizo Kusayanagi conducted with Mrs Onishi. It is possible that Mrs Onishi may have exaggerated her husband's initial

opposition to Special Attack Forces. After all, not long afterwards Onishi told a *Mainichi* war correspondent (Yukio Togawa): 'If every one of us exerts a *tokko* [special attack] spirit, even if Japan should be defeated, it would not bring about the destruction of our nation.' But it is also possible that Onishi had two faces, one for the public and another for his intimates.

[2] A wooden fin was devised to be mounted on an aerial torpedo so that the torpedo would not dive deep. Together with allowances made for dive-bombing, the attack on Pearl Harbor was thus given the go-ahead.

11

LAST POEMS AND LETTERS

Many Japanese today, when remembering the Kamikaze pilots sentenced to a watery sepulchre, involuntarily find their eyes brimming with tears and they can't help saying, 'How cruel.' In Japan after the war, when peace was restored and there was the development of a healthy democracy, many diaries and letters belonging to youths who had died in suicide missions were found, or brought out of obscurity by families of the deceased. Some of the men had fallen in the Philippines, others in the waters off Okinawa. One father, whose student son died in Iwo Jima (Sulphur Island), had written the following epitaph:

'A most painful fight he fought – and a bitter end he suffered.'

After many decades of putting out of mind the inhumanities of the Pacific conflict, new history books and feature films revived memories of the war. But some aspects of the war continue to rankle, including the use of young men as suicide weapons, mainly the Special Attack or Kamikaze pilots, but also the *Kaiten* 'human torpedoes' and the manned *Ohka* (Cherry Blossom) missiles which were dropped from an aircraft at some distance from the target. With few exceptions all of these weapons became the pilots' tombs.

For years, the Special Attack pilots and other suicide units were scorned, some people saying, 'They died like dogs' or 'They were forced to be killed'. A part of the general public continued to bear resentment towards the Imperial Army and Navy for promoting Kamikaze tactics, a phenomenon without parallel in history.

Once inside the cockpit, the young men had taken off proudly. Many left with garlands of flowers or small branches of cherry blossoms filling the cockpit, handed to them at the last minute by girls who worked at the airfields. It was a custom all the pilots adopted. The cherry blossom is an ancient Japanese symbol of transience and perfection.

According to the *World Almanac*, 1,174,474 Japanese combatants died and over 600,000 civilians lost their lives in air raids and at various battle fronts. At least 5,000 but perhaps as many as 7,000 Kamikaze pilots (in organized units or as individuals) never returned. Today, at every Air Self-Defence Force base in Japan there is a small museum displaying letters, wills, swords, military tunics and other personal items left by Kamikaze flyers. There were no remains of the suicide pilots. What was left behind were the letters and poems they wrote, some clothes, often a lock of hair for their families or girlfriends, sometimes nail clippings wrapped in a piece of paper. Very few of the pilots were married. Some of their letters and poems are preserved at a dozen museums dedicated to Kamikaze pilots in different parts of Japan.

From the letters and poems, as well as diaries, we know that many of the Special Attack pilots firmly believed that after they were gone, life, family, the nation, even the world would go on, perhaps for the better, maybe helped in that direction by their sacrifice. Some of the letters reveal a remarkable independence of thought. Invariably, the pilots mention mothers fondly but rarely fathers. There is in the Japanese language the expression *Bokoku* (Motherland) but there is no word for Fatherland.

In Japan, whereas fathers invariably demand discipline from children, mothers are generally the ones who protect and generate love. Fathers are more harsh; they expect children to compete against each other. Nevertheless, the Japanese have not imposed a father-image on the country. The highest Shinto deity is Amaterasu Omikami, the sun goddess – in other words, a she-god. On their final sortie, many Special Attack pilots carried pictures of their mothers. It may even be said that Japanese culture is basically feminine. In 1004, Murasaki Shikibu wrote: *Genji Monogatari* (Tales of Genji), which was mankind's first novel written by a woman. There were many illustrious women writers, such as Seisho Nagon, Izumi Shikibu and Sugawara Takasuenomusume, who were Murasaki's contemporaries. In that period, women all over the world with few exceptions were illiterate and subservient to men. The first novel written by a woman appeared in the West in the eighteenth century, and much later on the Asian mainland.

SOME LAST POEMS

An imperishable bond lit up this fleeting world
As mother and son spent the entire night
Exhausting their thoughts to each other.

Lieutenant Junior Grade Yuzuru Ogata.
He died piloting the *Ohka* or '*Baka* bomb'.

*

My mother taught me tenderness and sincerity
And now I shall scatter[†] and remain fragrant
In the skies over Yamato.[††]

[†] *A reference to falling cherry blossoms*
[††] *Another name for Japan.*

Ensign Toshiro Washimi died on April 6, 1945
in the Okinawan waters, taking off from Kanoya
Naval Air Base on Kyushu. He was 23 years old.

*

How can I tell my ageing mother
who waits for me in my hometown,
not knowing that her son is about to perish?

Second Lieutenant Shigeru Nakata died on
May 28, 1945 in Okinawan waters, taking off
from Chiran. He was 21 years old.

*

I am wondering how mother is faring
with her chilblains on her frail hands,
as I look up to the sky where spring is gathering.

Lieutenant Senior Grade Hiroshi Murakami died near
Iwo Jima on February 21, 1945. He was 24 years old.

*

Mother bravely smiled at me as we parted,
suppressing the unbearable pain of bidding farewell
to her child about to go on a journey of death.

Second Lieutenant Toshio Kobayashi died in
Okinawan waters on April 6, 1945, taking off
from Nyutabaru Air Base on Kyushu

*

I am deeply grateful for mother's benevolence,
as I smash and obliterate the enemy fleet.

Ensign Kunio Otani died on May 4, 1945
in Okinawan waters. He was 23 years old.

LAST LETTER TO HIS DAUGHTER

Here is a short last letter written to his daughter Motoko by 25-year-old Ensign Motohisa Uemura, who died in the Philippine campaign on October 26, 1944:

Motoko – I am taking on my plane the doll you liked so much after you were born. So, you will be with me until the last moment. I just wanted you to know that you were with me.

Dad

'I WILL NOT FLINCH'

In 1966 the Japanese government, for the first time since the war, posthumously decorated more than 500 Special Attack flyers. (More fallen pilots as well as those who perished other than in the air were decorated in subsequent years.) Among them was Army Captain Takashi Komecha, who died on April 1945, as a second lieutenant, when as a 22-year-old pilot he took off from Bansei Air Base for Okinawan waters.

When Takashi was posthumously decorated by the government in 1966, his father, Sotaro, said: 'Nothing pleases me more. My son did not die in vain.'

Sotaro was then 69. He and his wife, Kinu, 68, Takashi's mother, lived in the same house where Takashi grew up in Amagasaki City, near Kobe. Takashi was awarded an Order of the Golden Eagle, the equivalent of America's Purple Heart medal for bravery.

Takashi graduated from Osaka College of Foreign Languages in 1941 and joined the Army Air Force. His aspiration was to work for a trading firm and he was accepted by the giant firm, Mitsui & Co. But he deemed it his duty to serve as a pilot, took up flying as a student and had already become proficient in handling gliders when he was in high school. Takashi met with his parents for the last time at Kakogawa Air Base, near Kobe, on March 31, 1945. He smiled as he told his parents: 'I am going to die in a very expensive coffin, an aircraft.' Here is the last letter he wrote before his final sortie:

Dear Parents,

Plums, peaches and cherries are ripening in the orchards on the hills. I must write to you the most lamentable news. We lost our Air Wing Commander and Second Lieutenant Sugita in accidents. I was relying on both of them so much. I find it hard to write about them. But your Takashi will not flinch any more. You have a much stronger son, spiritually. I would not be cowed even if every other man in the wing were lost. I will exert my utmost despite the mounting difficulties. I will be brave. Actually, I am enjoying the challenges before me and I feel am leading a truly meaningful life. Very soon I will dive into the enemy carrying the Wing Commander's ashes.

Believe me, I am sorry that I could not reciprocate all the kindness you both bestowed upon me. I thank both of you most profusely. I will go to heaven before you. I will look for a nice house here and shall wait for you.

Your Takashi

Postscript: I spent my last few days at Kikuyu Ryokan, 371 Ogawamachi, Shimonoseki City, and Kikuko Tao, the proprietress of the inn and her mother treated me so nicely. Please drop by at the inn when you can in the future. They can tell you what pleasurable days I spent there.

'SPOILED AND SELFISH'

From Captain Ryoji Uehara of Nagano Prefecture, who was 22 years old when he was killed in action as a member of the Army Special Attack unit, his target being American shipping in Kadena Bay, Okinawa:

To my dear Father and Mother,

I am so lucky ever since I was given life some 20 years ago to be brought up never being deprived of anything. Under the love and affection of my loving parents, and younger sister, I was so fortunate to spend such happy, youthful days. I say this despite the fact that at times I had a tendency to act in a spoiled and selfish manner. Throughout my youth, of all your children, I was the one who caused you, Father and Mother, the most worry. It pains my heart that my time will come before I can return, or try to return, any of the favours I received. But in Japan where loyalty to the Emperor and filial piety are considered one and the same thing, and total loyalty to the nation is a fulfilment of filial piety, I am confident of your forgiveness.

As an active pilot, I spend each and every day with death as a premise. Every letter and each word I have written constitutes my last will and testament. In the sky so high above, death is never a cause for fear. Will I in fact die when I hit the target? No, I cannot believe that I am going to die and there was even a time when I felt a sudden urge somehow to dive into a target. The

fact of the matter is that I am never afraid of death. To the contrary, I even welcome it. The reason for this is my deep belief
that, through death, I'll be able to get together again with my
beloved older brother, Tatsu. To be reunited with him in heaven
is what I desire the most. I do not have any specific attitude to
life and death. My thinking is that the cultivation of a specific
attitude towards them would amount to an attempt to give a meaning and value to death, something that may stem from a person's
fear of an uncertain death. My belief is that death is a passage
leading to reunion with my loved ones in heaven. I am not afraid
to die. Death is nothing to be afraid of when you see it as just a
stage in the process of ascending towards heaven.

Briefly said, I have always admired liberalism, mainly because
I felt that this political philosophy was the only one to follow
if Japan were really to survive for eternity. Perhaps this sort of
thinking seems foolish, but it is only because Japan is currently
drowned in totalitarianism. Nevertheless (and this state of affairs
notwithstanding), it will be clear to any human being who sees
clearly and is willing to reflect on the very nature of his or her
humanity that liberalism is the most logical ideology.

It seems to me that a nation's probable success in the prose-
cution of a war would, on the very basis of that nation's ideology, be clearly evident even before the war was fought. It would
in fact be so obvious that eventual victory would clearly be seen
to belong to the nation that holds a natural ideology, i.e., an
ideology which in its way embraces human nature itself.

I once had a desire to help make Japan like the British Empire
of bygone days. But that hope has been dashed. At this point
in time, I will gladly give up my life for Japan's liberty and
independence.

While the rise and fall of one's nation is indeed a matter of
immense importance for any human being, the same shift
dwindles to relative insignificance when and if that same human
being places it within the context of the universe as a whole. Exactly
as the saying has it, 'Pride goeth before a fall' (or, those who savour
victory will soon find themselves in the camp of the defeated).
And even if America and Great Britain turn out to be victorious
against us, they will eventually learn that the day of their own
defeat is imminent. It pleases me to think that, even if they are
not to be defeated in the near future, they may be turned to dust
anyway through an explosion of the globe itself. Not only that,
but the people who are getting the most fun out of life now are

most certainly doomed to die in the end. The only difference is whether it comes sooner or later.

Please note: in the drawer, right side of my bookcase, in the annex of the house, you will find the book I am leaving behind. If the drawer does not open, please open the left drawer and pull out a nail – then try the right drawer again.

Well, then, I pray that you will take good care of yourselves. Then, goodbye. *Gokigen-yo* [Farewell].

Goodbye for ever.

Ryoji Uehara

'THIS IS MY LAST DAY'

Last letter from Flying Petty Officer First Class Isao Masuo:

Dear Parents,

Please congratulate me. I have been given a splendid opportunity to die. This is my last day. The destiny of our homeland hinges on the decisive battle in the seas to the south [evidently, in Okinawan waters] where I shall fall like a blossom from a luxuriant cherry tree.

I shall be a shield for His Majesty and die cleanly along with my squadron leader and other friends. I wish that I could be born seven times, each time to smite the enemy.

How I appreciate this chance to die like a man! I am grateful from the depths of my heart to the parents who have reared me with their constant prayers and tender love. And I am grateful as well to my squadron leader and superior officers who have looked after me as if I were their own son and given me such careful training.

Thank you, my parents, for the 23 years during which you have cared for me and inspired me. I hope that my present deed will in some small way repay what you have done for me. Think well of me and know that your Isao died for our country. This is my last wish, and there is nothing else that I desire.

I shall return in spirit and look forward to your visit to the Yasukuni Shrine. Please take good care of yourselves.

How glorious is the Special Attack Corps' Giretsu Unit, whose Suisei bombers will attack the enemy! Our goal is to dive against the aircraft carriers of the enemy. Movie cameramen have been here to take our pictures. It is possible that you may see us in newsreels at the theatre.

We are 16 warriors manning the bombers. May our deaths be as sudden and clean as the shattering of crystal.

This is written at Manila on the eve of our sortie.

Isao

'WILY POLITICIANS'

From Ensign Teruo Yamaguchi:

Dear Father,

As death approaches, my only regret is that I have never been able to do anything good for you in my life.

I was selected quite unexpectedly to be a Special Attack pilot and will be leaving for Okinawa today. Once the order was given for my one-way mission it became my sincere wish to achieve success in fulfilling this last duty. Even so, I cannot help feeling a strong attachment to this beautiful land of Japan. Is that a weakness on my part?

On learning that my time had come I closed my eyes and saw visions of your face, mother's, grandmother's, and the faces of my close friends. It was bracing and heartening to realize that each of you wants me to be brave. I will do it. I will.

My life in the service has not been filled with sweet memories. It is a life of resignation and self-denial, certainly not a comfortable one. As a *raison d'être* for service life, I can see only that it gives me a chance to die for my country. If this seems bitter it probably is because I had experienced the sweetness of life before joining the service.

The other day I received 'The Philosophy on Life and Death' written by a Lieutenant Otsubo which you so kindly sent. It seems to me that while he appears to have hit on some truth, he was concerned mostly with superficial thoughts on the service. It is of no avail to express it now, but in my 23 years of life I have worked out my own philosophy.

It leaves a bad taste in my mouth when I think of the deceits being played on innocent citizens by some of our wily politicians. But I am willing to take orders from the high command, and even from the politicians, because I believe in the polity of Japan.

The Japanese way of life is indeed beautiful, and I am proud of it, as I am of Japanese history and mythology which reflect the purity of our ancestors and their belief in the past – whether or not those beliefs are true. That way of life is the product of all the best things which our ancestors have handed down to us. And the living embodiment of all wonderful things out of our past is the Imperial Family which, too, is the crystallization of the splendour and beauty of Japan and its people. It is an honour to be able to give my life in defence of these beautiful and lofty things.

Okinawa is as much a part of Japan as Goto Island. [Lying off the western coast of Kyushu, Goto Island was a gateway to Japan for the entrance of Chinese culture.] An inner voice keeps saying that I must smite the foe who violates our homeland. My grave will be the sea around Okinawa, and I will see my mother and grandmother again. I have neither regret nor fear about death. I only pray for the happiness of you and all my fellow countrymen.

My greatest regret in this life is the failure to call you *chichiue* [revered father]. I regret not having given any demonstration of the true respect which I have always had for you. During my final plunge, though you will not hear it, you may be sure that I will be saying *chichiue* to you and thinking of all you have done for me.

I have not asked you to come to see me at the base because I know that you are comfortable at Amakusa. It is a good place to live. The mountains north of the base remind me of Sugiyama and Magarisaka on Goto Island, and I have often thought of the days when you took Akira and me on picnics to Matsuyama near the powder magazine. I also recall riding with you to the crematorium at Magarisaka as a youngster, without clearly understanding then that mother had died.

I leave everything to you. Please take good care of my sisters. One setback in its history does not mean the destruction of a nation. I pray that you will live long. I am confident that a new Japan will emerge. Our people must not be rash in their desire for death.

Fondest regards before departure.

Teruo

Postscript: Without regard for life or name, a samurai will defend his homeland.

ABORTED FLIGHT

Lieutenant Shunsaku Tsuji twice had to abort a suicide mission, the first time on April 12 and again on May 13, 1945. The delays were punishing for Tsuji, from Toyama Prefecture on the Japan Sea coast, who took off on these sorties together with three fellow pilots: Shizuka Imano, Tadao Shiraishi, and Hisamitsu Inaba. Each of them flew a single-seater *Hayabusa* (Peregrine Falcon) fighter. Tsuji wrote several letters before his last mission, and his final days are vividly described by Mie Yuhashi, a young woman who worked at the base canteen and had befriended the youthful pilot.

On both of Tsuji's aborted missions, after flying 600 kilometres towards the seas off Okinawa Island he and his fellow pilots failed to spot an enemy task force owing to poor weather conditions and returned to their base. On their third try, taking off from Taiwan's Hualien Air Base at 5 p.m. on May 17, they did not return, having, says an official report, 'successfully engaged American targets'. A US official 'Kamikaze score card' for that date says the destroyer *Douglas J. Fox*, which was cruising between Taiwan and Okinawa, was hit by the enemy and was 'so badly damaged that it played no further role in the war'. It is likely that the destroyer was the target of Tsuji's sortie.

An hour before taking off on his earlier unsuccessful sortie, on May 13, Tsuji wrote the following letter to his parents:

Dear Parents,

On this day, May 13, I am taking off to attack the enemy around Okinawa. My heart holds no doubts or disbelief about what I am doing. On my last sortie, unfortunately I failed to find the enemy due to very poor weather. I turned back, cursing my bad luck. But this next time I am going to accomplish my task; that is, although I will quit this life, I will take with me a 'big prize'.

I received a piece of news that elated me. Lieutenant Tadamasa Fukuzwa is flying with us to verify the results of our mission. He is from our village and studied at the Toyama Teachers' College side by side with me for two years. How happy I am that he will be witnessing my dive into an aircraft carrier, observing how the carrier explodes and sinks.

I have no more time for writing. I only wish for the luck to strike a carrier. Goodbye, Dad and Mom! Mom, I am taking your photograph with me. Don't lament! I pray for the prosperity and the health of our family. Please pass to our neighbours our best wishes.

Shunsaku

When Tsuji's second mission was aborted, he wrote another – his final letter. It was dated May 17th and mentions his sister, Ritsuko:

Dear Parents,

I just received the good news from you that Ritsuko was accepted by the Prefectural High School. I had eagerly waited to hear about her success! Now I can depart with a glad heart. Congratulations to Ritsuko!

We will take off shortly, at 5 p.m. This time I know I am going to succeed. Ritsuko, you must take good care of our parents on my behalf.

Shunsaku

After Tsuji's death, his parents received a long letter from Mie Yuhashi, the young woman at the canteen who was also a volunteer at the barracks, where she helped clean the premises and mend the pilots' uniforms. She lived close to the air base with her family. Here is the letter sent by Miss Yuhashi to Tsuji's parents on the day following his death:

To the parents of Lieutenant Shunsaku Tsuji:

The season of bright green foliage is upon us. I trust you are all in good health. I met your son often and got to know him quite well. I was asked by Shunsaku to mail to you the enclosed notes, just before he departed on his last mission. I am working at the billets where Shunsaku spent his days after he arrived from another base on Taiwan.

At that time I knew your son only by the name on the list. A few days after he came back from his first unsuccessful sortie, he visited our station and chatted for a while. During the conversation, he said he lost his Rising Sun *hachimaki* [headband], which he tied over his flyer's cap, when it was blown away while he was flying towards Okinawa.

When I promised to make him another *hachimaki* for him, he was delighted. And I did make one for him.

That day he came to our home for a visit. I had a younger brother of Shunsaku's age who was also serving in the Air Force, and therefore I felt a special affinity towards Shunsaku. I tried my best, as if I were in your place, to comfort him.

I wish to tell you that all the Special Attack pilots I have met are pure-hearted and jovial. It is difficult to conceive that, momentarily, they are about to meet their end. But I have yet to encounter any of them who walk with an air of gloom. I have always wondered how young people could come to such a saintly state of mind so they can face death wearing blissful smiles. They seemed, also, so manly and terribly attractive.

All of these young men were kind-hearted and were emotionally tied to their families.

Plate 1   A master pilot – Takeo Tagata in 1940

Plate 2   College student flyer
Hichiro Naemura in 1942

Plate 3   Tagata prepares for
action from a Taiwan airport
in a Hien ('Swallow') plane on
October 12, 1944

Plate 4 Seasoned pilot Hichiro Naemura (at left) with friends beside his assault plane outside Tokyo, Japan in November 1944

Plate 5 'Father of the Kamikaze' – Admiral Onishi (Kyodo News Photo)

Plate 6 Before his epic flight. The first official Kamikaze pilot, Lt. Yukio Seki, on October 25, 1944 (Kyodo News Photo)

Plate 7 Their last picture: youthful Kamikaze pilots with mascot

Plate 8 General Tominaga and son, Yasushi, a Kamikaze pilot

Plate 9 Yasushi Tominaga, before his suicide mission

Miss Yuhashi added:

> All the while I attended the men of the Special Attack Corps,
> I felt wistful and was overcome by untold sadness. But at the same
> time, I learned how precious is the spirit of sacrifice carried out
> for the good of the people. They were possessed by true altru-
> ism. That I have been acquainted with such a noble spirit will
> remain a priceless treasure for the rest of my life. I shall tell and
> spread the story for as many people as possible.
>
> When Shunsaku came to visit us for the first time, my mother
> and I made a bowl of *udon* [special Japanese noodles] for him.
> He was so delighted that he exclaimed: 'Oh! This is my favourite
> dish. I searched for this when I was at my last base but couldn't
> find it. Boy! I like it so much! I feel so satisfied!'
>
> Shunsaku finished three bowls of *udon* one after another that
> evening. We were all filled with joy as we never expected to please
> him so much. Then Shunsaku said to me in a serious voice: 'I
> have a favour to ask of you. After my death is confirmed, would
> you inform my family that I departed on my last mission full of
> joy after I had feasted on *udon*? My last thoughts go to my par-
> ents. They would be consoled by knowing how I had departed.'
>
> I promised Shunsaku I would do so and he gave me a broad
> smile while shedding some tears.

Here the letter ends.

Miss Yuhashi vividly remembers how Shunsaku Tsuji walked out of
his barracks towards his plane. 'He was smiling, as if going for a walk
in the neighbourhood.' Here is her last recollection:

> At 5 p.m. on May 17, 1945, Shunsaku's plane took off for good.
> It was figured out that Shunsaku would probably encounter an
> enemy vessel sometime between 7.40 and 8 p.m. As the hands
> of the clock approached that time, I went to a nearby Shinto shrine
> and prayed that he and the others would succeed in their mis-
> sion. The next morning, I learned that Shunsaku had crashed into
> an enemy vessel. According to the escort pilot who flew along to
> confirm the results, Shunsaku capably led his formation and
> when the time came each plane banked its wings in farewell and
> dived towards their target.

Miss Yuhashi added a postscript to her letter: 'Let me wish you the
best of health. From Taiwan, I pray for your family's prosperity.'

Later, Shunsaku's sword and uniforms were entrusted to the Special Attack Corps' *ihingakari* (the place for articles left behind by the departed) to be forwarded to his parents.

According to the official report, Shunsaku perished at 7.35 p.m. on May 17, 1945.

12

SECOND THOUGHTS

From the beginning there were flyers who did not agree with suicide tactics. For example, Lieutenant Commander Tadashi Minobe, flight leader of a group of night fighters in the Philippines, was openly sceptical of Special Attack operations. But in spite of Admiral Onishi's announcement that he would not tolerate dissent, the admiral never forced Minobe and the men under him to take part in Kamikaze missions. A memorable Onishi–Minobe confrontation took place, however, and, not long after that, Minobe was transferred to Japan where he fulfilled his duties as flight leader of the 131st Air Group until the end of the war.

The confrontation occurred in mid-November 1944 when Minobe was summoned to Clark Airfield near Manila to report to Onishi. Minobe flew in from Cebu Air Base where his unit was stationed. When Minobe arrived at headquarters, Onishi was standing in front of a map spread on a table and he asked Minobe how he proposed to attack a US amphibious air base in the Kossal Passage in Palau.

'That's easy,' Minobe replied. 'I have four Zero fighters. From Cebu to Kossal is about 600 miles. I will raid them and destroy them with a single stroke.'

'No, don't use Zeros,' Onishi said. 'They are being saved for Leyte. Use Gekko (Moonlight) planes.'

'Admiral, we cannot use the Gekko because they are equipped with slanted guns.'

'Then let me use the Gekkos for Special Attack missions,' said Onishi.

'Admiral, I do not intend to talk back to you, but I do not agree with the idea that Kamikaze operations are the answer in every case. If I can fulfil your aim by employing other means, I believe it would be so much better. I believe we should try other methods with all our might.'

Onishi listened intently. Minobe continued.

'First of all, suicide operations are outside military tactics. No commander should choose to employ them. I have my own tactics and I am not going to obey you in using my unit for that purpose, sir!'

Surprisingly, Onishi nodded. 'I am impressed. You are a commander with firm determination and experience. Good! I am not going to ask your unit to take part in Special Attack operations. But do not send Zeros to the Kossal Passage. Please attack the torpedo boat and amphibious plane bases there.'

Minobe personally led the attack and succeeded in razing the amphibious base.

There were some flyers who, seeing the ruins of their cities and feeling the loss of thousands of their fellow pilots, were seized with inner doubt about the official optimism on the course of the war. Ryuji Nagatsuka, a suicide pilot who survived and published an autobiography in 1973 called *I was a Kamikaze*, saw suicide aircraft attacks as ineffective and even foolhardy because towards the close of the war there were no escort planes to protect them. While death might be meaningful if it accomplished something specific and worthwhile, the suicide missions were seen by pilots like him as a squandering of young lives. Another Special Attack pilot who had been sceptical of the official view of events (he was killed when his plane was shot down in the last months of the war) left behind a poem with these non-conformist lines:

Cease your optimism
And open your eyes
People of Japan.
Our nation is heading towards defeat.
. . . .
[But] a new road to reconstruction
Will be ours to build.

Ryozo Ban was uneasy with what he saw as a disproportionate zeal among his companions waiting to be called up for suicide missions.

Ban was of two minds about his own imminent sortie. On the one hand, he had volunteered as a Special Attack pilot out of selfless patriotism and knew that the time was fast approaching when his life would be snuffed out. On the other, he had a yearning for life and was torn by regrets at the thought of giving it up so easily. As a 26-year-old pilot with four years of flying experience, he had doubts about the wisdom of his superiors who regarded pilots like himself as expendable. But a big majority of his companions were novice pilots with only a few hours' flying experience, and many were still in their teens. After they had volunteered for a suicide mission, they were selected to join one of the special attack units in preparation for what was termed their *tai-atari*, or body-crashing, flight.

In August, 1944, Second Lieutenant Ban was transferred to Narimasu Air Base in Tokyo from Jinzhou in Manchuria where he had completed his flight training. At Jinzhou, he was assigned to the 26th Air Training Squadron where Type 97 fighters were used to train pilots.

'I remember that bright August day when we were transferred,' wrote Ban, who survived the war although he had been assigned to a Kamikaze unit that intercepted the giant B-29 bombers:

> I and two other second lieutenants, Akira Matano and Nobuo Sugimoto, flew on a transport plane over the Korean Straits and landed at Narimasu Air Base. As we landed we heard the roar of engines as Type 2 fighters began to take off. The sight of these planes made me a bit nervous because I was not sure I could fly such a state-of-the-art fighter plane.

Ban remembers a later day in November when all of the flyers were assembled at the canteen. A senior officer of his air wing was speaking:

> Enemy bombers are expected to conduct raids over Tokyo in force in the immediate future. The 10th Air Division has decided to launch *tai-atari* attacks in order to break his morale and also to inflict severe damage on him. Each one of you who desires to volunteer is asked to fill out the form that is on the table in front of you. After filling out the form put it into the nearby envelope and seal it tightly.

Says Ban:

> Although we were aware of fierce air battles raging in the Philippine theatre, there was not yet a sense of emergency in the

Tokyo area. But I had to fill out the form. I brooded for some moments, then circled the first line that said 'enthusiastically wish'. As the war situation was heating up, some of us were called upon to die and we, the officers, had a duty to die ahead of the men, so I thought. As for me, I was fortunate in that I had brothers who could take care of our family.

As it happened, the first four Kamikaze flyers were chosen from the men who had circled the words 'enthusiastically wish'. But Ban was not one of the four chosen:

On November 24, we were alerted that a large formation of enemy bombers was flying northward towards us. We expected a full-scale bomb attack. As we finished lunch in haste, the order was blared through the public address system that our unit should take off to intercept the approaching planes.

The announcement was followed by the order: '*Tokko-tai shutsudo!*' ('Special Attack Corps, sally!'). Ban writes:

We were ordered to climb high above the skies of Tokyo. Our company, with 12 Type 2 fighters, took off and when we reached an altitude of 9,000 metres over Hachioji, we spotted approaching B-29 formations. We were above the enemy. This was going to be my first taste of battle. I swooped down on a formation of ten B-29s firing my cannons. The bombers were firing at me with all of their weapons. But I failed to hit any of the B-29s. I executed a sharp turn but it was difficult to close in again. I was surprised how fast the B-29s flew. I followed them and managed to catch them off the coast of Choshi as they were heading back to Saipan. I attacked them again but again was not successful. As my fuel was running quite low, I returned to the base.

The first suicide attack on B-29s by Ban's air wing was delivered that day. One 'kill' by the *tokko* unit was confirmed:

We were stunned by the feat [Ban says]. We were all caught up in a solemn mood. That evening, as I was playing a game of *go* with Second Lieutenant Ichiki Omori at the officers' billet, the adjutant to the wing commander came over and said: 'We received an order from Division Headquarters to form two more Special Attack units of eight planes each.'
Saying this, the adjutant left immediately.

I knew the adjutant well as he was from the same class I attended at the Army flying school. That night I was not able to sleep well because I kept thinking that he came to let us know that officers like myself were required to lead the Kamikaze units.

Ban continues:

The next morning, as I went to the airfield, maintenance crews were busy removing cannons from my plane. I cannot adequately describe how I then felt. How miserable to see a fighter plane being stripped of its cannons! It was no longer a fighter but a simple flying machine. And I was being told to die in that aircraft! Jousting in the air was supposed to be my job but now my pride as a fighter pilot was shattered.

When I returned to pilots' quarters, First Lieutenant Yoshizawa asked me to fetch Sergeant First Class Masumi Kou. I went to the non-commissioned officers' quarters and asked him to come with me. Yoshizawa ordered us to stand at attention. We saluted him. He looked embarrassed as he said, 'To tell the truth, I wanted to be selected, but you two men were chosen for a Special Attack mission.'

I thought: this is my death sentence. It is an order to die. I heard myself say '*Hai*' in a choking voice.

Kou answered, '*Hai, yarimasu!*' ('Yes, gladly!') in a buoyant tone.

His youthful courage surprised me. Although I was calm I thought I could not match his stoutness. I was informed about the other members of my unit. I also learned that Lieutenant Sugimoto was leading the other unit, although his sortie was later cancelled. In my heart I felt displeased that such an important order had not been delivered by the wing commander in person.

Now I had to face certain death. Before this I'd thought of death often but only in abstract terms, never as a reality. That day I lost my appetite completely. But my vanity forced me to gulp down my food. I did not want to be seen as a coward who was so scared that he could not eat. In my mind I approved of the Kamikaze squadrons, but I could not detach myself so easily from an ardent desire to live. I tried to console myself with the thought that my death could contribute towards saving my family and our homeland from destruction by our enemies.

Once I made up my mind to die, the temporal world became a completely new world. It lost all sensuality for me. Ordinary emotions like laughter, anger, happiness and sorrow all belonged to the other world in which people aspired to continue their lives. My life became void of emotion. My fellow pilots turned into men belonging to a world apart. I could not even join them in normal conversation. It suddenly occurred to me that flying, conducting firing exercises and other training were all intended to help you survive against the enemy. Now I lost interest in keeping myself physically fit. I did not want to swallow food. A new sorrow enveloped me when I realized that I could not leave behind me a child to continue myself in the world. I now completely gave up all earthly desires and only waited for that last moment when I would meet the enemy in a body-crashing attack.

Meanwhile, Kamikaze attacks against B-29s continued. Sergeant Kou crashed into a B-29's left-wing engine soon after he sent a radio message saying, 'Sergeant Kou executing crash attack!' He sent two of the planes plunging to earth. Many Tokyoites saw Kou's plane crashing into the intruding plane and took photographs. But many on the ground did not know that Kou had himself perished along with the crew of the American plane.

Daredevil pilots soon became adept at ramming American B-29 'flying fortresses'. These ramming attacks by interceptor units gradually increased from the spring of 1945 as B-29s began flying at lower altitudes for precision bombing. Ban later wrote that he voiced opposition to continue what amounted to suicide tactics against B-29s as they were flying lower and thus could be effectively attacked by normal means. At the same time, American carrier-born fighters began regular raids on the Kanto (Tokyo–Yokohama) area. Reports said they attacked civilian targets in order to break the will and the morale of the population; and that because of this, the need to intercept the carrier-based fighters became extremely important. Against these fast, incoming planes, Ban did not consider body-crashing tactics at all worthwhile.

Ban sallied on a suicide mission only once. But because of thick clouds, all the Special Attack planes failed to engage the enemy. From December, delivery of the new Type 4 fighters began and the wing then needed officer-flyers to lead the advanced fighter squadrons. Therefore, Ban and Sugimoto were removed from the Kamikaze units and once more they became conventional interceptor pilots.

13

EYEWITNESSES

LAST MESSAGE

Often the last moments of a Special Attack sortie were not known even to headquarters because the observer planes or escort fighters were themselves destroyed or had never accompanied the doomed pilots in the first place. Every suicide pilot knew he would never find out if his mission was a success. In addition, very few last-minute messages were received from the pilots. However, here is one that was sent by Tsunesaburo Nishio, commander of the Fugaku Air Unit of the Japanese Army's Special Attack Corps, in mid-November 1944 before his unit dived against Allied naval targets east of Luzon Island in the Philippines:

5.47 p.m. All the planes are ready to attack.
5.50 p.m. All the members are in high fighting spirits and morale.
6.02 p.m. We have spotted an American task force and are now peeling off to smash them. . . .

Here Nishio's message stopped. Members of the Fugaku unit were reported to have sunk one US warship near Luzon on the evening of November 13.

TAGATA'S KAMIKAZE STUDENTS

Flight instructor Takeo Tagata witnessed his first Kamikaze sally on March 22, 1945 and his second two weeks later when he was present at the Matsuyama Air Base in Taipei, the Taiwanese capital. Tagata's students were not yet members of a suicide unit, though they were determined to fly such missions. Tagata has described what happened:

On March 22, 1945, the Eighth Air Division, to which my unit belonged, ordered our unit to conduct a Kamikaze mission against the US fleet in Okinawan waters. Twenty-one officers, two warrant officers, 80 non-commissioned officers and men volunteered for the mission. Including myself, they represented the entire corps of pilots.

That morning, a bugle sounded and the 103 pilots gathered on the grounds of our unit. They were divided into three companies. Some 500 ground crews also lined up in formation. Major Yoshiharu Kobayashi, our commanding officer, accompanied by his adjutant, Captain Kiichi Kobayashi, came out of the command post and the major mounted a podium carrying some papers in his hand.

'I hereby order a *tokko* mission in accordance with Divisional Orders!' Major Kobayashi shouted.

His voice trembled as he read from the list of names he carried.

'Second Lieutenant Tomio Hatakeyama, step forward! You are ordered to lead the 120th Makoto [roughly, 'faithful in duty'] Squadron!'

Hatakeyama exclaimed '*Hai!* [yes]' and stepped two paces forward.

'Sergeant First Class Akio Hotta, Corporals Mitsuo Hagino, Eiji Tanaka and Kazuo Higashitsubone. You are assigned to the 120th Makoto Squadron!'

The men stepped forward, each shouting '*Hai!*' as their names were called. They stood at attention behind Lieutenant Hatakeyama.

'Second Lieutenant Taiso Gomi! You are ordered to lead the 116th Makoto Squadron!'

Lieutenant Gomi instantly smiled and, shouting '*Hai!*', stepped forward.

'Privates First Class Shigeru Arai, Shigeo Tanaka and Kensuke Ichimaru! You are assigned to the 116th Makoto Squadron!' The three men, shouting at the top of their voices, '*Hai!*', stepped forward, taking their position behind their newly appointed squadron leader.

Then the squadron leaders replied.

'Second Lieutenant Tomio Hatakeyama and five of us respectfully report to you that we were assigned to Tokubetsu-Kogeki [Special Attack] 120th Squadron, sir!' Hatakeyama barked.

'Second Lieutenant Taiso Gomi and five of us respectfully report to you that we were assigned to Tokubetsu-Kogeki 116th Squadron, sir!' Gomi shouted.

Major Kobayashi acknowledged the reports and then said:

'Warrant Officer Takeo Tagata! You are ordered to oversee the transportation for Lieutenant Hatakeyama and the men who are transferred to the Divisional Headquarters in Taipei from your embarkation place to the Kagi Station, leaving at 10 a.m. on March 23!'

Since all ten men were Tagata's students, he was grateful to the commanding officer for letting him accompany them to the station to bid them farewell. At 1 p.m. a send-off party was given in the auditorium of a primary school which the unit was using. Hatakeyama, representing his squadron, was the speaker:

We were ordered to fly *tokko* missions today. Now that we were chosen to spearhead the Special Attack, we all realize the gravity of the responsibility that rests on our shoulders. Frankly, we are still immature as pilots, but we will exert our best. Officers, non-commissioned officers and men may differ in rank in our squadron. But we are united by a fierce sense of love for our Motherland.

The lieutenant paused, then addressing the men who would be left behind, added:

'Once the war is over, please reconstruct our nation as a peace-loving, righteous and spiritually rich country that will contribute to the creation of a better world. Please take good care of the families of our men.'

Lieutenant Gomi followed him, saying: 'I am sorry to be given this honorary order in place of many senior officers. But I entrust all of you to fight for the Motherland.'

Then, taking turns, each of the squadron members delivered parting words.

Tagata recalls:

> I saw streaks of tears running down the cheeks of many men
> who were listening to the ten departing flyers. But we had to
> look cheerful. The gods forbid that we should appear wistful!
> Curiously, there was, I noted, a stark contrast in the men's reac-
> tions. While the Special Attack flyers appeared very much at ease,
> smiling or laughing from time to time (perhaps because they had,
> as it were, made their peace with the world), those who were
> remaining behind looked tense and uneasy. It seemed that it was
> not the *tokko* flyers who were putting themselves through a great
> ordeal but those who were left behind. Clearly, those who sent
> the *tokko* flyers out looked plaintive. But while their eyes were
> moist, the eyes of the departing flyers seemed to burn with inten-
> sity. I was astonished at their joviality. Such scenes were repeated
> again and again. There was something sacred, something exalted
> about being close to death by your own choice. To the men it
> was death for a lofty cause. In a word, these flyers radiated an
> energy which overwhelmed us.

At 4 p.m. Tagata returned to his apartment near the base in order
to prepare a dinner for Sergeant Hotta and seven men. They were to
come at 7 p.m. He asked the cook to prepare the best meal possible.
At 6 p.m. he went over to a photo studio to ask for the photographer
to come to his place. On the way, passing the Hokko Shinto shrine,
he saw Corporal Hagino praying before the shrine just as the sun was
going down. ('I thought I had never seen anyone who looked more
saintly.') The corporal was only 19 years old but had the dignity of an
older man. Tagata decided not to disturb him. When the men, led by
Hotta, arrived, they avoided all talk about the Kamikaze mission, all
of them simply enjoying the evening.

But it was far from easy for Tagata. 'When we exchanged toasts we
did so without saying that they were our farewell toasts.'

The next morning at 10 a.m. Tagata and the pilots boarded a truck
which took them to the railway station. The station master at Kagi Station
and a group of military police were waiting to pay their respects to
the Special Attack flyers, whose ages were between 18 and 24. They
chatted until the train pulled into the station bound for Taipei.

Tagata shook hands with each of his students.

As they were parting, Hotta said:

'Throughout history, young men like us defended our Motherland.
We are called upon to follow them. We are gladly sacrificing our lives

for the good of our nation. I am convinced that those who survive this war will rebuild our nation and that they will be leaders in a better world!'

A fortnight later Tagata landed in Taipei from Pingtung in the south piloting a Hayabusa (Type I) fighter at around 9.50 a.m. He was ordered to go to the Air Divisional Headquarters in Taipei to receive official papers for his unit. He returned to Masuyama Air Base in the afternoon after collecting the documents. Shortly before 5 p.m. he went into the tent for conventional pilots and crews. Everyone getting ready to fly would wait in that tent which was next to another tent reserved for Kamikaze pilots about to take off. Tagata noticed that there were five Hayabusa fighters parked on the apron already loaded with bombs. At this moment five pilots came out of the 'Kamikaze tent' led by a very young second lieutenant. All of them wore a *hachimaki*, the headband with a red circle in the middle over their flight caps. It was reminiscent of the samurai who went into battle wearing a similar headband. Tagata:

> The five pilots were smiling naturally, looking very much relaxed under the circumstances. They lined up as the divisional commander appeared accompanied by staff officers. The five pilots saluted their general. He in turn, looking very tense, returned the salute and gave a short farewell talk in a voice that was almost choking. The Kamikaze pilots were going to attack a US task force near the island of Okinawa. They planned to reach the target area just before sundown.

Tagata makes an interesting observation. He says that although the divisional commander, with the rank of general, far outranked the young pilots, the latter appeared more calm than their commander. The general looked anxious, as if he were addressing not his subordinates but his superiors. When the general went over to each pilot and shook hands, his facial muscles remained taut, unlike the pilots who seemed to smile genuinely as they shook hands with him.

Next, small ritual cups of sake (which are more like tiny plates) were handed out by an adjutant to each pilot. The general also took a cup. Sake was poured, the general wished all the men success in their mission, and the cups were drained. Then each flyer turned and headed for his plane.

'I stood by,' Tagata says, 'completely awed by what I had seen. I was unable for some time to forget the contrast that I had observed at that farewell meeting.'

On the airfield the planes started to taxi, one by one.

Tagata recalls the scene: 'We who watched, formed a line, waving frantically at the planes. And we continued to wave for some time after the planes disappeared from our sight.'

FOUR BALLS OF FIRE

As the war drew to a close more and more suicide pilots and their aircraft were immolated in the fireballs thrown up by Allied naval guns. Often the escort pilots, too, were killed in action. Three months before Japan's surrender, an escort pilot saw the elimination of his entire Kamikaze squadron, then returned safely to his base and reported the details of the mission.

This account is taken from the notes of the escort pilot, Lieutenant Takashige Sakamoto:

On May 17, 1945, at 1600, I lined up with four *tokko* pilots at Hualien Air Base on the east coast of Taiwan. I yelled to the wing commander:

'The Sakamoto formation will now take off to attack enemy vessels off Kerama Islands [of the Okinawa group]. The estimated time of crashing into the enemy will be 17.30!' We all were saluting at the same time. The wing commander, returning the salute, tersely replied:

'Do your utmost. I wish you success.'

I felt unease, thinking: success? What a cruel way to send them off. But I knew that severity reigns when one is close to the battleground. I also told myself that there are those who sally forth and those who bid farewell. How can their minds meet?

In a short while the engines began roaring. Maintenance crews were busy making last-minute adjustments.

I regained my composure. I wished that all the planes would fly to their targets without mechanical trouble.

My orders were to guide the four Special Attack (*tokko*) pilots to their destination and, after confirming their results, to return to the base. I was not myself a *tokko* flyer but I knew very well that most of the guidance, or escort, planes failed to return, having to engage swarms of enemy fighters. Anyway, I knew the four pilots well. They were all lieutenants junior class: Hisamitsu Inaba, Koreshizu Ima, Tadao Shiraishi, and Shunsaku Tsuji. All were graduates of a teacher's college. Their *Hayabusa* planes were stripped of cannons and radios and carried only enough fuel to fly for three hours to reach their targets, because of the acute shortage of aviation fuel.

The four flyers were green and therefore they were not able to fly a long distance or fly in formation. I was full of deep admiration for them. Just before boarding their planes, I confronted the four young men. They all appeared outwardly tense but showed no deep-set fear at all. In fact, they looked normal. This was my first time to act as a guide for Kamikaze planes. These would be my last words to them. I wanted to boost morale but I was at a loss what to say.

I swallowed my saliva and said firmly, almost in one breath:
'Have confidence in me and follow my lead. That's all!'
'Yes, sir!' They replied in unison.
I pressed each one's hands strongly.

The flyers would reach the target area by 17.30 just as dusk began to set in. This was the best hour to strike at the enemy. And just before they dived into their targets they would pull the safety pin on their bomb loads.

'A member of the ground crew lowered a red flag which was the signal to take off.'

About Sakamoto: in 1939 he had learned to fly as a member of the Kansai University Flying Club, where he won first place in an essay contest held by the *Asahi Shimbun* newspaper on the subject of aviation. The winning prize was a glider. In the spring of 1941, while he was in college, Sakamoto volunteered as an Army Air Force cadet and saw action during the next four years. As a fighter pilot during the last year of war, he also performed duty as an observer of suicide missions, although he sometimes acted as fighter-escort. But his primary duty was to guide the young aviators to their naval targets. Sakamoto continued his account:

A staff officer ordered us to commence our sortie at 5.30 p.m. Frankly I hated staff officers. This one had no experience as a flyer. He had come from an infantry unit and in issuing orders he always sounded bureaucratic. For this mission no escort fighters were to be provided. In the event we encountered enemy planes, the pilots were given orders that if there were no other means of escape, to ram into the enemy planes. Meanwhile, I was to engage them conventionally. More than that, I was under orders to defend the four Kamikaze pilots, should they be attacked.

Once we reached Ishigaki Island, we were to descend quickly, skimming the sea at zero altitude.

It took two hours and a half to reach Okinawa. The last hour and a half, we breathed easily as we skimmed over the ocean to avoid radar detection.

I was physically exhausted after skimming the waves for an hour and a half. My muscles were completely stiff. Although the sun was about to go down the sky was still bright. Now the sea turned a dark blue. It became difficult to tell our height above the sea. I was flying, relying solely on the compass for two hours now. I saw the shadow of an island just ahead of me. To my left the shadow of another island became larger. It was Kumejima Island.

I signalled by hand to the four planes following me to remove their safety pins. All four did what I had ordered and I saw brass particles flying in the air. This meant that their bombs were now activated.

Each pilot now waved his arms in farewell to me. I banked my wings violently, ordering them to commence their attack. Our formation now broke up. Each pilot rose sharply in the direction of Okinawa. I saw the [outlying] Kerama Islands in the dark. There were a few hundred enemy vessels appearing as black dots floating on the silvery sea.

I shuddered.

The time was 19.30. Darkness was gathering quickly. I dropped my fuel tanks and test shot my cannons. My four pilots reached their designated altitude and were now flying horizontally.

Three kilometres to go to reach the targets.

Suddenly a quartet of red, blue, and purple fireballs lit up the sky. The flak from a few hundred vessels had started. My plane was lifted by the jolts from exploding anti-aircraft shells all around me. The noise was deafening.

In front of me was an eerie sight. The four balls of fire from concentrated flak were enveloping the four attacking planes. The scene was like an impromptu display of fireworks. Only, these fireworks were deadly: as if an angry god had unleashed thunderbolts.

I looked at my watch. It was 1935. I veered momentarily towards the main Okinawa Island. When I returned my gaze to our planes, I saw there were now only three balls of light. The remaining three pilots were still flying horizontally. Then, one of the three planes was hit and I saw a huge flaming ball fall towards the sea. It broke up and disappeared into the black water. Two planes forged ahead at a height of about 1,000 metres. Both started their dives. I couldn't see them but the concentration of anti-aircraft fire told me where they were. A few seconds later, one of them scored a clear hit, though I wasn't able to distinguish the type of vessel it had crashed into. The plane had exploded on impact.

I was hoping that the vessel would also be enveloped in flames. But it did not happen. The other plane also scored a hit. The two target vessels appeared quite big but I was not able to tell the scale of the damage at all.

Now I was left alone in a hostile sky.

I broke radio silence. Using Morse code, I sent out a message, '*chi-gu-go*', which meant that the guide plane had accomplished its mission.

Now I had to report the results. I could not tell what type of ships received hits or the scope of the damage. But I reported that two of the planes were lost while two inflicted damage to medium-sized cruisers. This was not accurate, but I had to say something.

I started my return to Hualien Air Base at 20.00.

Before Sakamoto took off from Hualien, his thoughts turned to home. In quick succession, he says in his notes, the face of his wife (he was newly married) and the image of the war memorial, Yasukuni Shrine, in Tokyo's Kudan district, crossed his mind. The idea of being deified at this most famous of all the Shinto shrines was strongly imprinted in the mind of every soldier. '*Yasukuni de aou!*' ('Let's meet at Yasukuni!') was the catchword among the officers and men. A popular Second World War martial song (it is sung even by young people today) has these lines:

> Cherry blossoms are blooming at
> Yasukuni Shrine in Kudan,
> Let's bloom side by side on the same twig.[1]

Sakamoto, after observing the four suicide planes perish in battle, sent signals to his home base and then turned around, heading for Taiwan. He had never felt so tired. It was his first experience to guide a Kamikaze mission and to observe its results. He was assailed by a desire to fall asleep and, from time to time, he dozed momentarily. He was surprised how physically exhausted he was.

A seasoned pilot, Sakamoto had previously flown for over seven hours in a single flight. But witnessing the last moments of four Kamikaze pilots had debilitated him.

Later when he saw the red lights of Hualien Air Base that marked the runway, it was past 22.00. A beam of light appeared in the dark sky to guide Sakamoto's landing and he automatically turned on his lights and banked his wings. After landing, Samakoto jumped out of his cockpit and, feeling the weight of his recent mission, staggered over to his wing commander, who waited eagerly by the runway. He saluted. Then he reported:

> The Sakamoto formation successfully delivered an attack on the enemy! All the planes reached their target area in the Okinawan waters, but two were lost to fierce anti-aircraft fire. Two crashed into American vessels at 19.35, scoring hits on two medium-sized cruisers. I am sorry that because of the darkness and the A-A fire, I was not able to clearly ascertain the results, sir!

'A job well done, lieutenant!' replied the wing commander, looking into Sakamoto's eyes. 'We heard your signals from the Okinawan waters clearly! Now take a good rest.'

In July 1944, Major-General Kiyaro Yoshida, Commander-in-Chief of the 10th Air Division, based near Kyoto City, issued an order to seven air wings under his command to form Special Attack units. Each air wing was ordered to form a unit of four fighters. Three air training divisions were also placed under General Yoshida's command. Lieutenant Colonel Shizuma Matsumura, a divisional staff officer, took a liaison plane and flew to each air base, delivering the order.

At the same time, Admiral Onishi announced that he had a victory plan, a summary of which was published in the newspaper *Yomiuri* on July 19, 1944. It said: 'We have weapons called aircraft. If one is willing to crash a plane into the enemy, we need not fear the enemy's mobile units.'

The summary ended with these words: 'Those who would make body-crash attacks without heed for their lives deserve the name of godlike soldiers.'

NOTE

[1] For the Japanese, becoming a deity is not a promise of an afterlife or a reunion at the 'pearly gates'. Shinto lacks such a clear vision of an afterlife. There is no heaven or hell. Becoming a *kami* (god) means achieving the respect of the nation. It means being worshipped at Yasukuni Shrine. It may be noted that probably in no other country in the world are military songs sung so widely among the population as in Japan. Even today, young people

break into these songs over wine or beer. But this ought not to be interpreted as a sign of militaristic spirit. Most Japanese songs have a wistful quality. Incidentally, most Japanese of all generations believe that only a well-armed Japan in the nineteenth century saved the country from being dominated by Imperial China (the Sino-Japanese War of 1894) and Czarist Russia (the Russo-Japanese War of 1904–5).

14

THE KOREANS

Admiral Onishi's 'godlike soldiers' are given full honours at the Chiran Peace Museum, in southern Kyushu, which contains the richest collection of Kamikaze artefacts in Japan. At the entrance to the museum there is another attraction: over 1,000 shoulder-high stone lanterns that commemorate 1,036 boyish Kamikaze pilots (the majority were between 17 and 19 years old) who flew from Kyushu bases on their one-way missions against Anglo-American targets. A close-up look at these lanterns shows that each one bears the name of a fallen pilot, as well as the raised image of a Kamikaze: an aviator's cap pulled over a chubby face. Hushed visitors mingle among the endless rows of lanterns, some of them stopping at a particular lantern, looking at one of the names. Some visitors, observing the photos of the flyers, express the thought that the pilots were freed from the process of ageing ever since the hour they took off on their last mission towards Okinawan waters. The youthful flyers, it has been said, all look like Peter Pans.

A helpful guide points out that in the main exhibition hall there is one photograph for every lantern: 1,036 photos altogether. The guide informs that 11 of the photos are of fallen Korean pilots.

During the war 202,341 Koreans served in Japan's Army and Navy.[1] Out of this number 22,183 perished. In 1938, Koreans, except for the elite who joined the Japanese officer corps, were for the first time accepted as volunteers for military service. In 1941, whereas the

Army announced it would accept 3,000 Korean volunteers, 145,000 young Korean men enthusiastically filled out applications. In 1942, more than 250,000 applied for another 3,000 openings. Then, in 1944, military conscription began in Korea. All of the Koreans who fell in the war are deified at Yasukuni Shrine.

Koreans often had to wrestle with the problem of identity. Many Koreans who felt self-conscious about being different tried to become invisible within the Japanese community. At the same time, many educated and well-to-do Koreans sought to assimilate.

A museum guide points to the photo of Captain Kim San Pil, a Korean who led a formation of seven Kamikaze planes against the American fleet off Okinawa on April 3, 1945. The eight flyers took off from Nyutabaru Air Base in Miyagi Prefecture, north-east of Chiran, on Kyushu. A second lieutenant at the time of his sortie, Kim was promoted posthumously to the rank of captain, jumping two ranks, as was the custom for Special Attack pilots. The story of Kim San Pil is interesting not only because it tells about the life of a suicide pilot but also because it reveals how a Korean-born pilot coped with the question of identity.

According to Kim's elder brother, Kim San Yol, San Pil told him after joining the Japanese Army Air Corps: 'I must become more Japanese than the Japanese in order that we Koreans may gain their respect.' It seemed that one way to accomplish this was to attain proficiency in the martial arts. Right away, therefore, San Pil took courses in Kendo, becoming an expert at the sport.

Kim San Pil was born in 1921 in Korea. Upon graduation from Yon Hi College in Seoul (the city was then called Keijo), in 1943, he volunteered for the Imperial Army Air Corps which accepted three Koreans that year from the college, including Kim San Pil. Yon Hi College was a prestigious private school, founded by Christian missionaries in Korea. After Korea regained its independence, the school was renamed Yonsei University.

For his pilot training, Kim San Pil attended the Tachiarai Army Flying School in Kyushu. After he heard that five more Yon Hi College students were accepted by the Army Air Corps, Kim wrote a letter to Gyo Karashima, the Chancellor of the college, in which he said:

I am writing this letter to you with a feeling of joy but also with a trembling hand. A deep satisfaction overwhelms me, helping heal the physical exhaustion from the strenuous training I am receiving. I pledge to you that I will fight bravely and set an example to the lower classmen by shedding my blood in the sky as a guiding beacon in order that they may follow me.

There is another letter sent by San Pil to Karashima that includes these words: 'Every day is devoted to learning how to fly. Thanks to able instructors, I am now at the level of a chick sparrow. It will be some time before I become an eagle.'[2]

The first time he went on leave, Kim took time to visit his alma mater. Aware of his visit, every student chipped in to buy a present for Kim: a samurai sword. Asked to give a 'pep talk' to all the students, Kim took off his jacket, mounted a platform and barked: 'Follow me!'

That was all he said.

Then he got down from the platform and immediately began running. Every student followed him through the fields and woods, running up and down hills for about an hour. It was truly an exercise in youthful vigour as well as stamina.

Many Yon Hi students followed Kim's example and joined the Army Air Corps. After he finished his flying course at Tachiarai, Kim served briefly in Manchuria, afterwards returning to Kyushu by way of Korea. The last meeting between the brothers Kim took place in Pyongyang (then called Heijo) at an inn where San Pil was staying on February 15, 1945. San Pil had already put in a request to volunteer for a Kamikaze mission. At that time his elder brother San Yol was a practising dentist in the port city of Chinnampo, on the coast of the Yellow Sea. (Chinnampo, called Nampo, is now located in North Korea.)

Having learned that his brother and his men were spending two nights in Pyongyang, San Yol rushed to that city to see his younger brother. When they met, San Pil, suppressing his emotion, confided to San Yol that he would shortly embark on a suicide mission.

'Tonight will very probably be our last meeting,' the younger Kim said. 'But please do not tell our mother.' In fact Kim San Pil had six more weeks to live. But it was the last time the brothers met. On April 3, San Pil and his men, who were all Japanese teenagers, perished on a suicide mission.

San Pil also told his brother that he had paid some women to spend the night with his younger fellow pilots because 'I felt sorry for the boys to die without tasting women.' San Pil added: 'The boys were all highly satisfied after the experience. They looked very cheerful in the morning.'

San Pil's last days have been documented by Karashima and the proprietress of an inn where San Pil was staying.

From February to March 1945 San Pil spent a month in Matsumoto City on Honshu. Since Kyushu was exposed to severe American air raids, his squadron was moved to a mountainous region to continue its training. Kim San Pil and 14 Kamikaze pilots stayed at an inn called the Hinomeyu Ryokan, along with 13 members of a maintenance crew.

Mrs Kazu Nakano vividly remembers Kim. She was then the young bride of the innkeeper's son. San Pil is remembered as an 'extremely handsome young man with a well-built physique'. Mrs Nakano says that the maids at the inn 'adored' his appearance. According to her, Kim and four other officers who stayed at the inn 'were all extremely correct and serious. If they drank and sang songs, they did not do it to excess and, anyway, they always were up early in the morning and went off to the airfield. Most of the time they would all turn in after the evening meal.'

While the group was at Masumoto, their planes were refitted to carry a 500-kilogram bomb instead of the normal 250-kilogram bomb.

At the Hinomeyu Inn a piece of paper is still preserved on which each of the five officers wrote words of farewell before their departure for their Kamikaze base in Kyushu. Kim San Pil wrote: 'I am a Korean. So I will write in Korean.' He wrote in Hangul, or Korean letters: '*Eguk* (patriotism)' and '*Chonwha Peha Mansei!*' ('Long Live His Majesty the Emperor!') Then he added in *katakana*, or Japanese phonetics: '*Aikoku*' (patriotism) and '*Tenno Heika Banzai!*' ('Long Live his Majesty the Emperor!')[3]

In the evening darkness of April 3, Kim San Pil, as squadron leader, led six planes piloted by his teenage protégés in an attack on US Navy ships off Okinawa. But this was not San Pil's last sortie. After seeing his men dive towards their targets, he himself landed at Okinawa's Minami (South) Air Base which was still held by Japanese forces. Jumping from his plane, he ran to the sheltered command post and smartly saluted the base commander, to whom he reported his men's success. That done, he boarded his plane and took off, shortly afterwards hurtling himself at the target below: a huge American off-shore fleet.

All the while fierce land battles were raging on the island.

On May 11, 1945, Korean pilot Second Lieutenant Tak Kyon Hyen took off from Chiran Air Base. Tak was a graduate of Kyondo Medical College in Korea and had also volunteered to join the Army Air Corps. He, too, was trained at Tachiarai. On the night before he flew his last mission, he visited a friend at Tomiya Ryokan. That evening he opened his heart to Tome Torihama, the proprietress of that restaurant and a mother-figure to all the young flyers. She remembers him saying: 'You know I am from Korea. I want to go on a Special Attack mission at the earliest possible moment for our Empire. Mama, please live a long and rewarding life on my behalf! Now, allow me to sing for you a Korean song.'[4]

Then Tak began to sing a wistful folk song, 'Ariran', which depicts a young man who is separated from his lover, climbing a hill alone. (Ariran is the name of a Korean mountain pass.) Tak, who was 24, sang the song again and again. Tak's compatriot, Kim San Pil, when he was drinking, had often sang 'Ariran' with his fellow Japanese officers, the latter singing also martial songs.

> *Ariran, Ariran, Arahriyo* . . . [the song began]
> You are going over the Ariran pass
> Forsaking me,
> Your foot will hurt before very long.

Among the Korean flyers whose pictures line the walls at the Chiran Peace Museum, the youngest was Sergeant First Class Park Ton Fun, who was only 17 when he took off from Okinawa's Central Air Base on March 29, 1945. The Americans landed on Okinawa forty-eight hours later.

NOTES

[1] At least that many also worked in Japanese coal mines and industrial plants. Also, thousands of Korean 'comfort women' worked alongside their Japanese counterparts in military brothels in Manchuria and also accompanied the troops in China and South-east Asia. There were also Chinese 'comfort women'. Many prostitutes from brothels in Japan and Korea were attracted by higher payments as 'comfort women' for the troops. Incidentally, prostitution was then legal in Japan, Europe and in parts of the US.

[2] In 1964, Karashima, then retired, wrote about Kim San Pil for the April issue of the popular Japanese monthly journal, *Bungei Shunju*.

[3] In 1910, the last Korean Emperor signed a treaty under which Korea was annexed to Japan.

[4] Some Japanese scholars argue that Korea was not, technically speaking, a Japanese colony, claiming that the two countries had virtually merged. In any case, many high-ranking Korean officers served in the Japanese Imperial Army, including generals under whose command Japanese soldiers fought. However, at war's end, a robust Korean nationalism reasserted itself.

15

THE LAST BANZAI –
THE FINAL TOLL

The Kamikaze phenomenon proved to be the most murderous and spectacular aspect of the Okinawan campaign. Seen first during General MacArthur's invasion of the Philippines, it became a nightmare for the US Navy in its giant amphibious operation at Okinawa. In the Battle of Okinawa (between April and June, 1945), wave upon wave of suicide planes created a rain of death, sinking or damaging almost 200 American ships. A US observer described the scene at Okinawa as 'the world's greatest madhouse'. US journalist Homer Bigart wrote in late June: 'Not since Pearl Harbor has the US Navy taken such losses.'

Situated about 560 km (350 miles) from Japan's home islands, Okinawa was the scene of some of the most intense sea, air and ground fighting between American and Japanese forces and was the last major campaign of the war. Many episodes of the struggle have been vividly portrayed but one that is still mired in controversy is the sinking of the pride of the Japanese fleet, the world's largest battleship, *Yamato*.

During the battle for Okinawa, *Yamato* was sacrificed in a vain effort to defend the strategic island. Many books, employing copious detail, have portrayed the sinking of the 67,000-ton ship as a true Kamikaze exploit. It was not. But there is ample controversy over *Yamato*'s last sortie in April 1945.

The battleship *Yamato*, with her sister ship *Musashi*, was sometimes derided by men in the Army and Navy during the war as 'One of the world's three useless colossi' along with the Egyptian pyramids in Giza and the Great Wall of China. Vice Admiral Takijiro Onishi, who was known as an illmannered visionary, often told his superiors to 'scrap' the two ships. Never one to conceal his opinions, Onishi advocated abolishing the Navy and converting it into an air force. He even called for replacing the Navy's emblem of the anchor with a propeller.

The two giant battlewagons were launched soon after the outbreak of the Pacific War in anticipation of a decisive battle between opposing surface fleets, vaguely reminiscent of the First World War. The best and brightest in the Japanese Navy went into gunnery service. '*Taikan Kyoho-shugi*' ('Big Ship, Big Gun-ism') prevailed within the naval leadership for some time after the commencement of the war. However, both *Yamato* and *Musashi* were nicknamed 'hotels' by sniggering naval officers because they did not participate in the action until October 1944, in Philippine waters.

Nevertheless there was a halo around *Yamato*. 'Yamato' is the ancient poetic name for Japan. The construction of *Yamato*, *Musashi* and *Shinano* was conceived after Japan was forced into accepting a 5-5-3 ratio at the pre-war London Treaty on the Limitation of Naval Armaments – with Britain and the United States allotted the bigger shares.[1] The strength of *Yamato* was in its 18.1 inch (46 cm) guns which could out-distance US or British battleships. (During one engagement a single barrage from the dreadnought's biggest guns knocked out an entire squadron of US planes.) *Yamato* was launched in December 1941, *Musashi* in August 1942, and *Shinano*, which was converted into the world's largest aircraft carrier, in November 1944.[2]

Compounding the controversy over whether *Yamato*'s last sortie was a suicide operation, there is also a dispute among naval historians as to whether *Yamato* was only given fuel for a one-way journey to Okinawan waters. One report has it that before her final sortie, staff officers arranged to collect extra fuel to fill the bunkers of all the vessels so that they would have the means to return to port if the opportunity arose. But the naval leadership knew the unpleasant truth: that the mission was doomed from the outset. In that sense, the sortie by *Yamato* was suicidal; that is, it was a kind of pseudo-Kamikaze attack. In fact, it was called '*Kaijo tokkotai*' – roughly translated as, 'maritime Special Attack squadron'. Such a sobriquet served to boost the morale of Kamikaze flyers. Admiral Seiichi Ito, who led the sortie, was told by the Chief of Staff of the Commander-in-Chief of the Combined Fleet (who flew over from Yokohama to deliver the order) that Ito's fleet 'should lead the way of *ichioku tokko* ["100 million *tokko*", meaning that every Japanese should be ready to perish as Special Attack Forces – a popular slogan of the time]'.

Since there existed a slim chance for survival of *Yamato* and the rest of the fleet (slim is putting it mildly as it was generally believed the chances were only one in a thousand that *Yamato* could reach Okinawan waters and bombard US vessels), this was, then, not a Special Attack, or Kamikaze mission, in the strict sense of those words.

Meanwhile, the naval leadership believed that Japan should not be allowed to capitulate with the battleship *Yamato* intact or lying half-damaged in port. The pride of the fleet had to go down in a gallant battle to convey to future generations that the nation had fought to the very end. The orders given to Vice Admiral Ito, commander of the Second Fleet which comprised *Yamato*, the light crusier *Yahagi*, and several destroyers, by the Commander-in-Chief of the Combined Fleet, were to 'annihilate the enemy' and to 'bequeath the glory of the Imperial Navy's surface unit to eternity'. Again, although it seems like splitting hairs, the mission was a 'suicidal' one but not a purely 'suicide mission'.

On April 7, 1945 the US Command found its naval target and hundreds of American carrier-based planes hit Ito's fleet, sending more than a dozen bombs and torpedoes ripping into *Yamato*. By late afternoon *Yamato* and *Yahagi* had been sunk along with several of the destroyers with heavy loss of life. Some reports say *Yamato* went down with almost 2,500 out of her total crew of over 3,000 men.

Since the war *Yamato* has been glorified by Japanese youth. The most popular comic strip, '*Uchu-senkan* Yamato' ('Space Battleship *Yamato*') was made into a hugely successful animated film. Hideaki Kase once heard an officer of Japan's post-war Navy (called the Maritime Self-Defence Force) say: 'If *Yamato* had been captured by the Americans after the surrender, we [the MSDF] could not have inherited the spirit of the Imperial Navy.'

Admiral Ito, who went down with his flagship, had served as Chief of Staff to the Commander-in-Chief of the Combined Fleet and as Deputy Chief of the Navy General Staff of the Imperial High Command. A graduate of Yale University, he had served as an assistant naval attaché at the Japanese Embassy in Washington between 1927 and 1930 where he got to know some of the US admirals he would be pitted against in the Pacific, including Raymond A. Spruance.

When Ito left his house prior to his last mission his wife, Chitose, jokingly told her husband: 'I will not let you through the door if you lose the forthcoming battle.' They smiled at each other. On the day before the fateful sortie, Ito wrote a last letter to his wife:

My dearest, most adored Chitose,

I am in high spirits as I am about to sortie, having been given a worthy mission. I am determined to exert my best and fight to the end so that I can make a requital to the nation even in a small way.

At this juncture, as I look back to the days you and I shared, I remember that they were replete with happiness. At the same time, I thank you from the bottom of my heart that, as a fighting man, I have no reluctance in departing and I congratulate myself for being so lucky, because I can leave everything behind in the hands of my most beloved, you.

I trust you to understand what thoughts I have at this moment and to know that I was filled with joy until the very last instant. I hope that this could help soften the loneliness through the rest of your life.

I wish most earnestly for your happiness.

Seiichi

Lieutenant Commander Nobuo Fuji, a graduate of the Naval Academy, tells the story of how he directed a mortal Kamikaze attack one month before the war ended, using the slowest and oldest aircraft on hand: eight stubby biplanes that did not fly more than 100 miles per hour. The biplanes, popularly known as *Aka-tombo* (Red Dragon Fly), were intended for training purposes but the 29th Air Wing on Taiwan which had been formed in June 1945 converted these planes so that each could carry a 250-kilogram bomb.

With the loss of thousands of planes during the last year of the war, aircraft of every type, even sluggish biplanes, were used for Kamikaze attacks against the huge concentration of American vessels in Okinawan waters. But these actions could not be decisive, and most of the senior leadership knew that victory was in any case out of the question. With the nation taking punishing blows from Allied ships and planes, the suicide attacks had become the principal means of demonstrating the people's will to resist.

On July 24 the eight painfully slow biplanes took off from Taiwan, with Fuji accompanying them in a Zero fighter, and landed at Miyakojima Island near Okinawa. Before departing, they had the usual ceremony, with their commander pouring sake into their sake cups. The young pilots wore their dashing Rising Sun headbands over their flying caps. After the toasts, they posed for a group photograph.

On July 28 a message was received from headquarters on Taiwan ordering a suicide sortie against enemy vessels in Okinawan waters that night. All the pilots were assembled and the planes were ordered to take off for Okinawa at 9 p.m.[3]

Fuji went to the pilots' billet at around 7.30 p.m. and saw the men seated on the floor, forming a circle and singing children's songs and folk songs. Shortly after 8.30 p.m. the eight pilots formed a line at the airstrip. Fuji gave them a formal order, said a few words of farewell, and shook each one's hand. The eight slow-moving, obsolete planes disappeared into the north-eastern sky.

But half an hour after their takeoff, Fuji heard a drone from aircraft coming from the north-east and, one by one, the eight biplanes landed back at the airstrip. They had all discarded their bombs before landing as they were instructed. The pilots, says Fuji, alleged that their engines had developed abnormal noise. Fuji had his maintenance crews check the engines but they were found in good order. Fuji thought the pilots were all too tense and mistook normal engine noise for a serious fault. He was ready to abandon the attack altogether, but the eight men pleaded with him to be given another chance.

Fuji dispatched a cable to headquarters, explaining the failure of the mission and adding that the men were eager to try it again.

An order was received from headquarters in the morning of July 29 to resume the suicide attack that night. The eight planes took off. Some time later, Fuji again heard the drone of airplanes. Four of the planes returned. The pilots, looking very serious, said the engines were again 'not running normally'. They said: 'Permit us to take off as soon as the trouble is fixed.'

'Understood,' Fuji snapped. 'I will let you give it one last try. If you come back, you will not have to sally again.' At 10.40 p.m. the four biplanes took off again. This time, only one returned. Fuji told the pilot that he would not have to join in the attack.

Fuji returned to Taiwan the next morning. Upon his return he heard that a reconnaissance plane that took off from his base at Xinzhu had reached Okinawan waters at 12.40 a.m. that morning and observed a tall column of flame shooting up from an American destroyer. Fuji's training planes were the only Kamikaze aircraft launched that morning. After the war, Fuji learned from US war records that USS *Callaghan* was sunk after she received a direct hit by a Kamikaze plane on one of its turrets at 12.41 a.m. The bomb had exploded in the engine room, setting the vessel on fire and igniting the ammunition stores.

Other official reports back up Fuji's information. They say a biplane flew unharmed through a hail of anti-aircraft fire and crashed into the 'No. 3 upper handling room' of the destroyer; that the bomb ripped through the deck, exploding in the engine room and killing all hands there. Five minutes later the ammunition stores exploded, killing and injuring many men trying to control the damage. A few minutes later the ship sank, 47 of her crew members being lost, over 70 wounded. Before going down the destroyer had shot 13 Kamikaze planes out of the air.

Obsolete or not, the slow Red Dragon Fly plane that hit *Callaghan* had caused appalling casualties. *Callaghan* was the last officially reported American vessel to be sunk by a Kamikaze attack.

AN ADMIRAL AS SUICIDE BOMBER

On the day Japan surrendered, Vice Admiral Matome Ugaki, commander of the Fifth Naval Air Fleet headquartered in Kyushu, himself chose a crash-dive death. Shortly before 5 p.m. on August 15, 11 Suisei twin-seater dive-bombers took off from the Oita Naval Air Base on Kyushu. Crammed with another passenger in the lead plane was Ugaki. Piloted by Lieutenant Tatsuo Nakatsuru, the additional passenger was Master Sergeant Shushou Endo. The 56-year-old admiral had insisted on sacrificing his life together with the much younger crew members. Ugaki and Endo shared a single seat in the small aircraft. (Incidentally, Lieutenant Nakatsuru was a classmate of the first Kamikaze pilot, Yukio Seki, belonging to the 70th Class of the Naval Academy. They had graduated in November 1941 in a class of 432. Nakatsuru and Seki were among only five officers from that class who became dive-bomber pilots.)

Ugaki's Fifth Air Fleet had previously carried out extensive Kamikaze operations against the American fleet. At noon on the sweltering day of August 15, Emperor Hirohito had made a broadcast to the nation saying that Japan had accepted the Potsdam Declaration, which meant capitulation to the Allies. The admiral, like another, Takijiro Onishi, could not accept the idea of surrender.

Ugaki had narrowly escaped death on April 18, 1943, when American fighter planes ambushed two Japanese naval medium bombers, shooting them down and killing Admiral Isoroku Yamamoto (he acquired fame as the planner of the Pearl Harbor attack) over New Guinea. Ugaki, who was in the plane following Yamamoto's, was severely wounded when his plane crashed into the jungle. Yamamoto and Ugaki had been on their way to an inspection tour of a naval air base in New Guinea when they were spotted and attacked in mid-air.

Tough, determined, without a trace of fear, Ugaki is said to have embodied the spirit of the samurai. On the day when the date for the Pearl Harbor attack was decided upon, Admiral Ugaki, who was aboard ship, entered two poems in a diary in which he announced his readiness to die for his country. The day was Emperor Meiji's birthday, a national holiday, and the ship was decked out with flags. (Meiji was the founder of modern Japan.) Here are Ugaki's two poems:

The upper deck was warm. Comfortable in the sun.
I recognized a school of horse mackerel in the water below.
I fetch my rod. Men soon follow my example, dipping lines into the water.
Men sharing this delectable hobby stand side by side.
We caught only a dozen or so fish but we had fun.

And:

Mackerels swimming.
The men crowd around to admire them on our full-dressed ship.
Holding our rods we attain self-effacing moments.
We [now] await the gathering storm.
[Ugaki evidently refers to the impending conflict with America.]

Ugaki's diary continues:

At 8 p.m. a signal was received that the Commander-in-Chief was returning to Kure [Kure harbour, near Hiroshima] tomorrow afternoon. The meeting at the [Navy] Minister's official residence ended sooner than expected, enabling him [the Commander-in-Chief of the Combined Fleet, Admiral Isoroku Yamamoto] to get back to the flagship a day earlier. It meant a formal decision was made. Later, the Chief of the First Section [of the Navy Ministry] telephoned to say that an agreement was reached with the Army that a day was selected between the 8th and 10th [of December 1941, as the date for commencing the war]. We are fully ready. Everyone should [be ready to] sacrifice his life. Let everybody be prepared to die. I too will dedicate my life for the good of the nation.[4]

In mid-August 1945 when Ugaki got wind of Japan's imminent surrender, he made up his mind to die. He had to insist that he be allowed to join in what was perhaps the last Kamikaze attack on the US fleet. On August 14, Commander Hiromu Miyazaki, senior staff officer to Ugaki, was summoned by the admiral and told to draft an order for a Kamikaze sortie to be led by himself. Stunned by what he heard, Miyazaki declined. But Ugaki was adamant and Miyazaki hurriedly left Ugaki and consulted with the chief of staff and two other officers. All of them joined Miyazaki in an attempt to dissuade the admiral. But they, too, failed. Ugaki, a meticulous diarist, made this entry on August 15:

> Foreign broadcasts have reported that the [Japanese] Empire was surrendering unconditionally and that His Majesty was personally going to make a broadcast. I gave orders to ready five Suisei [attack planes], saying that I would personally lead the Special Attack against enemy vessels in the Okinawa area.

Early in the morning on August 15, shortly before 4 a.m., Ugaki summoned the staff officer in charge of operations, Captain Masaomi Tanaka, to his office in the command bunker. Ugaki again gave orders that five planes be readied for an attack in the Okinawa seas. By then, the Naval High Command had already ordered the Fifth Air Fleet to cease firing against the US and Russian forces short of a provocation by the adversary.

Tanaka wavered. Seeing this, Ugaki smiled and said, 'I am going. Please do what I have ordered.'

But still Miyazaki and the other officers gathered around Ugaki and pleaded with him to retract the order. Ugaki, now looking very stern, did not give in. He said, 'Give me a chance to die honourably as a fighting man. I must join the ranks of men under my command who perished gladly, believing in the ultimate victory of our nation. Let me go!'

At noon, all hands were lined up on the parade ground outside the bunker, facing a public address system and listening to the Emperor's broadcast. When Ugaki returned to his office, he entered these words in his diary:

'14.00. I assembled all staff officers. We exchanged our last toast. Thus I close for ever my war diary.'

The suicide attack led by Ugaki was conducted by 23 men aboard 11 planes.

After Ugaki and his fellow officers raised small sake cups, he removed his grade insignias and, taking a samurai dagger given to him by Admiral Isoroku Yamamoto, the co-creator with Admiral Onishi of the Navy's Air Arm, emerged from the bunker and boarded a sedan. A five-minute drive took him to the airfield. Arriving at the command post at the eastern end of the airfield, he saw 11 Suisei planes instead of the five he had ordered, their engines roaring. Their 22 pilots and crew members stood in front of the planes in two files. Suddenly, Miyazaki ran after Ugaki, pleading that he be allowed to go with him.

'No,' Ugaki said flatly. 'You remain here and attend to your duties.'

Ugaki then climbed onto a chair facing the 22 men. Most of them had tied a white *hachimaki* headband over their flyer's caps just as samurai warriors had done before engaging an enemy.

'Gentlemen,' said Ugaki, 'the Fifth Air Fleet to date has carried out operations with a determination to wage Special Attacks to the last man. We are forced to terminate the war by His Majesty's words. However, I am now leading the final attack on our enemies in Okinawa.'

Ugaki stepped down. He accosted the 24-year-old Lieutenant Nakatsuru, who was the leader of the 701 Flight Squadron. All 22 men belonged to this squadron.

'This is not what I had ordered,' Ugaki said.

'No, sir!' Nakatsuru shouted excitedly. 'I gave instructions to ready five planes. But the men did not follow the order. Because you are personally leading the mission, they felt five were not sufficient. The men were adamant in joining the mission. They said they will follow you even if it meant disobeying an order!'

Ugaki listened silently. When the young officer ended his plea, Ugaki nodded.

'Permission granted,' Ugaki said. 'I revise the order. We attack the enemy fleet in Okinawa with eleven Suisei planes'.

Hearing these words from Ugaki, the men still standing at attention cheered and uttered exclamations of joy.

The next moment all 22 men scrambled to their planes. Ugaki walked to Lieutenant Nakatsuru's plane and found Master Sergeant Endo already ensconced in the rear, or navigator's, seat. Ugaki shouted at Endo to give his seat to him. Endo pleaded warmly with the admiral to be allowed to go along on the one-way mission. Ugaki finally consented and climbed into the rear seat. Due to the small space, Endo had to squat between the admiral's legs.

That done, Ugaki stuck out his arm from the cockpit and signalled to the formation to take off.

One by one, the 11 Suisei planes climbed into the air, while everyone left behind, at the order 'Wave caps!', frantically waved them in farewell.

Of the 11 planes, three almost immediately began to have mechanical problems and ditched along the way, causing the death of one crew member. At 8.24 p.m. there was a radio report from Ugaki's plane, saying that it was diving towards an enemy target. Seventeen men in eight planes reached the target area and ended their lives.

It was later confirmed that the plane carrying Ugaki, Nakatsuru and Endo had not scored a hit but had crashed on Iheijima, an islet off the northern tip of the main island of Okinawa, after skimming the top of a US landing craft (an LST) berthed near the beach. Three unidentified bodies were recovered from the scattered debris of the plane.

Six hours after Ugaki's death, Admiral Onishi committed suicide, disembowelling himself in a traditional rite at his Tokyo residence.

An American vice admiral, C.R. Brown, who served in the Philippines and at Okinawa in the war, has taken issue with Onishi, who spoke of the Kamikaze pilots as 'already gods without earthly desires'. Brown doubts if these pilots actually thought this way. Rather, he likens the 'special attacks' of these youths as another form of the suicidal 'Banzai charge' made by Japanese soldiers on the battlefield who would not accept the bitter pill of defeat. (In Japanese the Banzai charges were called '*Gyokusai kogeki*,' where '*Gyoku*' is a 'precious gem stone' and '*sai*' means 'to explode into pieces'. The description may seem much too poetic for the gore of a battlefield, but the Japanese are often said to be a romantic, even an emotionally highly charged people.)

The sixteen men who perished with Ugaki were not given the posthumous promotions which was the rule for honouring all Kamikaze pilots. This was because Ugaki's action had violated the order not to attack the enemy except in self-defence, although in Ugaki's case the official ceasefire was yet to be imposed.

But these men have not been forgotten. On April 23, 1983, a ceremony was held to uncover a monument commemorating Ugaki and his men at Ohzu Park, the old site of the airfield in Kyushu where they had taken off for the last time. Attending the ceremony was Tomeaki Nakatsuru, the 87-year-old father of the *tokko* pilot Lieutenant Nakatsuru, accompanied by his granddaughter, Suzuko. His only son, Lieutenant Nakatsuru, had married and his daughter, Suzuko, was born on July 22, 1945, less than a month before her father set off to die. Suzuko was only seven days old when her father visited their house, a short drive from Oita Air Base, and saw her for the first and last time.

After the unveiling ceremony, the elderly Nakatsuru told a television interviewer: 'Throughout the years after the war, I cursed Mr Ugaki all the while. Why didn't he shoot himself with a pistol or something? The war was over. Why did he take young men with him? But time has passed and now I forgive him.' He explained his reconciliation, saying that if Ugaki were to be blamed, his son Lieutenant Nakatsuru must share the blame for allowing his own men to take part in the one-way sortie.

THE KAMIKAZE WHO WAS A GOOD SAMARITAN

Second Lieutenant Shinya Shibata took off from Chiran Air Base as a Kamikaze flyer on April 13, 1945 for Okinawan waters but because of engine failure he was forced to ditch on the beach of Kuroshima, an islet on the way to Okinawa. Kuroshima (Black Island) is about 425 kilometres north-west of Okinawa. Shibata's plane caught fire and he was badly burned. But there was no medical doctor on the small island and the islanders did their best to save the young pilot. They even killed one of their precious horses and applied its oil to ease his burns. Toward the end of April, another pilot, Lieutenant Tadashi Yasube, ditched his plane on the sea near the beach after it developed engine trouble on a suicide sortie after takeoff from Chiran. Yasube was not injured.

On the island he learned of Shibata's desperate condition. Seeing his suffering and eager to resume his mission, he asked a young islander, Katsuya Yasunaga, to row a boat with him to Kyushu. Fearing American planes and submarines, no ship dared call on the island. Yasube promised that once he reached Kyushu he would fly on another Kamikaze mission but he would first drop medicines for Shibata on his way to Okinawa. Yasube and Yasunaga left the island in a small sail boat. A few hours later, a gale hit them and they relied on a compass to find their direction. After 31 hours in which each of them manned the oars, they finally reached Kyushu.

Yasube took off from Chiran on May 4 on a Special Attack flight. As his formation neared Kuroshima, Yasube made his way to the islet and after circling and banking his wings, he dropped a small chute with a package containing medicines. He banked his wings again and headed south for Okinawa.

Thanks to the medicines, Shibata recovered and returned home after the war. He died in April 1998 at a ripe age. Yasube was 21 when he died. He was a graduate of Meiji University in Tokyo.

BASEBALL PLAYERS AS KAMIKAZE PILOTS

Twenty-two-year-old Ensign Shinichi Ishimaru, who was a student at Nippon University, died piloting a Zero fighter on May 11, 1945, in Okinawan waters. He took off from Kanoya Base on Kyushu on that clear, sunny day. Just before taking off, he asked a fellow officer, Ensign Oiichi Honda, to put on a catcher's mitt. Ishimaru pitched ten times and each time Honda cried out: 'Strike!' Thereupon, Ishimaru said, 'That's it, I'm satisfied.' He ran to his plane. He was a pitcher for the popular professional team Nagoya in 1942 while he was attending a night college course. (Today the team is called the Nagoya Dragons.)

Honda died as a suicide pilot, taking off from Kanoya three days later, also in Okinawan waters. He was a baseball player for Hosei University where he was a first baseman.

At the Tokyo Dome, the largest indoor baseball stadium in Japan, there is a monument commemorating 69 professional baseball players who died in combat. Two of them (Ishimaru and Second Lieutenant Shizuka Watanabe) were popular players for professional teams and went to their deaths as Kamikaze pilots.

THE FINAL TOLL

A new type of war fear was born between between October 1944 and January 15, 1945 when approximately one in four Kamikaze aircraft were making strikes, hitting the American fleet at sea and ships of the amphibious force in Leyte Gulf. The suicide aircraft sank 16 vessels and damaged almost 90 others. The American losses included 2 carriers, 3 destroyers and 5 transports, while damaged were 23 carriers, 5 battle-ships, 23 carriers, 9 cruisers and 28 destroyers and destroyer escorts. Japanese losses included over 700 suicide Army pilots from General Tominaga's Fourth Air Army and almost 500 pilots from Admiral Onishi's Air Fleet. Thus, approximately 1,200 pilots lost their lives in a vain attempt to halt the US invasion of the Philippines.

The first successful suicide operations took place on October 25 against American vessels in the Leyte Gulf. Coming out of an overcast sky six Zero suicide planes dived at the US escort carriers, some almost straight down, just as the carriers were launching their own planes. The Zeros headed for the carriers *Petrof Bay* and *Sangamon* but were turned away by anti-aircraft fire and instead went for two other carriers, *Santee* and *Suwannee*. Both were hit by suicide aircraft whose bombs ripped their flight and hangar decks. Emergency repairs, however, enabled the damaged carriers to resume flight operations the same day.

But on the morning of that day (October 25) suicide pilots went after more US carriers commanded by Admiral Clifton Sprague, doing considerable damage to *Kitkun Bay* and *Kalinin Bay*. One Kamikaze aircraft smashed through the flight deck of *St Lo*, detonating bombs and torpedoes on the hangar deck. Blown apart, *St Lo* sank before noon.

In spite of severe losses, the Japanese by mid-November had 70,000 troops on Leyte against 100,000 Americans who were then advancing on the island. US forces were increased but by early December US resupply convoys were hit hard by Kamikaze planes. The destroyer *Mahan* and the high-speed transport *Ward* were so severely damaged they had to be abandoned and sunk. Meanwhile the destroyer *Reid* was hit by a suicide plane, which sank it.

It was evident that the Kamikaze pilots were receiving better instructions, thus raising the peril for Allied sailors. Sometimes for ten hours running a succession of Japanese planes with their pilots bent on their own death aimed their aircraft at the sea targets.

By the end of the Leyte campaign, 68,000 Japanese lay dead on the island. US casualties were 3,500 killed and 12,000 wounded.

Here is a Kamikaze scorecard for only one day during the US invasion of the Philippines:

January 6, 1945:
> *Long*, destroyer (USA), sunk
> *Shropshire*, cruiser (Australia), near miss
> *Richard P. Leary*, destroyer (USA), near miss
> *New Mexico*, battleship (USA), damaged
> *Mississippi*, battleship (USA), near miss
> *California*, battleship (USA), damaged
> *Australia*, cruiser (Australia), damaged
> *Walke*, destroyer (USA), damaged
> *Allen M. Sumner*, destroyer (USA), damaged
> *Brooks*, destroyer transport (USA), damaged
> *O'Brien*, destroyer (USA), damaged
> *Barton*, destroyer (USA), near miss
> *Columbia*, cruiser (USA), damaged
> *Louisville*, cruiser (USA), damaged

Three days later *Mississippi* was slightly damaged by a Kamikaze plane; *Columbia* was hit a second time by a suicide attack (also three days later) and suffered extensive damage and heavy casualties; HMAS *Australia* suffered suicide hits on three consecutive days, January 6, 7 and 8, and was so badly damaged that it played no further role in the war.

The big carrier *Lexington*, the flagship of Vice Admiral John S. McCain, the commander of Task Force 38, was the victim of a Kamikaze attack on November 5, 1944 that killed 50 members of the crew and seriously injured 132 others. McCain (the father of current US Senator John McCain) was forced to transfer his flag to the carrier *Wasp*. November 25 was a black day for American aircraft carriers in the Philippine Sea. Hit by Kamikazes were *Cabot* (36 killed and 16 wounded), *Intrepid* (69 killed and 35 wounded) and *Essex* (15 killed).[5]

Another carrier, *Hancock*, was hit but no casualties were reported. (However, *Hancock* was hit again when a Kamikaze crashed into its deck on April 7, 1945, killing 72 men. The Japanese raids of April 6–7 were the first of ten massive Kamikaze attacks launched against the American fleet and shipping off Okinawa. In addition there were smaller-scale raids by both conventional and suicide planes nearly every day.)

Deeply worried by the heavy toll to the carriers from suicide attacks, Admiral William 'Bull' Halsey, commander of the Third Fleet, said that further exposure of the carriers to such danger 'did not appear profitable' and would occur only after improved defensive techniques were perfected, or the carriers were part of a great force – or when their presence was indispensable. But Halsey admits that he had earlier never believed that the Japanese 'for all their hara-kiri tradition' could gather enough recruits to make a Kamikaze corps effective. When in the month of October 11 US aircraft carriers (including two giant carriers, *Intrepid* and *Franklin*) were hit by suicide attacks, Halsey scratched a planned raid on Tokyo.

The damage to the Allied invasion fleet off the Philippines created by the Kamikazes in the month of January did not prevent a successful landing but it was big enough for US Admiral Jesse B. Oldendorf, the commander of a huge armada of over 100 vessels, to appeal for help with these words: 'Enemy attacks heaviest morning and evening especially around 17.00 [5 p.m.]. Additional damage may seriously and adversely affect this as well as important subsequent operations.'

Mother nature also pounded the US fleet. On December 15, 1944 the Third Fleet was temporarily put out of action by a powerful typhoon east of the Philippines. Three of the fleet's destroyers sank, almost 200 planes were washed overboard, and 800 men lost their lives.

Approximately three months after the sanguinary Philippine campaign, in the operation to capture Okinawa, a far greater number of Anglo-American ships were lost or damaged in Kamikaze attacks than had occurred in the previous campaign. On some particularly bad days – in April and May – the list of ships sunk or damaged was longer than the list for January 6. For example, 27 ships were sunk or damaged on April 6; the total for April 12 was 18, for May 4 it was 22.

This was a favourite trick of Kamikaze planes: two would come in together and then, when within range of multi-barrelled pompon, Oerlikons or Bofors anti-aircraft guns, split up to make separate dives on the ship. Despite some dazzling displays of shooting, Allied ships could hardly survive without air patrols.

Between April and June of the Okinawa campaign, suicide planes seemed to rain down on the American fleet, scoring high rates of success. For example, during action on April 6–7, a two-day operation called *Kikusui*-1 (Floating Chrysanthemum, No. 1) Japan lost 450 pilots and their planes. However, 34 American ships were sunk or damaged. In addition to the sinking of 2 US destroyers and 4 auxiliary ships, 2 carriers, 1 battleship and 15 destroyers were damaged, as well as a number of smaller vessels. Five days later suicide planes damaged 3 US battleships, *Idaho*, *Tennessee* and *New Mexico*, the latter two receiving extensive damage and heavy casualties.

US ships were often unable to tell until the very last minute if the approaching planes were conventional or Kamikaze. And when two (or more) suicide planes dived from opposite directions at various angles, this greatly increased the chances of a hit, despite desperate efforts to destroy the intruder or take evasive action. There was no survival for pilots once they aimed for a target or crashed into the sea. Some of the largest Japanese planes, such as the Mitsubishi bomber codenamed 'Betty', had a seven-man crew. The reader can imagine the gruesome scenes left behind on the ships hit by the Kamikazes. (A diarist aboard the US cruiser *Montpelier* which was attacked for three hours in late November 1944 by suicide planes – at least four scoring direct hits – wrote that the deck close to his gun mount was running with blood, knee-caps, scalps, brains, hearts, tongues and arms.)

The total Japanese activity in the air in the Okinawan campaign was unprecedented. There were almost 900 Japanese air raids against Allied forces at Okinawa. Approximately 4,000 Japanese planes were destroyed in combat, 1,900 of which were Kamikaze planes. The intensity and scale of the suicide air attacks on naval forces and shipping have been called the most spectacular aspect of the Battle of Okinawa. In the Kamikaze defence of that island between April and June 1945, at least 35 American vessels were sunk and over 300 damaged. In addition to organized raids, there were sporadic small-scale suicide attacks directed against the American fleet by both Army and Navy planes. The success of the air attacks is indicated by the damage inflicted on the American forces. The 'tin cans' – or destroyers – sustained more hits than any other class of ships. But some of the bigger vessels suffered heavy damage from suicide dives and the cumulative explosions that often caused great loss of life. The crews of US ships had a jittery existence as the Kamikaze planes flew at a distance, stalking their ships. On one carrier, *Franklin*, that came under attack in the Pacific in March 1945, a Catholic priest, Father Joseph O'Callaghan, remembers vividly (in a memoir) that as death was about to strike, 800 men (out of a crew of 3,200) were drawing their last breath. He recalls the billowing smoke, the 'snake-tongued flames', the scourging of those men who had thought, mistakenly, that they were at a safe distance from the destruction. The carrier *Bunker Hill*, the flagship of Admiral Mark Mitscher, was struck down in May 1945, losing 353 dead with 43 missing. Another 264 men were badly injured. Mitscher survived and transferred his flag and personal staff to another carrier, *Enterprise*, which was also crashed into by Kamikaze planes a few days later. Mitscher survived his second suicide attack in four days but had to transfer his flag again, this time to the carrier *Randolph*. Both *Bunker Hill* and *Enterprise* were so badly damaged that they played no further part in the war.

To thwart the suicide attacks, Admiral McCain, among other top-ranking officers, took a number of countermeasures. These included improving the accuracy of weapons, adding more fighter planes to the carriers while reducing the number of bombers, increasing patrols over the carriers, and sending fighters to Japanese airfields to stop big-scale Kamikaze attacks.

The British Pacific Fleet which supported the massive US amphibious invasion of Okinawa included two dozen ships and almost 250 aircraft. Between April 1 and May 9, 1945 Kamikaze planes damaged the British carriers *Indomitable, Formidable, Victorious* and *Indefatigable*, while one plane strafed the battleship *King George V*. But the reinforced steel decks on the British carriers proved an immense advantage over the American carriers with their wooden decks in dealing with crash tactics. For example, despite the hit on *Indefatigable* caused by the wing tip of a Kamikaze and the explosion of its 550-lb (250 kg) bomb on the flight deck, the carrier was able to operate aircraft again after a few hours. Ships from the Royal Australian Navy played an active part in the invasion of the Philippines, joined with the US Seventh Fleet for operations at the island of Borneo but were too late to save the lives of 2,000 Allied prisoners, mostly Australians, who died on a death march from Sandakan to Mount Kina Balu.

Rear Admiral Etsuzo Kurihara, Chief of Public Affairs of the Navy General Staff, taunted the US over the presence of the British Navy, claiming but not providing supporting evidence that the US Navy was not strong enough to engage its Japanese counterpart alone. Said Kurihara:

Although the enemy has been saying he will fight the Pacific War singled-handed, his inability to do so is seen in the fact that he has been aided by the British forces in the Okinawa operations. The British Fleet is aiding the Americans to a considerable extent. Several British battleships, including *King George V*, and regular aircraft carriers and other auxiliary warships are engaged in the naval operations around the Okinawa islands. We may say that the combined Anglo-American fleets in their entire strength have come to the Pacific Ocean to fight this country.

The month of May 1945 was one of the worst days for American radar picket vessels off Okinawa. Kamikaze planes would take off from bases in Kyushu and Taiwan and US sailors would watch the suicide planes coming in, which they identified as Kates, Peggys, Sallys, Dinahs, Vals, Judys, Lilys and Bettys, not to mention Oscars, Franks and Zekes. The Zekes, incidentally, were the US codename for Japan's famous Zero fighters, while the others were assorted fighters and bombers, including sea planes. The Bettys carried the Ohka piloted bombs.

Several ships were sunk or damaged by the Ohka human bombs released by Betty bombers.

The story of the US destroyer *Laffey* gives a mirror image of the Pacific carnage. In 80 minutes on April 16, 1945 *Laffey* had been attacked by 22 planes, she had been struck upon by eight of them, and four bombs. She had shot down nine planes herself. Corsairs from a carrier had taken care of another 16 and several landing craft a mile away shot down two more. As a result *Laffey* was slowly sinking. She was down by the stern, her rudder jammed. Only four of its 11 small-bore guns continued operating. But she didn't sink, although she had to be withdrawn from service.

In the Okinawa campaign, Japanese losses were staggering. Previously, during the ten months from January to October 1944, the Japanese Navy lost over 5,200 pilots, or 42 per cent of the total in service at the start of the year. This meant that more inexperienced pilots were thrown into action, with predictable consequences. Since the pilots had to die anyway, according to Admiral Onishi at least this way they would 'die splendidly'. But Americans also had to lick their wounds. At Okinawa the Kamikazes caused the greatest losses ever suffered by the US Navy in a single battle, killing approximately 5,000 men.

In the end, Kamikaze attacks could not made a difference in the outcome of the war. The Kamikazes failed to sink any large aircraft carriers – their main targets. But they were capable of doing immense damage. US admirals concluded that one in four Kamikazes were hitting their targets, that one in about 35 were able to sink a vessel. The suicide planes also caused a huge psychological shock to the Allies. US historian Samuel Eliot Morison speaks of the 'flaming terror', not to mention the painful burns and searing death caused by the suicide onslaughts. (Morison cites the courage and fighting spirit, unparalleled in history, he says, of American crews. The same may also be said of the crews of British and Australian warships that came under the same aerial attack.) The principal Kamikaze strategist, Admiral Takijiro Onishi, had rationalized the use of suicide warfare, saying it would perpetuate Japan's eternal spirit, that the victors were not always those nations that won wars, that as long as citizens were willing to give up their lives for a noble cause a nation would not perish. Onishi would have agreed that the Kamikazes were more important for the spirit of resistance they symbolized than for the damage – though extensive – they inflicted.

Nevertheless, in retrospect, many historians would fault the Japanese High Command for continuing the struggle against hopeless odds, thereby making the war toll heavier.

The Special Attack fury gave rise to some acts of pitiful self-destruction that seemed outrageous even by Kamikaze standards. Two of them took place in Manchuria. In the first, as Russian tank forces approached the town of Jinxian, Army pilot Second Lieutenant Teruo Iwasa visited his fiancée at the house where she lived with her mother and informed them that he and the men at the base were taking off shortly to execute crash-dive attacks on the advancing tanks. He understood that both the mother and his fiancée had decided to take their own lives. They died in his presence, throwing themselves on daggers they held in their hands. In the second incident, two young women chose to end their lives together violently in the company of their men. Asako, the newly wed wife of Lieutenant Tetsuo Tanifuji, squeezed herself into the cockpit of her husband's single-seater plane and, in a second small plane on the same mission, Sumiko, the fiancée of pilot Second Lieutenant Iwao Okura, sat on his lap. Both men were Kamikaze pilots. Both planes took off from a base near Jinxian and crash-dived into the advancing enemy, Russian tanks.

NOTES

[1] As a young diplomat, Toshikazu Kase was made the press officer of the Japanese delegation to the Naval Conference. Officiating at a press

conference he handed out British '555' cigarettes to attending reporters, saying he 'regretted very much' that there was no '333' brand.

[2] *Musashi* was sunk by US carrier-borne planes in Philippine waters in October 1944. *Shinano* was torpedoed and sunk by a US submarine a few hours after it left Yokosuka port on a trial cruise after launching in November 1944.

[3] Lieutenant-Commander Fuji supplied these details to Hideaki Kase.

[4] *Intrepid* survives today as a permanent museum, tied up on a New York City Hudson River pier.

16

EXOTIC WEAPONS

The sky over Otsujima in Japan's inland sea was clear and bright on the morning of November 8, 1944. A few thin white clouds floated in the sky and the autumn air was balmy. Three black submarines were moored at the pier, supporting on their decks 12 human torpedoes, the Kaitens, also painted jet black. Each Kaiten (the name means 'reversing fortune') was 14.75 metres long. Each was fastened to the deck by four steel bands. The Kaiten had a range of 23,000 metres and a top speed of 30 knots. Here was a new suicide weapon which the Navy hoped would soon blast many Allied ships out of the water.

For each submarine, taking on board the four human torpedoes presented great danger. Each Kaiten was packed with 1.55 tons of high explosives and eight cylinders of high-pressure oxygen that propelled the converted midget sub. The enemy's depth charges could easily destroy the parent submarine. For example, the I-47 submarine with a crew of 90 was carrying on her deck more than six tons of high explosives.[1]

In the spring of 1943 Japanese naval officers and architects were finishing plans to create a human torpedo that would travel at a speed of 40 knots, be armed with a 3,000-pound (1,360 kg) warhead and be capable of hitting the fastest enemy ships. In the battle for Okinawa, the Kaiten torpedo finally made its debut. Each torpedo, sometimes described as a cigar-shaped coffin, was manned by a single pilot. One of several exotic weapons used by the Japanese forces, the Kaiten proved to be surprisingly effective: within a short period of time the US Navy is said to have lost a dozen ships as a result of Kaiten attacks. But as a suicide weapon the Kaiten had at least one major defect: a short periscope. Consequently, it could not dive deep enough to hit a targeted vessel well below its draught line. With a large ship like an aircraft carrier or battleship, the most vulnerable area was five or six metres below the waterline.

Twelve young officers who were to board the human torpedoes, accompanied by 12 maintenance crew members, descended from the hill after offering a prayer at the small Shinto shrine which was built on the hilltop looking down towards the calm inland sea. On the I-47 the four Kaiten officers and four maintenance crews were added to the already crowded space on the submarine. After the four officers boarded the mother ship, Lieutenant Sekio Nishina spoke on behalf of his men to the submarine's commander and other officers:

'We are sorry that we are depriving you of precious space. Thank you for providing us with very comfortable beds. And please bear with us, for it will not be for long.'

Nishina was the co-inventor of the Kaiten and was a Naval Academy graduate. Other Kaiten officers were Lieutenant Junior Grade Hitoshi Fukuda, and Ensigns Kozo Watanabe and Akira Sato. They had all volunteered as Kaiten pilots. Fukuda had graduated from the Naval Engineering Academy. He was 22. Five days before their sortie, on November 3, Fukuda visited his mother at their home in Gannosu in Kyushu. (The Navy had provided a seaplane for the round trip.) That night he slept by his mother's side. He had not done so since he entered junior high school.

At 8 a.m. a bugle played the national anthem, '*Kimigayo*' ('Bless Your Reign'), as the three submarines raised the brand-new men of war at the sterns. The new day dawned at the Kaiten base. At 4 p.m. the 12 young offices stood at attention in a line. The first Kaiten unit was named '*Kikusui-tai*' ('Chrysanthemum and Water', an ancient symbol). Lieutenant Senior Grade Nishina commanded the unit. Vice Admiral Shigeyoshi Miwa, Commander-in-Chief of the Sixth Fleet, addressed the officers. He told the young men:

'I am handing to you daggers which were given to the members of the sallying Kaiten pilots by the Commander of the Combined Fleet.' Daggers in white wooden sheaths, on which a set of two characters, '*Go Koku*' ('Safeguarding the Nation') were inscribed with a brush, were given to each officer in solemn manner. Each officer held the dagger horizontally by two hands at the height of his shoulders and bowed.

'I wish that you will succeed in your missions,' concluded Miwa. The commander of the base, Miwa's chief of staff, a staff officer, adjutant, commanders of the submarines and officers and sailors, high school students, both boys and girls who were mobilized to help in the factories on the base, gathered for the ceremony.

As dusk gathered, a farewell party hosted by Admiral Miwa was given at the officers' mess that stood on the slope of the hill. On the menu were grilled sea bream, dried abalone, chestnuts and seaweed. It was the same menu that appeared in *Heiji Monogatari*, a well-known saga of samurai, published in the thirteenth century, before they departed for the battlefield. A formal toast was proposed by raising cups of sake. Then, before the meal began, everyone sang patriotic songs.

After eating, Nishina summoned all the students he was training as Kaiten pilots to meet him on the hill.

'We are going to perish for the Motherland and for our descendants. If ever Kaiten develops mechanical failure as I head for the enemy, I shall open the hatch and swim with all my might, board the enemy vessel and create havoc with my sword!' exclaimed Nishina, his long hair swishing as he turned his head.

The next morning, the 12 officers ran down the hill after paying homage at Kaiten Jinja. The officers and men helped the young men put on their Rising Sun headbands. They then walked to the pier through the throngs of officers, sailors, factory hands and high school students. The girls were also wearing *hachimaki* with Rising Suns on them. The previous day the high school girls had placed colourful cushions that they had made in the small cockpit of the Kaiten torpedoes. The 12 men boarded a motor launch. Three submarines, I-36, I-37 and I-47, each carrying four Kaiten manned torpedoes on its deck, awaited the arrival of the pilots.

Nishina, on boarding the launch, carried a box on his chest, containing the ashes of Lieutenant Kuroki who died in an accident while testing the Kaiten torpedo, wrapped in white cloth and strapped from his neck.

Nishina was born in Otsu City, by Lake Biwa, the largest lake in Japan, neighbouring Kyoto. His hobby was mountain climbing.

He met with his mother for the last time on November 3, 1944. He had given his mother short notice. Hatsue, his mother, spent the day cleaning house in Otsu City all day long, waiting for her son's return. Sekio's father was away in Nagano Prefecture to look for a house where the couple could evacuate if necessary. The doorbell rang shortly after

10 p.m. and there stood her son. She had just heard the news over the radio that five Kamikaze pilots had bodily smashed into US aircraft carriers in Philippine waters. She was thrilled to see her son alive.

Hatsue served her son a late dinner she had cooked. While they were eating, Hatsue said:

'It is a real pity that young men are smashing into enemy ships. Isn't there a more reasonable way to win the war?' Her son did not answer. They chatted about the family. Hatsue noticed that her son looked exhausted.

'You look haggard,' she said.

'Yes, I'm sort of tired,' Sekio answered.

Sekio was unusually reticent that night. The next morning, when Sekio was leaving, he said: 'I'll come back soon.' Mother and son hugged each other.

Sekio had graduated from the Naval Academy in 1942. Two years and 10 months later the war ended. Of his 581 classmates, 329 perished in the Pacific War. The attrition rate was 56.7 per cent.

After the 12 officers boarded the submarines and stood on the decks, Admiral Miwa approached on a launch. The 50-year-old admiral boarded each submarine and shook hands with the young officers, saying: 'Do your best!' Miwa was in tears while the young men smiled at him.

A bugle sounded the order 'Get ready for sea!' followed by another bugle, 'Anchors away.' The three submarines, each displacing 3,500 tons and covered by special paint to prevent radar detection, began to move slowly. Thin white smoke from their diesel engines rose in the clear morning air. On the two sides of the bridge, Kikusui symbols were painted below the Rising Sun and the serial number (I-36, I-37 or I-47). Torpedo boats, launches and small crafts accompanied the submarines to see them off while seaplanes hovered above, banking their wings in farewell.

Lieutenant Nishina, who had boarded I-47, ran down from the bridge and stood on the rear deck. He unsheathed his samurai sword and brandished it. He was acting out the message that if the Kaiten should fail on its way, he would storm the enemy ship single-handed like the defenders who boarded the Mongol ships as they approached Japanese shores in the thirteenth century. The three officers who remained on the bridge also wielded their swords which reflected the rays of the bright morning sun. Probably never before in the history of the Japanese Navy had men brandished naked samurai swords as they sallied forth to battle.

After the three submarines reached the outer sea, the flagship I-36 sent out the following message: 'Break up the formation. Each boat is to proceed according to orders.' Japanese reconnaissance planes had previously flown over Ulithi in the Caroline Islands and seen a lagoon full of American ships. As a result, four Kaiten manned torpedoes were now going to execute attacks against vessels in the lagoon on the early morning of November 20. To reach their destination they had to cover 1,450 nautical miles. The dozen young Kaiten officers had 12 more days to live.

Nishina had been meticulous in keeping a diary until the very last day. On the evening of his first day aboard the mother submarine, he had written:

> There is only one path ahead of me,
> And this day has been a splendid beginning.
> It started with a drizzle – surely
> Inappropriate tears for our mission.

On November 18, the I-47 was closing in on Ulithi atoll. Submerged, the air-conditioning and ventilation systems on the submarine were shut off to keep noise to a minimum. It became unbearably hot for the men and everyone stripped to the waist. Fifty minutes after sundown the submarine surfaced. Through binoculars, the bright lights of Ulithi base were observed. Commander Yoshitsugu Orita, the captain of the I-47, recalled seeing the lights of San Francisco in December 1941 when he was weapons officer on another submarine that was then operating off America's West Coast.

For the last dinner for the Kaiten officers, the chef had prepared the best meal possible, including ice cream. Captain Orita was surprised that the chopsticks of the four officers did not tremble at all. They ate well.

The submarine was now moving at 12 knots for the site at which it would release the human torpedoes. In the meantime the four men went into the shower room and cleansed themselves. (Cleansing with water is important to Shintoism, as it is to the Islamic and Jewish religions. It is noteworthy that instructions to the Al-Qaeda warriors involved in the September 2001 suicide attack stressed cleanliness and washing before prayers and carrying out their mission.)

At 4 a.m. the submarine reached the designated point and Orita spoke over the intercom to the four men. 'I wish you a big catch!'

The last steel bands that held the Kaitens to the submarine were released electrically and all four Kaitens headed for the atoll. Through the periscope a huge fireball rising from Ulithi atoll was lighting up the sky. One of the Kaitens had hit a large oil tanker loaded with fuel.

Although maximum energy went into planning, testing and construct-ing the 'exotic weapons' including the Kaitens and Ohkas, the actual results were less than expected. The suicide boats sank an estimated eight small ships and damaged a dozen more. The Kaiten torpedoes are recorded to have sunk two ships: the destroyer *Underhill* and the oil tanker *Mississinewa*. But over 80 Kaiten pilots lost their lives. The Ohka (Cherry Blossom) missiles were less effective although they had greater explosive impact (a half-ton of high explosives) than regular Kamikaze planes and could fly faster (reportedly 600 miles, 960 kmh, per hour).

THE OHKA MISSILE

Since we were pilots, sooner or later we would die.
I didn't want to die without being able to offer some resistance.
It was better to go out with a challenge.

Statement by a pilot volunteering for Ohka duty

At Okinawa in April 1945 the Japanese Command began using a number of Special Attack weapons in addition to the Kaiten torpedoes. They included human mines, crash boats and human bombs called the Ohka (Cherry Blossom), also mockingly called *baka* (idiot bomb) by the Americans. But this rocket-propelled 'idiot bomb' was regarded as potentially the most dangerous weapon the Japanese had and because of its speed the most difficult target for gunners and pilots.

The Ohka missile, which carried a half-ton of explosives in its nose, was attached under the body of a twin-engine bomber and, after being separated from the mother plane, was guided to its target by a suicide pilot. The pilot had no means of escape once the missile was fastened to the aircraft that would launch it. The Ohka pilot would ride in the bomber until the launch area was approached, at which time he would climb through the bomb bay and into the narrow cockpit of the bomb. The mother plane usually flew at an altitude of over 25,000 feet (7,500 metres) and at more than 50 miles (80 kilometres) from its tar-get, the missile would glide to within a few miles of its target before the pilot turned on its rocket engines, accelerating the speed to 600 mph (960 kmh) in its final dive.

But many of the attacks by Ohkas ended ignominiously. Thus on March 21 when three American carriers were spotted off Kyushu, 18 Japanese 'Betty' bombers, 16 of which carried Ohka missiles, took off, escorted by 55 Japanese fighters. More fighters had been requested because the Japanese pilots were of limited skill and ability, being no match for pilots of America's Grummans. Of the fighter escorts, 25 were unable to get off the ground or had to turn back due to engine trouble. A worse fate awaited the mission when some 50 Grummans suddenly appeared and concentrated their efforts on the Okha-carrying bombers. All of them jettisoned their Ohka missiles but still failed to escape, 15 of them being shot down in quick succession. The three remaining mother planes dived into a cloud bank but they too never made it back to base. The Ohkas had better luck in April and May, damaging several destroyers and minesweepers and assisting a Kamikaze plane in sinking a destroyer. Some Ohka pilots lost their lives before they could board their rocket-propelled craft. It is reported that almost 200 mother planes used in Ohka attacks were destroyed at a cost of over 400 Japanese pilots.

The US destroyer *Abele* was the first Allied ship to be sunk by an Ohka bomb. (*Abele* was simultaneously crashed into by a suicide plane.) Eyewitnesses said the sinking vessel looked like a torn sardine can. The crew saw the plane and its pilot blown into a thousand bits and scattered among the wreckage. The destroyer's toll was high: 79 killed and missing, 35 wounded.

Another destroyer, *Stanly*, was on routine patrol near Okinawa when it found herself the prey of Kamikaze planes that hovered above like angry bees. Suddenly what looked like two strange planes with short, stubby wings, headed straight for the ship. An anti-aircraft shell from the ship's guns ripped the wing off one of the Ohkas as it made a steep dive. It careened over the destroyer and side-swiped one of the stacks before exploding a safe distance away. But the other Ohka hit the bow of *Stanly* and went right through the hull, coming out the other side and exploding. The designers of the Ohka had made the missile capable of piercing the heavy armour of large warships. It was a serious hole but the ship did not sink.

NOTE

[1] The oxygen-driven torpedo, or Type 93, adopted in 1933, was launched from surface vessels. It was 9 metres in length, 61 centimetres in diameter and had an astonishing range of 40,000 metres at 36 knots or 20,000 metres at 48 knots. It left no wake in the water. Only Japan succeeded in developing an oxygen-driven torpedo during WWII. The Type 93 torpedo was converted into the 'notorious Kaiten'. Type 95 was the submarine-launched version of Type 93.

17

HIROHITO, HIROSHIMA AND THE RUSSIANS

TWO DAYS IN HIROHITO'S LIFE

As the nominal Commander-in-Chief, Emperor Hirohito was informed of major developments during the war. When the sensational news of the highly successful first Kamikaze attack was reported to Hirohito – one US escort carrier sunk, six damaged on October 25, 1944 – his reaction was ambiguous. 'Was it necessary to go to this extreme? But they have certainly done a good job.' What follows are two candid portraits of the Emperor, one on New Year's Day, 1945; the other on a critical day in August of the same year.

JANUARY 1, 1945

It is only five hours since 1945 dawned. The trees at Fukiage Gardens on the spacious Imperial Palace grounds in the heart of Tokyo are still shrouded in darkness waiting for the dawn. A crimson-coloured Mercedes Benz waits before the entrance of the Imperial bunker, idling its engine. The exhaust pipe is leaking thin white smoke in the chilling early morning air. The steel doors of the Emperor's concrete bunker, deep below the palace grounds, have been opened. The bunker is called, in coded language, Gobunko (Imperial Library).[1]

Now, the Grand Chamberlain, Naotoku Fujita, wearing a black uniform, steps out. An *udoneri* (an ancient term in court language for the Emperor's bodyguard) dimly light's Fujita's path with a flashlight covered by a black cloth. An air raid alarm was issued at 4.50 a.m.

Emperor Hirohito appears, led by a court chamberlain. He is dressed in an Army uniform with the golden insignia of Grand Field Marshal on the lapels and a decoration bar (in green, yellow, red and white) of the Grand Order of the Chrysanthemum on his chest.

Flashlights are turned off as soon as the Emperor and the Grand Chamberlain have boarded the limousine. Followed by cars carrying chamberlains and the chief military adjutant officer, the limousine drives out of the gate of Fukiage Gardens and turns right.

The Three Sacred Shrines[2] stand next to Fukiage Gardens. Hirohito has already taken a ritual bath in the bunker's bathroom. He then changes into ceremonial Heian period costumes at the Ryokiden Hall of the Sacred Shrines. After this he steps onto the garden and performs the first Shinto ritual, called 'Shihouhai' (worshipping in four directions) before sunrise.

When the motorcade was a few hundred metres from the gate of Fukiage Gardens, a shrill siren wailed, its sound being heard all around the palace. Fujita was seated on a jump-seat facing the Emperor.

'Air raid, Your Majesty,' said Fujita. 'We must return to Gobunko.'

Hirohito, who had turned 43 the previous year, simply nodded. Fujita through an intercom instructed the driver to return to the bunker.

It had been a moonless night and the skies were still dark. Suddenly several rays from searchlights criss-crossed the heavens, lighting the bottom of vaguely discernible clouds. The limousine executed a U-turn. As it was about to reach the entrance to the bunker, they saw through tall trees in a north-easterly direction faint scarlet patches in the sky. Eight hours earlier, on the last day of the year, two B-29 'flying fortresses', dropping incendiary bombs from high altitude, set more than 500 homes afire in Tokyo's Shimoya, Kanda and Asakusa districts.

Hirohito entered the bunker accompanied by Empress Nagako and together they went down the stairs to the underground air raid shelter. He listened to minute-by-minute reports of the advancing American planes from an adjutant. But Hirohito was more concerned about the 'Shihouhai ritual'. It was his religious duty to conclude the ritual before sunrise.

Hirohito muttered, 'We should not wait; the day will dawn soon,' as Fujita reiterates that the air raid was still going on.

At 5.20 a.m., the B-29s headed out towards the sea. Although the air raid alarm was still on, Hirohito decided to venture outside.

At 5.25 a.m. the intelligence unit of the 10th Army Air Division, located at the Dai-ichi Seimei Building (the same building was later used by US General Douglas MacArthur for his headquarters in Japan), across the moat from the Imperial Palace, monitored and recorded a signal from a departing B-29, repeating the ironic message: 'Happy New Year! Happy New Year!'

Shortly afterwards, Hirohito arrived at the Three Sacred Shrines and performed the first ritual of the new year. The Emperor prayed for the peace and prosperity of the nation and the world at Shihouhai.

At 8.15 a.m. Hirohito performed *Haregozen no gi* (a ceremonial first meal) in the dining hall of the bunker. For the ritual he touched with chopsticks an array of cooked food but did not eat. Right after this ritual, Hirohito inspected a typical last meal offered to Kamikaze flyers. This consisted of a piece of cooked red freshwater bream, rice cooked with red beans and vegetables in a small wooden lunch box, and a small bottle of sake. (The bream and red beans are thought to bring good luck.)

AUGUST 15, 1945:

This day, on which the Emperor made his surrender broadcast, marked the end of Kamikaze sorties. For some days after the surrender, the plaza outside the Imperial Palace, in the centre of Tokyo, was stained red with the blood of military and civilian suicides who killed themselves as an apology for defeat in the war and for causing humiliation to the Emperor.

At five minutes past midnight, the Emperor returned to the Gobunko where he and Empress Nagako lived as American air raids over Tokyo intensified, after recording his broadcast to the nation that Japan was terminating the war by accepting the Potsdam Declaration. There was no reference to surrender or capitulation. He had made the recording at the Ministry of the Imperial Household building situated within the Imperial Palace compound.

The historic broadcast had been recorded at 11.25 p.m. the day before when Hirohito arrived at the Ministry building. No Emperor in the past had personally addressed the nation over the radio. It was a short broadcast, taking about five minutes. The NHK, the national radio corporation, had installed the recording system for the occasion.

On his first attempt, Hirohito misread the script, which was an Imperial Rescript drafted and approved by the Cabinet, in several places. He tried again and asked Kainan Shimomura, Director of the Information Agency: 'How did it go this time?'

'It went very well, Your Majesty,' Shimomura replied, although Hirohito had again misread the script, this time in two places.

Time was pressing. The recording was played back. Hirohito listened to it and was pleased.

'It went quite well, didn't it?' he exclaimed and laughed.

Masaharu Kikuchi, an *udoneri* (imperial bodyguard) who stood right outside in the corridor and heard the Emperor laugh, says he felt immensely relieved and deeply impressed that the Emperor was so much at ease despite the national crisis.

Upon returning to his bunker, Hirohito went straight to bed. Shortly after 3 a.m. two chamberlains rushed to the bunker in the dark from the Ministry building to report that the Imperial Guards Division had mutinied in order to prevent Japan's capitulation. The telephone lines to the Emperor's bunker were cut by the mutineers. It was learned that officers of the division had rebelled after killing General Takeo Mori, the Division Commander. Soldiers searched the building for the Emperor's recording but failed to discover it. At the imperial bunker two chamberlains on duty were surprised at the news. Two bodyguards on hand began locking the steel doors and windows. They decided not to wake Hirohito. At 5 a.m. Naotoku Fujita, the chief chamberlain, and two aides reached the bunker and became part of the defending force.

Fujita opened a steel window slightly and saw that the rebellious troops had completely surrounded the bunker. At this point the chamberlains decided to wake up the Emperor. Hirohito came out of the residential quarters wearing a scarlet nightgown and a pair of slippers. Chamberlain Yasuya Mitsui after bowing deeply told the Emperor that the Imperial Guards Division had mutinied and occupied the Imperial Palace.

'It is a *coup d'état*, isn't it?' Hirohito said. Then, in a commanding tone: 'Gather the troops in the garden. I will personally address them. I will tell them with an open heart what I believe.'

Hirohito then asked for his military aide-de-camp to be summoned and retired to his quarters to change into his army uniform.

In the meantime, General Shizuichi Tanaka, commander of the Eastern Army Group, arrived at the palace grounds and told the men that the commander of the Imperial Guards Division was murdered by staff officers and that the orders to the division were forged. Hirohito, already dressed in his army tunic, was now at his study in the bunker when a chamberlain reported to him that the mutiny was over.

Throughout the war, Hirohito kept busts of Abraham Lincoln and Charles Darwin in his study. He held the two men in admiration, Lincoln for liberating the oppressed and Darwin for his work as a marine biologist. There were no other busts or portraits in his study.

Before 11 a.m. Hirohito walked over to an underground conference room. There, a meeting of the Privy Council was called to approve the Imperial Rescript terminating the war. It was merely a formality. All 17 Council members wore swallow-tail coats. After the meeting, from noon, Hirohito heard his own broadcast in the adjacent room.

In the afternoon, Hirohito conferred with the Minister of the Imperial Household, Koichi Kido (who was also his private secretary) several times about the selection of a successor to Prime Minister Admiral Kantaro Suzuki. Suzuki came to the bunker to tender his resignation personally to Hirohito. At 6.35 p.m., Kido reported to the Emperor that he and Chairman Giichi Hiranuma of the Privy Seal Council had agreed to recommend Prince Higashikuni as Prime Minister. Hirohito was pleased. Because the fear remained that Army or Navy units might mutiny against the order to lay down their arms, presenting the nation with a serious danger, it was felt that only an Imperial prince could act on behalf of the Emperor in overriding the crisis.

Hirohito ruled as divine emperor until Japan's defeat in the Second World War, becoming a constitutional monarch after the 1946 populist Constitution was introduced under the American occupation of Japan. Considered an expert on marine biology, Hirohito died in 1989.

His role in the war, say some Western experts, remains unclear.

Hirohito made the following comment one year after the war:
The Special Attack operations were truly impossible to bear in terms of our natural human feelings but Japan having been put in an impossible position, those unreasonable measures were all that was left to us.

TAGATA IN HIROSHIMA

On August 6, 1945 a Japanese radio broadcast said simply: 'A B-29 raided Hiroshima City and released a special bomb, turning the entire city into flames and causing widespread damage.'

Later that day Tokyo Radio said:

The authorities are still unable to obtain a definite check on the extent of the casualties. Medical relief agencies from neighbouring districts could not distinguish – much less identify – the dead from the injured. The impact of the bomb was so terrific that practically all living things – human and animal – were literally

seared to death by the tremendous heat and pressure set up by
the blast. All the dead and injured were burned beyond recognition. Those outdoors were burned to death, while those indoors
were killed by the indescribable pressure and heat.[4]

Four days later, Takeo Tagata entered the city by train and saw for
himself the grim aftermath of atomic warfare.

'When I first heard the news on the radio I sensed that it was a kind
of atomic bomb,' says Tagata. 'A rumour had been circulating in the
Army for the last half-year or so that the United States was developing an atomic bomb.'

Two months earlier, with the roof falling in on Japan, Tagata had
been given a new assignment at a base near Kobe which didn't suit his
talent as a fighter pilot: reconnaissance duty. Disappointed, he was also
disillusioned when at the end of June 1945, he and his friends heard
the news that on Okinawa on June 23, 1945, two prominent generals,
Mitsuru Ushijima and Isamu Cho, ended their own lives with ritual hara-
kiri, each officer given a knife with the blade wrapped in white cloth,
the symbol of harakiri. (Ushijima was the Commander-in-Chief of the
32nd Army which defended Okinawa; Cho was his Chief of Staff.) On
the very same day Takeo Tagata had been transferred to Miki Air Base,
near Kobe.

When Tagata reached Miki Air Base to take up his new assignment,
he immediately went about seeking a change of duty:

As soon as I knew my new assignment, I telephoned the Air
Divisional Headquarters at Gifu, near Nagoya, and asked to be
transferred to a fighter squadron. I was flying Type 100 reconnaissance planes daily, combing the waters off Shikoku Island within
a radius of 150 kilometres looking for enemy surface ships and
submarines. There were 40 pilots in our unit but I was the only
seasoned flyer. I knew the unit commander regarded me as indispensable, but I kept on pleading for a transfer. On August
6 – the day of the Hiroshima tragedy – my wish was granted. I
was assigned to a fighter squadron at Metabaru Air Base in Saga
Prefecture, in Kyushu. I was to proceed to Metabaru by train.
But the rail link between Osaka and Kyushu had been disrupted
by the bomb dropped on Hiroshima on that very day.
  I boarded the first train that left Himeji Station for Kyushu
during the night of August 9. The train would pass through
Hiroshima. That day, a radio broadcast said that Russia had declared
war on Japan; that Manchukuo [Manchuria] was under Russian

attack, and that Nagasaki had received extensive damage from the second 'special bomb'. I had heard at Miki Air Base through our intelligence unit that the US B-29 that delivered the atomic bomb over Hiroshima had taken off from Tinian Island. This information was obtained by tracking the plane's radio signals. Our intelligence unit reckoned that the Americans possessed two more atomic bombs. How they came to this conclusion, I do not know. In my own mind I figured there was probably one more such bomb left.

The train was packed and Tagata was barely able to find standing room:

Most of the passengers were civilians. The train made stops at Okayama, Kasaoka, Fukuyama, Onomichi, Mihara and Kure before it pulled into Hiroshima in the morning. It was quiet in Hiroshima and we heard no air raid sirens. But we were confronted by widespread damage. The structure of the railroad station was almost entirely gone. I saw twisted pillars. There was debris all over. Where there had been a steel roof over the station there were now only the bare concrete platforms. Railroad cars were turned upside down. Our train stopped in Hiroshima for two hours. We saw railroad workers still working to replace twisted rails ahead of us. The rails looked like long twisted and melted candy bars. A conductor with a megaphone warned the passengers that they should not leave the train for long because of radioactivity. But the workers themselves braved the danger. Anyway, we walked outside the train.

Tagata says that despite the horror of the atomic bomb, the morale of the population was 'still high' and that this pleased him:

Hiroshima was flattened completely as far as I could see under the bright morning sun. But the Hiroshima Castle had disappeared, leaving only the ramparts. I saw dead bodies everywhere, including bodies of children. It was an incredible sight: the hundreds of dead bodies. The stench from rotting corpses was unbearable.

Those passengers – a few hundred of them – who had left the train were stunned. Many slowly shook their heads as if they were confronting hell. Many of them expressed disgust at the unspeakable atrocity. Multitudes were crying out loud, not caring to wipe their tears away. I thought: what an enormous sin has been committed by man! The shock I felt was heightened because I had been told that the Japanese Air Force was very strict about not hitting civilian targets.[5]

As a military man I was constantly gratified to see that the atomic strikes did not weaken the people's morale. An elderly lady who was one of the passengers on the train said to me: 'Officer! We are relying on you!' Others bowed to me, expressing their encouragement. 'We are behind you!' cried out another passenger. But although I was wearing a pilot's insignia, I felt ashamed that the air force failed to prevent the enemy from dropping the diabolic bomb.

Commander Masatake Okumiya, who was a staff officer in charge of air defence at the Imperial High Command, flew over Hiroshima on August 7, the day after the city was hit by an atomic bomb, to assess the damage. Strangely, he reported that he was 'surprised' that the scope of destruction appeared *less* than he had expected. He had in his position flown over Tokyo, Osaka, Nagoya and other major cities immediately after intensive American air raids and thought the March 10 fire-bombing of Tokyo's residential areas had brought far greater damage than what he observed, flying in an airplane, at Hiroshima as a result of the new weapon.

Okumiya spent August 8 and 9 on the ground in Hiroshima surveying the destruction. Dead bodies were still floating in rivers. He was shocked at the sight of incinerated bodies everywhere. The air was still suffused with the malodour of decomposing bodies. In other cities, says Tagata, the dead and wounded were removed in a matter of a single day. But this was not the case in Hiroshima.

RUSSIA AND THE BOMB

All of a sudden Tokyo was the recipient of a double shock. Two days after the first atomic bomb fell, Russia declared war on Japan. Before these events, the Americans and British believed that to force Japan's surrender with a huge invasion army would be very costly. Although confident of winning, their conclusion had been fixed: Russia's entry into the war against Japan was essential. And adding weight to this opinion was the scope of Kamikaze attacks in the Okinawa area and the threat of more of the same if a land invasion of the Japanese home islands got under way. The very ferocity of Japan's resistance seems to have been one of the reasons behind the decision to use the bomb. And it can not be excluded that the successes of Kamikaze strategy in the sinking and mangling of several hundred (mainly American) ships contributed to the decision to use atomic bombs on Hiroshima and Nagasaki.

Other problems arose. For instance, there was a noticeable lack of coordination between some of the Allies owing to deep differences between them. Initially Washington and London counted on an activation of military operations by the Chinese Army. But that had been stopped cold by an aggravation of the political struggle going on in China. As a result, the United States, Britain and China began to work persistently to involve Russia in the war against Japan. President Roosevelt made such an appeal to the Soviet government immediately after Japan's attack on Hawaii in December 1941. Moscow turned down the request, explaining that it needed all its strength to fight Hitler's Germany, its main enemy, and since it had to fight practically single-handed.

But Russia still kept dozens of divisions in the Far East, thereby holding down a part of Japan's armed forces on the mainland.

On the Chinese front, the operations against the Japanese forces were less than dramatic; and, after hostilities had broken out in the Pacific, they stopped almost completely. Although Japan had by then far less possibility to carry out large-scale operations against Chinese troops, China did not venture to launch a full-scale counter-offensive. Generalissimo Chiang Kai-shek's vacillations and China's internal squabbles stood in the way. Meanwhile, the ruling Kuomintang (the national-democratic party of China organized by Sun Yat-sen in 1912) was mustering its strength for a decisive battle with Mao Zedong's unpredictable army. This made it impossible for China to carry out active military measures against Japan's forces, while Mao's units only engaged in guerrilla warfare in the Japanese rear. Consequently, the operations they undertook could not change the course of the war.

In their plans for the defeat of the Japanese Army the Kuomintang leadership counted on the US and Britain to land their troops in China. But all along, the Americans and British were counting on Russian participation in the Pacific War.

At the Tehran Conference between the US, Britain and Russia (November 28–December 1, 1943) Stalin had promised to enter the war against Japan after the war ended in Europe. The promise brought great relief to the Allies and ended the awkward situation created by the earlier Cairo talks between Roosevelt, Churchill and Chiang Kai-shek held on November 22–26, 1943. During those talks Roosevelt and Churchill had tried to persuade Chiang to carry out a large-scale operation ('Buccaneer') in Burma in order to open up a new road to China. Chiang, for his part, wanted US and British troops to take part in the operation and demanded increased arms supplies and other assistance.

At the end of a heated argument the US President and the British Prime Minister agreed to comply with many of Chiang Kai-shek's demands. But when they returned to Cairo after Tehran they went back on their commitments to China and Roosevelt cabled the Chinese government informing it that operation 'Buccaneer' was being called off.

Churchill wrote in his memoirs that after Tehran and the talks with Chiang in Cairo the Western Allies lost much of their interest in the Chinese front and became less persistent in their attempts to activate it. Churchill specifically pointed out that one of the main reasons for this was Marshal Stalin's assurance that 'Russia would declare war on Japan the moment Germany was defeated'. This, the Allies felt, would give them better bases than those they could find in China.

The promise made in Tehran was subsequently repeated by Stalin during his meeting with Churchill and US Ambassador Averell Harriman in Moscow on October 5, 1944. In his message to the Russian leader of October 4 Roosevelt had asked Moscow to join together in crushing the Japanese military. A final agreement on the Far East was reached at the Yalta Conference of heads of government of Russia, the US and Britain, held in February 1945. Under the agreement Russia undertook to enter the war against Japan in about three months after the end of the war in Europe. But even after the agreement was concluded the US and Britain were not convinced that the USSR would come to their aid. At the end of May 1945, President Harry Truman, who became President of the United States after Roosevelt's death on April 12, 1945, sent his emissary, Harry Hopkins, to Moscow to find out if the Kremlin was going to enter the war and, if so, when. Stalin replied that Russia's armed forces would be ready for military action by August 8.

The Russian participation in the war against Japan was also the subject of a special discussion at the Potsdam Conference (July 17–August 2, 1945). Truman wrote afterwards (in his *Memoirs*): 'There were many reasons for my going to Potsdam, but the most urgent, to my mind, was to get from Stalin a personal reaffirmation of Russia's entry into the war against Japan.' Truman added: 'Our military experts had estimated an invasion of Japan would cost at least five hundred thousand American casualties even if the Japanese forces then in Asia were held on the Chinese mainland.' General MacArthur, Supreme Commander of the South-west Pacific Area, demanded that an agreement be reached with Moscow whereby the latter would move at least 60 divisions against the Japanese forces. Describing his talks with Chinese Prime Minister T.V. Soong shortly before the Potsdam Conference, President Truman wrote: 'I explained to Soong, as I had done previously, that I was anxious to see the Soviet Union come into the war against Japan early enough to shorten the war and thus save countless American and Chinese lives.'

Truman's remarks were made at a time when the testing of atomic bombs was getting under way in America. Nevertheless, top-ranking US military commanders, including Marshall, Eisenhower and Eaker, seeing the fierce determination of Japan's military forces on the ground and in the air to resist, invariably 'to the last man', did not think Japan could be overcome by air bombings alone. Instead, they believed that Japan would continue fighting even in the unlikely event that it lost its own islands because then the Japanese government could set up bases on Chinese soil and go on fighting from there since its armed forces had increased to nearly 7.2 million by August 1945.

In support of Truman, Dr Karl T. Compton, a scientist directly involved in the decision to use the bombs, has recorded his 'complete conviction that the use of the atomic bomb saved hundreds of thousands – perhaps several millions – of lives, both American and Japanese'.

Adding to America's apprehensions were analyses by military experts that appeared in the Japanese press which gave minute details of how and why an American invasion would end in failure. These analyses used ringing phrases such as 'the coming decisive battle' and 'the fate of the Empire'. One analysis, aimed at Washington and London, appeared in the English-language *Nippon Times* of July 11, 1945 and was entitled 'The Invasion of Japan – The Last Stage'. It explained why the country was confident of 'smashing' an enemy landing on the Japan's home islands. Some excerpts from the *Nippon Times*:

First may be mentioned our absolute superior fighting force in quantity. Whatever vast forces the enemy may attempt to land on our shores, his action will be restricted by his limited shipping capacity. American military commentator Hanson Baldwin has expressed the opinion that America will have to use three ships in transporting the same amount of forces and materials in the Pacific that she carried in the European battle with a single ship. Since the United States had to use 18 tons of shipping to transport each soldier in his landing operations in Europe, she will have to use 54 tons for carrying each man in the Pacific operations. But supposing that 18 tons is sufficient, the USA will need 18,000,000 tons to convey a force of 1 million men in their landing operations. They will need 54 million tons to convey 3 million men to the Japanese mainland. But the United States has only 5 million tons and can only use part of this tonnage in his campaign. The first batch of the enemy forces in landing operations can not exceed 1 million men. But wherever the enemy may land this number, we can send against him a force at least several times the number that the enemy may land . . .

The second formidable factor will be our air force. The enemy will undoubtedly challenge us by pouring forth his entire air force by utilizing aircraft carriers and air bases, but we have succeeded in accumulating enough aircraft in preparation for the coming decisive battle on which will depend the fate of our Empire . . .

When we succeed in destroying the enemy's fleet and the first wave of the enemy landing forces, he will be unable to send many more waves of invading forces in landing operations. If the enemy's losses are heavy enough, we can earn time while the enemy will be forced to reconstruct his fleet. It is not impossible to repeat such a feat every time the enemy should attempt such a landing operation.

Meanwhile, the US made plans to use the bomb to force Japan's surrender. This notwithstanding the evidence that conventional explosives against Japan were causing vast destruction. US air raids on Japanese cities grew in scale in the autumn of 1944 and became massive in the spring of 1945. Sixty-six Japanese cities were raided, and 100,000 tons of explosives were dropped on them. Japan had lost the power to retaliate. The nature of the raids on Japan was similar to that of the previous Anglo-American raids on German cities. Residential areas were hit without pity. The Japanese government reported that 2,200,000 dwellings were destroyed in the air raids, with a toll of 260,000 killed and over 400,000 wounded.

The scientists at work on the American bomb had emphatic instructions to have the bomb ready in August 1945, that is, at the expected time of Russian participation in the war. A date close to August 10 was named as the 'secret deadline' and the people who handled the technical end were supposed to complete work at all costs, irrespective of risks and expenses. The stock of fissionable materials at all the laboratories and projects was completely used up – of uranium for the first bomb dropped on Hiroshima, and of plutonium for the second bomb dropped on Nagasaki.

The atomic bombing of the two Japanese cities killed or wounded over 400,000 civilians.

In a memoir written after his presidency, Truman again defended the use of the atomic bombs, saying that in August 1945 there were still more than 4 million men in the Japanese armed forces to defend the main Japanese islands, Korea, Manchuria and North China, and that the Japanese were building up a 'National Volunteer Army' at home for a last ditch stand. There was little doubt, he said, 'that the last-ditch militarists in Tokyo were ready to sacrifice 10 or even 20 million Japanese lives'.

On July 12, Foreign Minister Shigenori Togo dispatched a cable to Ambassador Naotake Sato in Moscow. Victory over Hitler's Germany had come two months earlier and the Russians were busily transferring armies from the European sector to the Far East. Togo's cable said:

> His Majesty is extremely anxious to terminate the war as soon as possible, being deeply concerned that the further continuation of hostilities will only aggravate the untold miseries of the teeming millions, innocent men and women, of the countries at war. Should, however, the United States and Great Britain insist on unconditional surrender, Japan would be forced to fight to the bitter end with all her might in order to vindicate her honour and safeguard her national existence, which, to our intense regret, would entail further bloodshed. Our government therefore desires to negotiate for a speedy restoration of peace, prompted as we sincerely are by solicitude for the welfare of mankind. For this purpose Prince Konoe will proceed to Moscow with a personal message of the Emperor and it is requested that the Soviet government be good enough to accord travel facilities to him.

Meanwhile, American code-breakers had been hard at work. In 1941, the US had succeeded in deciphering Japan's diplomatic codes prior to the outbreak of the Pacific War. In July 1945, Washington knew that Japan was prepared to end the war and it is generally agreed that the US was reading every diplomatic cable sent by the Japanese Ambassador in Berlin, Hiroshi Oshima, thus obtaining Hitler's secrets. Some experts say it is safe to assume that the US read Togo's message to Sato.

The Japanese Army was adamantly against capitulation. In February 1945, Hirohito met with each *jushin* (factions of former premiers and key politicians) in succession to hear their opinions how the war should be terminated. A majority urged the Emperor to stop the war. Some Army leaders said Japan should 'sue for peace' only after a victory was secured in the Battle of the Homeland. (The fact that such a victory would have been a Pyrrhic one apparently did not weigh heavily on the minds of these officers.) Prince Konoe submitted a memorandum saying that the war was lost and the sooner peace was secured, the better for Japan. When Konoe met with Hirohito on February 14, he told the Emperor he believed that the US would not demand abolition of the Imperial family, but if Japan fought on they might do so. On April 7, Admiral Kantaro Suzuki became Prime Minister by recommendation of a group of *jushin* who advocated suing for peace. In appointing Suzuki, the Emperor told the 78-year-old veteran of the Russo-Japanese War to 'bring about peace'. Suzuki had once served as Hirohito's Chief Chamberlain.

The 'peace faction', led by Foreign Minister Togo, Privy Seal Koichi Kido, Prince Konoe, and some other *jushin*, was ready to capitulate on condition that the preservation of the Japanese *kokutai* (national polity), or Emperor system, was guaranteed. The consensus was that the unique features of Japan as valued by its citizens would disappear in the absence of the Emperor. The question was: how to bring the Army (the Minister of the Navy, Admiral Mitsumasa Yonai favoured suing for peace) to accept peace talks. Togo and Kido agreed to use the Russians as a ruse. Togo proposed that Japan ask Russia to play the role of broker in seeking peace. Moreover, there was some optimism that Japan might be able to obtain more advantageous terms by working through the Russians. On June 18 a meeting of the Supreme War Guidance Council was convened and the participants – the Prime Minister, the Foreign, Army and Navy Ministers, and the Chiefs of Staff of the Army and Navy, agreed to ask Russia to act as mediator. They called for the minimum condition of safeguarding the *kokutai* in seeking peace. Four days later, Hirohito presided over an Imperial Conference, attended by the same participants, and confirmed the decision taken by the Supreme War Guidance Council.

But Russia turned down Prince Konoe's proposed visit. Stalin had already given his pledge to enter into the war against Japan. When Moscow declared war on Japan, it was, say Japanese historians, a violation of the Russo-Japanese Non-Aggression Pact signed in 1941, a pact which was valid until 1946. But Washington through various channels knew that Japan was preparing to surrender. For instance, in Switzerland the Japanese legation was making overtures to the US Office of Strategic Services which was run by Allen Dulles.

The Potsdam Declaration, subtitled 'Proclamation Defining Terms of Japanese Surrender', was issued on July 26, 1945 and stated bluntly: 'We will not deviate from [our terms]. There are no alternatives. We shall brook no delay.' Some Japanese sighed with relief because the terms demanded only 'the unconditional surrender of all Japanese forces' unlike the case with Hitler's Germany. In other words, the Declaration hinted at a *conditional surrender*.

But Tokyo's leaders worried that there was no specific guarantee for the continuation of the Emperor system. Finally, the Japanese government notified the Allies that Japan would accept the Potsdam Declaration with the understanding that it did not contain a demand to change the nation's political make-up. Looking back, there is reason to believe that if Washington had conveyed to Japan the promise that the US harboured no intention of abolishing the Emperor system, Japan would have agreed to stop fighting sooner.

The dropping of the atomic bombs on August 6 and 9, 1945 may have quickened Japan's surrender by a few days. The United States was planning to invade Kyushu ('Operation Olympic') in early November. It has long been argued that the bombs saved millions of lives. Nowadays, many historians contend that President Harry Truman was also eager to demonstrate the power of the new bomb to the Russians; that this may even have been an overriding reason for the destruction of Hiroshima and Nagasaki.

Winston Churchill favoured the use of the bombs, saying that they were needed 'to avert a vast, indefinite butchery'. Without the bombs, he maintained, the war might well have required 'the loss of a million American lives and half that number of British'. In the opinion of Justice Rolling of the Netherlands, this appeared to be 'deception of the public' on the part of Churchill.

On August 9 Russian armed forces began operations against Japan's Kwantung Army. On the same day, Nationalist Chinese leader Chiang Kai-shek sent a telegram to Stalin which said that Russia's entry into the war 'has aroused in all Chinese people feelings of great enthusiasm'. His concluding words were: 'I am confident that Japan, which is already in a hopeless position but is still carrying on its desperate struggle, will soon be finally brought down and defeated, and this will bring nearer the day when a lasting peace will be established throughout Eastern Asia.'

Lieutenant-General H.G. Martin, the military observer of the *Daily Telegraph*, wrote on August 10, 1945 that 'the [Russian] campaign may well last six months or more before the Russians can gain a final decision'. But in three weeks the campaign was over. Japan's Kwantung Army had been compelled to surrender. (In a footnote to history, a Russian marshal, Kirill Meretskov, one of the commanders of the Soviet forces in the war with Japan, says that Japanese Major-General Tokomatsu Matsumura told his Russian captors in September 1945: 'Capitulation is admission of defeat. I do not think that we would have been defeated if the Emperor had not ordered us to lay down our arms.')

Some US experts reached a novel conclusion: the *US Strategic Bombing Survey* in its 'Summary Report of the Pacific War', Washington, 1946, concluded:

> Based on a detailed investigation of all the facts, and supported by the testimony of the surviving Japanese leaders involved, it is the *Survey*'s opinion that certainly prior to December 31, 1945, Japan would have surrendered, even if the atomic bombs had not been dropped, even if Russia had not entered the war, and even if no invasion had been planned or contemplated.[6]

In any case, hostilities ended on September 2, 1945 when Japan signed the instrument of surrender.

NOTES

[1] The Gobunko was built to protect the Emperor and Empress from air raids and it became their residence in the last month of the war. The bunker was covered by a 3-metre-thick concrete roof.

[2] The Three Sacred Shrines are: the shrine dedicated to the sun-goddess, Amaterasu Omikami in the centre; the shrine dedicated to the spirits of past emperors; and the shrine dedicated to all deities in the country.

[3] The documentary sketches on Hirohito are based on interviews by Hideki Kase with *udoneri* (body guard) Kikuchi, Chamberlain Mitsui and other chamberlains, Hirohito's military adjutants, and other officials.

[4] Fifteen years after the raid on Hiroshima, Albert Axell visited the scene of the tragedy and on a city bridge saw the blackened outline of a human being who had been vaporized by the bomb.

[5] The Japanese have over the past decade or so become much less reticent about criticizing America. For example, some conservative leaders and commentators have sought to find an equivalency in the commission of Second World War atrocities. As to Japan's war record, periodically the so-called 'textbook controversy' rears its head. In the summer of 2001, a number of Asian neighbours, including China and South Korea, voiced protests against what they said was a tendency in Tokyo to 'whitewash its excesses' in China and elsewhere before and during the war. At issue is the appearance of school history textbooks containing revisions which some foreign critics say are unhistorical.

[6] On August 24–25, 1990, Hideaki Kase was invited to be a keynote speaker at the last reunion of the 509th Composite Group of the US Army

Air Force that dropped the atomic bomb on Hiroshima. The reunion took place at the former US Army Air Corps base in Utah. Says Kase: 'I told General Paul Tibbets, pilot of the plane that dropped the bomb, and the audience of about 800 veterans and their families that dropping the bomb on Hiroshima was not necessary because Japan had already decided to sue for peace.' Hearing these words, about four-fifths of the audience walked out of the hall into the corridor and started singing patriotic songs in protest. Those veterans who protested, says Kase, 'experienced a deep shock on learning that they did not save a few million lives by dropping the bomb but were themselves participants in a useless slaughter'. That evening a dinner party was held at the site of the old airstrip where the unit that dropped the bomb had made practice A-bomb runs before flying out to a Pacific isle and then on to Hiroshima in early August 1945.

18

FROM PILOT TO DIRT FARMER

Eight days after the first atomic bomb fell on Hiroshima, a bugle sounded on Tuesday, August 14, at the Army air base near Saga City in Kyushu. Officially the war was still on. Hardly anyone knew that in just a few hours Japan would agree to surrender. But at Saga Air Base another suicide attack was under preparation and everyone was ordered to assemble immediately in the yard that faced the headquarters' barracks.

The base, which was situated about 40 miles from Kuroki, Takeo Tagata's home town, was heavily camouflaged and surrounded by a forest of pine trees. Tagata had arrived at Saga only three days earlier, having been transferred to the base's 525th Air Unit. That unit had previously sent its entire complement of pilots on a Kamikaze mission against a US Naval Task Force in the vicinity of Japan and none had returned. Until the arrival of Tagata and his colleagues, the 525th Air Unit existed on paper only.

In terms of flying experience, Tagata ranked second at the air base only behind Major Kiyosuke Kono who had been flying for 11 years. Tagata had been flying for ten. Due to the air of excitement and commotion at the air base the entire 525th Air Unit knew that an imminent *tokko* operation was now being readied. Maintenance crews were toiling non-stop to prepare 22 *Hayabusa* (Peregrine Falcon) fighter planes to carry maximum bomb loads.

'In the yard we lined up in formation, each company assigned to its own place,' Tagata recalls.

Major Sakae Yamaguchi, the unit commander, had been Tagata's superior when the latter had served at two previous air bases and he was very pleased to see Tagata again. He was then 37 years of age to Tagata's 29. Not long after their reunion, Tagata told him of his wish to lead a Special Attack mission at the earliest opportunity. Due to a shortage of experienced pilots who were needed to lead ill-trained Kamikaze pilots on their last sortie, Yamaguchi approved Tagata's request.

Tagata's decision was his own. He had not informed his family; neither his parents or his wife, Teruyo, knew about it. He has explained his apparent negligence in these words: 'It was taken for granted that I would do this and they understood what I had done.'

Many *tokko* flyers did not reveal to their loved ones that they had volunteered for a suicide mission, so that in their last letters the flyers often berate themselves for keeping their decision secret until the end.

But why did Tagata, a married man with children, suddenly decide on an act of self-destruction? Tagata:

> On August 14, I volunteered for a Special Attack mission because I saw there was a shortage of seasoned pilots at our base who could lead 'green' pilots to their destination. Volunteering as a Kamikaze pilot came very naturally to me. I did not flinch and was not tormented at all by my decision. After all, so many men, including my students, had perished as *tokko* flyers. I thought it was my duty to the nation. It would have been shameful if I flinched from joining the ranks of Kamikaze flyers after so many good men had gladly sacrificed their lives.

At the same time he was aware of the huge death toll among ground forces; that the last bayonet charge the Japanese garrison troops on the Pacific islands often made against the Americans meant death to all the men.

Tagata adds: 'The thought that so many friends, high-ranking officers and my students had perished as Kamikaze flyers before me weighed down on me. How could I be different? Also, I was convinced that I had a definite role to play in the war.'

Tagata says he cannot establish the exact hour or day when he decided to volunteer for a Kamikaze unit. But obviously the idea had been ripening in his mind for some time.

He asks himself: 'Did I imagine the moment I would crash into an enemy ship after I volunteered as a Kamikaze pilot?' Answer: 'No, no, never. I have flown many combat missions. I knew that I could be shot down and killed. But I never imagined how I would suffer physically if I were wounded or my plane was destroyed. Courage and a sense of duty – together they can overcome the fear of death.'

On the subject of suicide, Tagata has this to say:

I believe that no Kamikaze pilot thought he himself was committing an act of suicide. For them it was not a case of suicide at all. A sortie that would end in self-destruction was looked upon as a noble, a calculated act. Actually, in battle you are often asked to sacrifice your life voluntarily. Such a norm is not restricted to the Japanese. It has happened many times in military history. For example it happened when HMS *Prince of Wales* was sunk by Japanese planes off the Malay Peninsula in December 1941 and the admiral went down with his ship. [Admiral Sir Tom Phillips lost his life when the *Prince of Wales* was sunk.]

On every island, from Attu in the Aleutian chain to Okinawa, which was contested by the American and Japanese forces, the Japanese troops refused to surrender and often fought to the last man. We pilots used to talk about the fate of the garrison troops on those islands, how everyone made their last stand and died. We felt great sorrow for them because they were forced to die in groups, after they exhausted their ammunition and were half-starved. They had been pushed into a corner. Consequently when we heard that Generals Ushijima and Cho had killed themselves, the news did not come as a surprise. [The bodies of Lieutenant General Mitsuru Ushijima, Supreme Commander of Japanese forces on Okinawa, and Major-General Isamu Cho, his Chief of Staff, were discovered under tombstones standing on the south-western coast of the main Okinawa island. They were both clad in their military uniforms. They had committed hara-kiri and their heads were cut off by an executioner, according to the prescribed ritual.]

Tagata pointed to a difference between soldiers on the ground and the pilots, as to 'the choice of death':

By contrast, we pilots were allowed to choose our own fate. A Special Attack pilot heads towards his last moment by himself, of his own free will. However dire the situation faced by the nation, it was the pilot's decision to end his life in order to help the nation. Moreover, a *tokko* pilot was able to know the timing of his death.

He had the luxury of spending some time on his own, calmly, before taking off for the mission.

Certainly, when we learned of Admiral Arima's heroic Kamikaze-style death [in the Philippines], we were deeply impressed. He was the first admiral to perish in a *tokko* attack.

But what truly made Tagata, a pilot whose instinct is to save his plane and his life, accept the reverse? That was the question we posed to the veteran pilot. This was his answer:

All flyers love their planes. You have to be a pilot to understand it. Piloting a plane high above the earth gives you a feeling that you have turned yourself into a bird. You feel that you and your plane are one. The plane is part of you and you are part of the plane. No pilot would gladly sacrifice his life if he were told to carry a bomb and charge into the ranks of enemies alone and blow himself up, taking the enemy with him.

But there was, Tagata readily admitted, 'a certain degree of romanticism in dying with your plane'. He continued:

By mid-1944, Japanese air power was hopelessly outnumbered by the Americans. We lost the bulk of the highly trained pilots who constituted the mainstay of our air force. We were producing superb planes, like the Army's state-of-the-art Hien fighter and the Navy's Shouki and Shiden fighters which were considered by many to be equal to or superior in performance to their American counterparts. But we were not able to produce enough of them. There was an acute shortage of experienced pilots. Consequently most of the green pilots, with pathetically few flying hours, would be mauled by the enemy each time they took to the air. Enemy planes were numerous and the skies were blanketed by enemy anti-aircraft fire. Each sortie was met by almost certain death. *Tokko* [Special Attack] was much more effective and rewarding. Your life is not wasted if you can sink an important enemy ship in exchange for your life. It was a more worthy way to dedicate your life.

I belonged to the 60th class of non-commissioned officers taking a pilot training course at the Army Tachiarai Flying School. There were that same number – 60 – of us who enrolled as students. Twenty-three were eliminated for lack of aptitude. Out of the remaining 37, one crashed and died before graduating from the course. Twenty-eight died in combat and three perished from accidents. Only five, including myself, survived the war. Attrition was high even among seasoned pilots.

In the last year of the war, the demarcation line between life and death became so thin as to be nebulous. Even civilians suffered. On Taiwan I have seen children and old people killed on the roads or wallowing in agony in the fields after being hit by machine-gun bullets. After I returned to Kyushu, I saw with my own eyes low-flying enemy planes shoot at any object that moved. Fire bombing or carpet bombing in civilian residential areas was often carried out against Japan. Death became a common commodity, lessening the fear of death. But these random killings by strafing or fire bombing civilian targets strengthens the popular will to fight, contrary to the expectation that such measures weaken the morale of people to carry on the war.

Another question we asked Tagata was whether Kamikaze tactics would have made a difference if Japan had kept on fighting after mid-August 1945. He gave this reply:

For the Battle of the Homeland, all experienced pilots would have been pitted against the enemy as Kamikaze flyers. They would have been far more effective than the green pilots we hurled against the enemy. But I doubt whether even the experienced pilots flying these one-way missions could have turned back the fortunes of war at the last moment. And once they were gone, Japan was deprived of her air power.

He added: 'We were also down to a minimum of vital energy supplies. I was told that the Army had only a 120-day stockpile of aviation fuel in early August, 1945.'

Major Yamaguchi now addressed the assembled men. It was, Tagata recalls, a humid day ('The sun was scorching and cicadas were wailing from the trees.'):

The enemy [began Yamaguchi] is at this moment bombing and strafing our homeland daily in preparation for his final landing on our shores. Enemy warships are bombarding our coasts. In flagrant violation of international law, with a satanic aim of annihilating civilians en masse, the enemy has just delivered atomic bombs on Hiroshima, on the 6th, and on Nagasaki, on the 9th. The Russians have joined the war in stark violation of the Russo-Japanese Non-Aggression Treaty.

A few months ago thirty-six of our pilots led by Second Lieutenant Asakura from our air base gallantly hurled themselves against an enemy task force off Okinawa that was a spearhead for the island's invasion. Our men meted out severe punishment.

The officer paused a few seconds, then barked: 'We must follow them!' He then added with unaffected gravity: 'You and I will live, at the longest, a few more months – until the autumn. It is a great honour for us, born into the Japanese nation, to dedicate our lives to the Motherland at her most perilous hours. Our ancestors have set many examples for us. I have nothing more to say except this: be prepared for a sortie against the enemy!'

The commanding officer inhaled deeply and said: 'From this moment you have all joined the *tokko-tai* [Special Attack corps]. You will await further orders.'

Tagata says that on hearing these words he felt as if he had had a 'supremely religious experience. I had gotten my wish to join the ranks of Kamikaze pilots and I now felt like a completely different man.' He adds: 'Suddenly the world around me seemed sacred and I experienced a tranquillity of mind. It wasn't that I was intoxicated; rather, I had feelings of liberation, of selflessness, even purity.' Fully accepting the fact that he would soon be giving up his life, he says that for the first time in his life he felt he had achieved complete bliss.

At that moment Tagata's family suddenly arrived at the base. All the families of all the pilots who lived in Kyushu had been notified of the impending mission and now the base canteen was full of reunions of the pilots and their families. 'At 3 p.m.,' says Tagata, 'I saw my wife, Teruyo, and my father. Teruyo was carrying our ten-month-old son, Hirofumi, on her back. She had been pregnant when I had sent her home the previous year when I was stationed on Taiwan.'

But his mother was absent and at the reunion he tried hard not to show the sorrow that he felt. Teruyo said she carried a message from his mother. It said simply: 'I didn't come because I could not bear parting with you.'

Tagata was shocked when he learned that his father and his wife, who carried their baby son, had both ridden over 40 kilometres to the air base from their home in Kuroki. It was midsummer and the hot sun was scorching:

My father and Teruyo were sweating profusely. The trains were no longer reliable and they had decided to bike all that distance. On the way, they were attacked by a lone US fighter which swooped down on them, firing its guns. They had narrowly escaped by rushing into the woods. Sitting down in the canteen, they now produced sweet bean cakes that my mother had made for me. Bean cakes were my favourite food.

The family sat across a table and Tagata ordered soft drinks. Then his father spoke. All his life Tagata's father had been a farmer, although he had occasionally worked in the forestry business.

'Takeo, you are finally going away . . . on a *tokko* mission.'

'Yes, very shortly,' Takeo replied. Takeo knew that his plane and those of the pilots with him would have barely enough fuel for an emergency return flight.

The father nodded. He was trying his best to hold back tears. But he didn't cry. In any case, remembers Tagata, it would have been inappropriate to exhibit too much emotion.

Tagata noticed that Teruyo's eyes were filled with tears. She had placed their tiny son on her lap.

'Take care,' she said. Then: 'Please do your best. I will take care of our son, I promise. Do not worry about that.'

Tagata responded with a lordly request.

'You must always be helpful to my father and mother, to my younger brother and sister on my behalf. I know you will do this.'

Teruyo was now close to losing her voice. Although she had choked up from time to time, she now spoke clearly: 'Your mother has asked me to give you her photograph, so that she could accompany you on your mission.'

Teruyo handed over the photograph. It showed his mother smiling.

'How very sweet of her to want to come with me on my mission,' Tagata said. Now he himself was almost on the verge of tears but he kept a tight rein on himself.

Teruyo stood up and came over to her husband.

'I held and embraced our son,' says Tagata. 'Not being able to understand what was going on, the little boy smiled brightly at me.'

'Do you have any last words for Hirofumi?' Teruyo asked.

'No, not that I can think of. But when he grows up, tell him his father died gladly, even proudly, defending his country.'

At this moment, Tagata took a small notebook from his pocket, ripped out a page and wrote a few lines of poetry:

> I am filled with delight to join the fray
> And proudly perish in the sky
> At the behest of our Sovereign.[1]

'That was the last thing I thought I would ever write in this life,' Tagata says.

As a child, Tagata had been taught to compose poetry by his brother, Toraji, who was older by nine years. (A government official in charge of forestry, he was not drafted into military service.) He also taught Takeo the art of kendo, and horseback riding. As his family owned a racehorse, riding had long ago become one of his pastimes.

Meanwhile, Tagata's father offered a few words of encouragement. 'Takeo, do your best!'

'I am always with you!' Teruyo chimed in.

Now they all went out of the canteen and Tagata's wife and father got on their bicycles and pedalled away.

Again and again his father and Teruyo looked back. As they were about to disappear from his sight they stopped for the last time and waved their arms.

Tagata took this moment to pray for their safe journey home.

During the family meeting, Tagata also had time to talk about family matters. But unlike some of the other pilots, Tagata did not discuss or write a last will. 'I felt very close to my family and I thought they knew well what were my last wishes,' he says.

After his father and Teruyo had left, Tagata shared his mother's cakes with his friends.

Meanwhile, other families were also leaving the base.

Shortly afterwards an urgent radio message was received from Tokyo: Japan had agreed to surrender. All Kamikaze sorties were cancelled and Special Attack training was to be discontinued immediately. However, some flight instructors ignored orders and went on teaching Kamikaze tactics. But when pilots inspected their planes on the following day they found many of the planes inoperable: the propellers and carburettors had been removed.

Tagata's fighting days were over. He says that if the war had gone on for a few more days, he and his fellow pilots would have carried out new orders for a suicide attack against a Russian fleet in Vladivostok.

On September 2, 1945 at 10.30 a.m. Tokyo time, the instrument of Japan's surrender was signed aboard the American battleship *Missouri* in Tokyo Bay. Signing the document were: the Japanese Foreign Minister Mamoru Shigemitsu and the Chief of the General Staff Yoshijiro Umezu. The signatories for the Allied Powers were: Supreme Commander-in-Chief General Douglas MacArthur for the United Nations; Admiral Chester Nimitz for the United States; the Kuomintang General Su Yung-chang for China; Admiral Bruce Fraser for Britain; General K. Derevyanko for the USSR; General Thomas Blamey for

Australia; General Jacques Leclerc for France; Admiral Conrad Helfrich for Holland; Air Force Vice-Marshal Leonard Isitt for New Zealand; Colonel L. Moore-Cosgrave for Canada. After the parties put their signatures on the surrender document, General MacArthur said: 'These proceedings are now concluded.'

Fortune had smiled on *Missouri* five months earlier, on April 11, the day before President Franklin Roosevelt died, when a Kamikaze plane nicked the 'Mighty Mo' causing slight damage. The unknown pilot's remains were scattered over the stern and a fire that broke out was brought under control in less than 15 minutes.

Tagata returned to his family home with two friends, a Korean and a Taiwanese, both corporals, who were from the Junior Flyers' School at Metabaru Air Base. Due to the chaos at the end of the war, the two junior pilots could not return to their own homes and Tagata invited them to live with his family. The young Korean flyer was from what is now North Korea. He stayed at the Tagatas for a year and returned to South Korea where he joined the police force. The pilot from Taiwan spent six months with the Tagata family before returning home where he opened a small business. At that time the Tagatas owned several acres of agricultural land and the two young flyers helped with the farm work. For Tagata, there would be no more flying as the Occupation authorities imposed a ban on all Japanese aviation:

At first I felt like I was being confined in an aviary [says Tagata]. But I had no choice and soon learned how to be a farmer. In fact, I found it wholly satisfying to be a farmer and I even developed a fascination for the daily chores. I saw it as something creative. Like the art of flying, you can't understand how stimulating farming is unless you experience it yourself. Together with my elder brother, we developed organic farming. That is, we avoided the use of toxic fertilizers and pesticides. It was exciting work. We were actually forerunners in the art of organic farming.

Tagata farmed for 15 years, growing rice, wheat, sweet potatoes, potatoes, tomatoes, cucumbers and spinach. He also harvested pears and persimmons. He sold rice and wheat on the market but kept the other produce for the family's consumption.

'Farming is the most honest toil there is,' he says. Perhaps he felt this way because, as he was fond of saying, farming 'was in my blood'. After all, he came from an old farming family.

Takeo Tagata has often thought about the horrible face of war and asked himself whether Kamikaze operations could be justified. 'I believe we had no choice but to resort to these tactics,' he concludes.

> Unfortunately, Japan did not train enough pilots because she did not anticipate waging a major war against the Americans. Yet, in the first phase of the war, our pilots were much better trained. Our pilots and planes were superior to our American or British counterparts. I was convinced that one Japanese fighter pilot could handle five American or British opponents. But as our experienced pilots were decimated, the fortunes of war turned sharply against us. The Special Attack Corps was our only effective fighting method. We would never have wrought such extensive damage to the Allied fleets short of Kamikaze tactics.

However, the veteran pilot admitted that lives were wasted in many cases. 'Green pilots were often not capable of reaching their targets once their guide-plane was shot down,' he said. Often they crashed into the sea.

Regarding his former adversaries, Tagata recalled some of the mutual misunderstandings that had prevailed at the start of the war. For example, he himself shared the common prejudice that, as enemies, Americans were 'soft', 'myopic' and 'barbarous', having obtained his illusions mainly from watching Hollywood films. This view was to prove costly when the two sides clashed in major naval battles in 1942. But it was reciprocated in the West, which had its own stock of myths. Thus, some junior British officers believed that the Japanese were unhygienic and susceptible to disease in a long campaign; that they were afflicted with poor eyesight caused by a poor diet which was also responsible for a prevalence of rickets in Japan. Therefore, it was alleged, their Army would be incapable of making a big dent in Allied defences.[2] With the outbreak of fighting, the unrealistic notion that Japanese soldiers would be a pushover for Anglo-American troops was to haunt the Allies throughout four years of struggle in East Asia and the Pacific.

On a visit to his birthplace in Kyushu in the year 2001, Takeo Tagata was accompanied by the authors of this book. We stopped at Tachiarai, a former air base where a small Memorial Museum for Special Attack pilots was opened a few years ago, and also at Chiran, where we toured the Peace Museum for Kamikaze pilots. We then drove to Kuroki ('Black Tree') where Tagata was born and where his family still maintains a home.

Before stopping for lunch at Kuroki's century-old riverside *Banzai* restaurant we passed by tea plantations as well as well-tended fields of grapes and strawberries for which the town of Kuroki is famous, and we couldn't help but marvel at the town's celebrated wisteria gardens. Tagata recalled his school days and the 40-minute walk he had to negotiate every day up and down steep hills thick with forests. At his comfortable ancestral home, Tagata was greeted by his elder sister, Sachiko (she was past 90 in the first year of the new millennium), who served us green tea and sweets. The house, where Tagata was born, has a black tiled roof and is surrounded by a long whitewashed wall that encloses several pine trees. Below the hill is a stream and, nearby, a reservoir.

Tagata remembered that after he received his 'wings' from nearby Tachiarai Aviation School, he made his first solo flight, and wishing to greet his family, flew at low altitude to Kuroki where his father, mother, sisters, brothers and neighbours all stood and waved to him. Because his house sits on a steep hill, when he banked his plane in order to fly in front of his home he suddenly realized that he was actually flying lower than his front gate.

NOTES

[1] It was the custom for each Kamikaze pilot to compose a farewell *waka* poem, a slightly longer version of the *haiku*, itself a short Japanese poem of three lines. These poems are at the core of Japanese culture. The *waka* and *haiku* have been a major, even a favourite, outlet for the people's emotion. It may be said that the Japanese tend to be more lyrical than philosophical. *Waka* poems had bound the people together from ancient times. In fact, the Emperor held national poetry contests from as early as the Heian Period (AD 794 to the twelfth century). The winners were invited to the court at the opening of each new year. Winners included farmers, fishermen and people in other walks of life. Everybody had their poems read in the Emperor's presence. It is still the custom today. The new year's poetry reading is called *utakai hajime* – the 'beginning of the poetry party'.

[2] Of course, not all British troops were so gullible. A few who had visited Japan found the information they received at military briefings inaccurate; they discovered that the Japanese were perhaps the most hygienic people in the world. Not only were the Japanese fond of their quotidian soak in a bathtub, but they wore face-masks when they had colds. Curiously Russian soldiers and sailors had widely contrasting impressions of the Japanese during the Russo-Japanese War of 1904–5. Once, on the Trans-Siberian Railway en route to the Far East, when talk centred on the Japanese people, a Russian soldier said they were a 'savage race' with primitive habits. But a sailor who had visited Nagasaki cut the soldier short, saying: 'They are a charming, clean people, far more cultivated than you or I.' (From Maurice Baring, *With the Russians in Manchuria*, London, 1905.)

19

VIEWPOINTS

EXPERTS' VIEWS ON THE KAMIKAZE PHENOMENON

From Ronald James Wren, who served with the British fleet in the Pacific War and was also a member of the Arctic convoys:

> When I was 20 years of age, serving in the Pacific, all I could see was idiots [the Kamikaze pilots] killing themselves. I had no other understanding. At 20 years of age when you see somebody tearing out of the sky in an aircraft, mainly to sink a ship, or whatever it is he's attacking, and then in desperation crash the aircraft on the ship, you think that there is going through his mind something which is not going through his mind; then you realize 60 years later that what you thought wasn't passing his mind at all.

The common opinion of numerous American, British and Australian experts is that the chances of hitting a suicide plane diving towards a target at full throttle were not great. From Admiral William F. 'Bull' Halsey:

> The psychology behind it [the Kamikaze attacks] was too alien to us. Americans fight to live, but find it hard to realize that another people will fight to die. We could not believe that the Japanese for all their hara-kiri tradition could muster enough recruits to make such a corps really effective. We were violently disillusioned the

very next day [October 29, 1944] when they missed the carrier *Enterprise* but hit two other carriers, *Franklin* and *Belleau Wood*.

From Captain Dixie Kiefer, commander of the ill-fated carrier *Ticonderoga*: 'It is fairly easy to manoeuvre away from other types of bombing but it is impossible to manoeuvre away from a bomb that is being steered. The Kamikazes scored four to five times the number of hits that normal aircraft could accomplish.'

Lieutenant Commander Tom Blackburn, USN, who shot down 11 Japanese planes: 'The most effective thing against the Kamikazes was that they [finally] ran out of pilots.'

A Swiss comment (from the *Tribune de Genève*) of July 9, 1945:

The systematized fighting method called the Special Attack is extremely costly in men and materials, but in its effect it far surpasses that of ordinary aircraft. On May 24 the Japanese Special Attack Corps carried out a furious attack on American warships and transports near the Okinawan islands. In this attack, Japan lost 111 pilots, but the Americans suffered a total of 11 warships and transports sunk. Personnel losses of the American Navy alone in the Battle of Okinawa reached 9,000 even according to the announcement of the Nimitz headquarters. The American Navy, having suffered extremely huge losses, was obliged to replace the Third Fleet with the Fifth Fleet. To kill the enemy without being killed is common sense in war, but to expect and to choose death often brings about maximum results. The death blow that faces the pilot who plunges himself onto his objective at a speed of 1,000 kilometres an hour is catastrophic. Yet such an enemy is to be respected.

From US Admiral Morton Deyo: 'The Kamikaze planes flew towards our ships like lonely, frightened ducks.'

From Rear Admiral Daniel Barbey, commander of the US Seventh Amphibious Fleet in Philippine waters in January 1945: 'They [the Japanese] had developed a deadly weapon in the suicide plane. As long as their numbers held out, we could expect heavy losses of surface ships as we came closer and closer to Japan.'

From a post-war comment by Admiral Kantaro Suzuki, who was prime minister of Japan in April 1945: 'Considered from the point of view of strategy, the suicide tactics were a product of defeat.'

US Admiral Chester W. Nimitz, in commenting on the first successful operations of Japan's newest weapon of war – the Kamikaze corps – during the US invasion of the Philippines, said the newly organized corps were composed of suicidally inclined pilots. He says many of the suicide pilots were ill-trained and therefore found it hard to penetrate American air defence. But at the same time he thought even novice Japanese aviators might prove highly effective if they flew the more sophisticated 'Zeke' fighters (the US Navy codename for the Zero; a frequently used suicide plane) armed with light bombs and smashed the planes into their targets. The suicide planes were, the Americans admitted, a terrifying means of challenging the US command of the seas.

From Pio Duran, a member of Philippine National Assembly, on November 3, 1944:

> The Special Attack Corps has brought terror to the American naval and air forces in the Leyte sector. . . . In addition, the bayonet charges made by the Japanese Imperial Army on Leyte Island are exacting a heavy toll among the enemy troops. . . . I wish to say that the Special Attack Corps represents the spirit of Asia and deserves the emulation of all East Asian youth. One thing that is most remarkable about the Corps is that it is fighting in defence not of Japanese soil, but of Filipino territory. Such noble sacrifice deserves the gratitude of all Philippine people and should make them ponder deeply on issues that have moved Japan into this titanic struggle. It should be clear to all Filipinos that Japan's motives in this war are unselfish. Sacrificing the flower of her youth she has no other desire than to liberate East Asia from its former masters so that all East Asians may live together in peace and harmony and pursue their natural destinies, unhampered and undeterred by alien rulers, who, despite their profession of humanitarianism, are nothing but selfish exploiters.

From Field Marshal William Slim, Supreme Allied Commander, South-east India: 'Everyone talks about fighting to the last man, but only the Japanese actually do it.'

US Vice Admiral C.R. Brown, who fought in the Pacific: 'True, the Special Attack Force – the Kamikaze – did tremendous damage. It sank a lot of ships and damaged a multitude of others. It killed and wounded thousands of men – inflicted more casualties in the US fleets off Okinawa than the Japanese Army did to the invading troops in the long battle ashore.'

From Ba Maw, wartime prime minister of Burma, in a speech at Hibiya Public Hall in Tokyo, November 18, 1944:

> The final issue in war will always depend upon the strength of the spirit behind the struggle. I say that the Kamikaze spirit, not

weapons, will decide the East Asia War. . . . The materialism of the Anglo-Saxons will not be able to overcome this spirit. I say that the issue will be decided not by planes and tanks, but by the spirit of man, by the spirit of the Kamikaze. In the East it will be decided by the Asiatic will to survive, the Asiatic will to live and conquer. And this struggle, as I read history, is at its roots the struggle of man's spirit against his environment.

In Japan in the new millennium there are those who look back and criticize the existence of the Kamikaze flyers as a waste of lives. There was of course a difference between those who voluntarily gave up their lives (the Kamikaze youth) and those who were commanded to do so (the other combatants). There are continuing arguments about the rights and wrongs of the war, about whether the sacrifices made by thousands of young pilots – who threw away their plans and hopes for the future – were worthy or not. The people at the time of hostilities were convinced that the fate of the nation depended on the outcome of the struggle and therefore they unquestioningly accepted, one and all, the 'Kamikaze spirit'.

From Ian Mutsu, whose grandfather was a prime minister of Japan. (His mother was English and as a youth he had attended school in Birmingham, England):

I feel irritation and anger at the waste of lives by the Army Air Force in a hopeless cause [and] the way the Army had the press and radio (only NHK at the time) get the masses to loudly applaud the so-called *gun shin* – the 'war gods'. This was the same term the Navy used for the pilots of the minisubs designed to attack US warships at Pearl Harbor. All of them failed in their mission. Towards the end of the war there was much reporting in the media of the Kamikaze suicide pilots. Admiration was widespread on the radio and in the press. But it is difficult to say how much of the Japanese people's thinking was heartfelt admiration and how much of it regret for wasted lives in a hopeless cause.

From an inscription by the former US Pacific Fleet Commander-in-Chief Chester W. Nimitz on a war memorial on a lonely Pacific island, Pelelieu, part of the Palau group of islands, where Japanese defenders put up a last-ditch struggle before the island was taken: 'Tourists from every country who visit this island should be told how courageous and patriotic were the Japanese soldiers and airmen who all died defending this island.'

20

STALIN'S KAMIKAZE PILOTS

Three years before Japan officially launched its suicide strategy, including ramming tactics against heavy bombers, the Russians, desperate to thwart Hitler's squadrons from bombing vital targets in Moscow and other cities, drew up written orders for pilots to crash into incoming Luftwaffe planes. The directives amounted, more often than not, to a sentence of death for these Russian pilots. Hundreds of them lost their lives when they crashed their small planes into German bombers. Since descriptive reports of successful rammings often appeared in Moscow newspapers, there can be no doubt that the Japanese Embassy in Moscow sent full details to Tokyo. Sometimes interviews with pilots who survived the rammings were also published in the Moscow press. Even in the United States, a photo essay on one of the Russian rammers was published in *Life* magazine.

Officially, the Russian orders on ramming (in Russian, *taran*) were taken off the books in September 1944. By that time Russian pilots dominated the skies and few Luftwaffe planes ventured outside German skies. But the evidence shows that wartime ramming was still possible and enforceable 15 years *after* the war; when Russian commanding officers could still give orders to initiate a ram attack, a tactic that often killed the pilot attempting it. There is the notorious case of May 1960 when a high-altitude American U-2 spy plane was spotted over Siberia. In a little-known sidelight, a Russian Air Force major was ordered to take off and ram the intruder. Although the pilot became airborne, he never made contact with the American U-2 which, he says, probably saved his life. Hit by a missile, the US plane crashed, its pilot, Francis Gary Powers, parachuting to safely. The order to ram the intruder was not made public until three decades after the event.

The first rammings took place during the very first hours of the invasion when Russian pilots stopped a number of incoming German planes by crashing into their wings or fuselage, sending them cork-screwing out of the sky. Each ram attack involved exceptional courage and great skill. In his popular wartime novel, *The Living and the Dead*, the author Konstantin Simonov has a character say, after hearing that a Luftwaffe plane was rammed over Moscow: 'Fancy smashing into another plane like that!' In reply, someone says the Luftwaffe have become less bold than previously; that the rammings had scared the German pilots.

There was some truth in this. On the opening day of invasion, six Russian pilots, having spent their ammunition, rammed Nazi planes, causing them to crash in flames. Hermann Goering's pilots who learned about the rammings could be excused if these reports raised an involuntary shiver.

A terse radio broadcast from Moscow announced the first ramming: 'At 05.15 hours on June 22, 1941, about 200 miles inside Russian territory, Flight Leader Junior Lieutenant Leonid Butelin rammed a German Junkers-88 bomber, severing its tail with the propeller of his fighter. This is the first ramming of the war.'

Rammings were supposed to be an expedient of last resort for Russian pilots. The Luftwaffe was all-powerful in the first weeks and months of the invasion and Russian air power was no match for it. German planes were generally superior and their pilots had the advantage of previous combat experience. But there was no shortage of Russian dar-ing. In the meantime, Russian pilots absorbed the tactics of ramming and some of them not only survived but went up and rammed again.

Russian wartime directives actually spelled out when pilots had to ram enemy planes. For example, a Combat Directive issued to the pilots of the 6th Air Corps during the defence of Moscow said: 'If machine guns jam in the air, if cartridges are spent prematurely, if the enemy is out to destroy an important state object, go and destroy the enemy by ramming.'

Here is how the Chief Marshal of the Soviet Air Force, A.A. Novikov, regarded the act of ramming: 'Any technique of air combat demands valour, courage and skill by the pilot. But a ram attack makes incalculably greater demands on a pilot. Ramming means, first of all, a readiness for self-sacrifice; it is a test of loyalty to the people, to the ideals of the Motherland.' Novikov went on to call ramming 'one of the highest forms of displaying a high morale that is inherent in the nation'. But he also spoke of the importance of ramming in the purely tactical sense. Looking back after the war, he said: 'The enemy pilots' fear of ramming gave our pilots advantages such as manoeuvring possibilities, and helped boost their growing superiority in air combat tactics.'

According to this directive, pilots were *not* being sent on suicide missions: 'To ram the enemy is an act of the greatest heroism and bravery but is not an act of self-sacrifice.' The directive added the injunction: 'You should know how to ram.' There followed four pages on the techniques of ramming. Pilots who had rammed enemy aircraft early in the war and survived taught others this 'act of total aggression' in the sky. The official reports said that ramming fatalities to Russian pilots were mainly the result of head-on collisions. Pilots survived, said the reports, if they were able to bale out or if they managed to land their damaged planes. Not mentioned was the detail that if and when both planes became uncontrollable after a ramming, their pilots were usually doomed.

The air ace Alexander Pokryshkin, who shot down 59 Nazi planes, and became an air marshal after the war, gave this opinion of the wartime directives that imposed ramming as a duty: 'Everything is correct; it was just like that. A strike by ramming is the weapon of fliers with iron nerves. In the defence of Moscow this method was rightly necessary.' Pokryshkin added:

> At short distances, behind the tail of an enemy bomber, our fighter was invulnerable. He got into the 'dead cone' of enemy fire, inched closer and cut off a section of tail, or a wing. One Nazi flier who bailed out after his bomber was rammed, said when interrogated: 'Rumours went around about rammings on the Eastern Front. But at first we did not believe in them. What a terrible thing it is!'

Apparently, ramming predates the Second World War. It is claimed that during the First World War a Russian pilot, Pyotr Nikolayevich Nesterov, was the first man in history to ram an enemy aircraft. This happened on September 8, 1914 during a dogfight with a German two-seater reconnaissance plane. But Nesterov was killed in the attack. According to Air Force Colonel Vladimir Amelchenko, a military writer, the ramming by Nesterov served during the Great Patriotic War as 'a symbol of selflessness, courage and valour' for Russian pilots.

There is this story of a 'Russian Rambo' that was confirmed by British pilots. Flying in northern skies, a Russian pilot had got into a dogfight with two German aircraft. He shot down one of them but, running out of ammunition, he rammed the second plane, sending it crashing to the ground. By chance his parachute landed near the downed two-seater German plane that he had engaged minutes earlier. Now the three air crew faced each other across frozen wastes on a part of the earth so desolate that you could walk for days without seeing another human being. Quickly the Russian dispatched one of his opponents with his revolver. But a boxer dog that the German crew had, for some reason, brought with them, leaped at him and he was forced to shoot the dog. Then, grappling with the other pilot, the Russia's face was slashed with a knife from forehead to chin and some of his teeth were knocked out. The contest ended when he fired a flare at the enemy's head from his Very pistol at point-blank range. The survivor then walked four days and nights in the snow with frost-bitten feet and with his face hanging open until he reached a hospital. A couple of British military men who knew the pilot visited him in a hospital and were able to check up on details of the story. In its toughness and determination, it represented in British eyes 'something near the heroic'.[1]

Moscow, as expected, became the main target for enemy air attack. Hitler's intention to level Moscow required hundreds of bombing planes. For this purpose the Luftwaffe formed a special group of 1,600 aircraft made up of the best squadrons. The leaders of this air fleet, which provided support for the Wehrmacht's Army Group Centre, chose bombers of the newest types, including the Heinkel-111 with high altitude engines, the Junkers-88, and the Dornier-215. Pilots in these raids were picked from famous squadrons, including the 'Condor', which had bombed Spanish cities including the Basque town of Guernica during the civil war, and others that had menaced the skies over London, Liverpool and Birmingham, or operated over Poland, Yugoslavia and Greece.

Moscow is an old city and its main thoroughfares are arranged in concentric circles – easily identifiable to unfriendly aircraft. To counter this, architects and artists altered Moscow's appearance. Roofs of houses were painted so they looked like a 'continuation' of streets; many squares 'disappeared'. Rivers on starry or moonlit nights can be easily recognized from the air. To alter the landscape, when darkness set in, barges with camouflage nets were moored at specific points on the Moscow River. 'New bridges' appeared and old bridges 'disappeared' under smokescreens and other means of subterfuge.[2]

In the first month of war the Luftwaffe made nearly 100 attempts to penetrate the skies over Moscow, clandestinely, one at a time, at a height of 8,000 metres (24,000 feet). Only a few planes got through. Between July and December 1941 there were approximately 120 raids against Moscow comprising over 7,000 Luftwaffe planes. Of this number only about 200 German aircraft succeeded in getting close to the capital. The rest were shot down or chose less forbidding targets. In the July–August period nine enemy bombers were lost due to ramming. Moscow's air defence proved to be of a high order.

On July 2, something unexpected happened. A Heinkel-111, equipped with a high-altitude engine, flew towards Moscow on an intelligence-gathering mission. On board was a colonel from the German General Staff who carried with him important documents including operational maps and codes. His aircraft was met by a Yak-1 piloted by Lieutenant Sergei Goshko. The Yak-1 was a wooden-winged plane with a top speed of over 450 kilometres per hour (279 miles per hour) which could outmanoeuvre some of the Luftwaffe's faster planes. Suddenly, after an indecisive aerial battle, the Russian pilot struck off the tail of the Heinkel with the wing of his fighter, sending the intruder spinning to earth. For his exploit, Goshko was decorated with the highest combat medal, the gold hero's medal. Goshko brought down six more German aircraft by conventional means, making his last flight over a defeated Berlin on May 8, 1945.

To safeguard Moscow as well as other cities, Russian pilots rammed Luftwaffe planes on at least 300 occasions during the war. Many of these rammings took place on the approaches to the capital.

On the night of July 22, 1941 Hitler launched his first massive air strike against Moscow, 220 bombers taking part. Marshal Zhukov says that only a small percentage of the enemy bombers reached the capital, most of the others being stopped by the Moscow Anti-Aircraft Defence System. About two dozen bombers were shot down outside the capital. This became the first of a series of aerial battles for command of Moscow's skies.

Erskine Caldwell, the American author of *Tobacco Road*, was in Moscow during the first month of the war and witnessed a series of air raids. This is how he described the night of July 23/24, 1941: 'I am unable to compare Moscow's air defence with that of London and Berlin; but judging from reports, if the Moscow defence is not superior it certainly must be every bit as effective in beating back air attacks as any air defence anywhere.' After watching repeated air raids, Caldwell said that in five nights of raiding Moscow the intruders 'have accomplished little more than the entire Swiss Navy accomplished in the First World War'.

At the beginning of August 1941 Russians crowded around a German aircraft that had been destroyed not far from the capital. Near the charred metal was a wooden signboard with the words: 'Tail of a Nazi bomber downed by Senior Lieutenant Yevgeni Yeremeyev'. The pilot, who worked at a research institute of the Air Force, was a pioneer in night flying. On the night of the first enemy raid on Moscow, Yeremeyev had shot down a German bomber with machine-gun fire.

'When I saw a report about night-time dogfights at the end of July 1941, I did not believe it,' says General Yevgeni Klimov, then commander of the 6th Air Corps. 'I called up Yeremeyev and he told me how it happened, and I recommended this hero of ramming to be decorated with the highest award.' The general adds: 'We were soon holding discussions in all units about Yeremeyev's exploits at night.' But the hero-pilot had only two more months to live. His life ended over Moscow when he was shot down by a Messerschmitt. However, among those who attended the discussions was Victor Talalikhin, a 23-year-old pilot, who was described by friends as 'short, unassuming with clever brown eyes'.

The Talalikhin saga began at 22 hours 55 minutes on the moonlit night of August 6, 1941 when enemy planes were trying to break through Moscow's air defences.

On that night his regiment was gathered at the edge of a forest revetment where fighter planes were concealed. Everyone was absorbed in his own thoughts. Mechanics were getting the planes ready for night flying. The war was only two months old and night fighters were few at that time; the regiment was just learning the rudiments of combat flying at night. To complicate matters, the regiment was short of experts to train pilots for night duty. After a briefing from the regimental commander, the pilots were ready to take off. Suddenly the quiet was disturbed by the dull crackling of anti-aircraft guns that covered the approaches to Moscow. Shells flashed in the sky high above the outskirts of the city. They burst sporadically, sowing splinters over wide areas. Searchlight beams probed the skies, intersecting in twos and threes and parting to pick out intruding planes and harass them across the sky.

The pilots leaped into their cockpits and began taking off into the darkness with orders to intercept the enemy. Talalikhin was airborne within three minutes.

Flying at 4,500 metres (14,000 feet) the young pilot saw the moonlight reflected on the fuselage of a hostile aircraft heading towards Moscow. Without further ado he pushed the throttle wide open to overtake the plane. The distance between them rapidly dwindled and Talalikhin banked sharply to approach from the rear. Then he saw a swastika on the tail of the aircraft and he recognized it as a twin-engine Heinkel-111 bomber. 'You will not escape me,' he thought. He held his breath until the Heinkel was centred in his sights and then pressed the firing button. The burst of machine-gun fire entered the starboard engine which immediately caught fire. The Heinkel did not answer and tried to escape. Its pilot increased speed, turned and dived to put out the flames. Talalikhin banked to starboard and fired another burst. But the Heinkel zigzagged, sharply changed course and began losing altitude. Evidently the pilot hoped to evade Talalikhin's fighter at low altitude, a manoeuvre with which the Russian was familiar. He followed the Luftwaffe plane, closing in on its tail. Falling to 2,500 metres (8,000 feet), he pressed the button again. After another turn he closed to within 15 metres (50 feet), intending to fire a point-blank burst.

Sensing the end, the German plane opened desperate return fire. As the enemy pilot was experienced, the pursuit went on, the pilot deftly manoeuvring towards hoped-for safety in the darkness. But Talalikhin doggedly followed. After a long burst his machine guns went dead – he was out of ammunition. His silence possibly gave hope to the crew of the fleeing plane. But Talalikhin was becoming agitated as he realized the enemy might escape. 'No, you shall not!' he said to himself. He was almost sitting on the enemy's tail. 'Now is the time!' he thought. 'He must not get away!' His decision was made: 'Ram him!'

Talalikhin's movements became more confident as he closed on the Heinkel's tail. The enemy gunner suddenly opened fire from a machine gun and bullets whistled on Viktor's right, some of them searing his arm. In response to the pain, Talalikhin pushed the throttle further open. His plane jerked up. There was a crash. The Heinkel burst into flames and plunged towards the ground. Talalikhin's plane also became uncontrollable. Releasing himself from the cockpit, he rolled overboard, dropping like a stone. He had to worry now about drifting out of the way of the falling planes. After a free fall of 1,000 metres (3,200 feet), he pulled the ring of his parachute. It paid out of the pack but he soon noticed that he was being carried towards a dense forest. Pulling at the lines he changed direction and landed in a shallow lake. Farmers who had gathered on the ground helped the pilot and took him back to his regiment.

The first night ramming attack by Talalikhin won him the highest government award, the gold hero medal. Meanwhile, his attack was written up in all the major newspapers. During the first four months of the war Talalikhin accounted for 27 German planes. But Talalikhin's luck ended on October 27, 1941 when he perished with his aircraft in a duel with three Messerschmitts.

As the front line moved closer to the capital enemy aircraft became more active and during October over 2,000 sorties were made; few bombers, however, got through to the city centre or the Kremlin. But General S.M. Shtemenko, at that time a member of the General Staff, remembers that on the night of October 28 a high-explosive bomb landed in the yard of the General Staff building. ('The building was shaken as if by an earthquake.') Several vehicles were destroyed; three drivers were killed and fifteen officers wounded, some of them seriously. A.M. Vasilevsky, one of the highest ranking officers in the Army, was injured by flying glass, although he was able to go on working.

Some of the aerial battles staggered belief. The 606th Air Regiment had wooden and canvas biplanes that were no match for metal aircraft. On October 7, 1941 Lieutenant Ivan Denisov, flying one of these biplanes, an R-5, crashed head-on with a Henschel-129. The twisted metal of the Henschel fell to earth. The biplane broke up, too, but the pilot parachuted to safety.

The last ram attack in defence of Moscow occurred on June 2, 1943. A Junkers-88 was flying at a height of 8,000 metres (26,000 feet). From a nearby airfield a MiG-3 piloted by Lieutenant Gennady Sirishikov went up to meet it. During the first attack the Russian fired two bursts which brought no results. The archive report says the pilot 'refused to leave the field of battle without winning'. He closed on the invader and, with his propeller, sawed off the tail of the hapless Junkers.

Some bizarre rammings took place in Arctic skies. Pilot Alexei Khlobystov rammed three German planes in the far north and survived. His exploits began in 1942 when the Arctic spring had set in. Heading for the northern port of Murmansk were 28 Luftwaffe planes. Khlobystov, a veteran pilot, took off with his squadron and saw one Messerschmitt crash. He now manoeuvred to help his less experienced colleagues. Suddenly he saw below him a two-seater Messerschmitt 110. He swooped down and closed in. Flying over the edge of a forest, he saw a hill loom up ahead and he decided to ram the enemy plane with his wing. The impact was strong and his own plane bounced around but the intruder plane crashed. However, something wasn't right with Khlobystov's plane as it climbed jerkily. When he turned his head he saw that his starboard wing was a foot shorter than the port one. Control of his plane was causing a problem although he could still fly.

Suddenly he saw two enemy planes heading right for him. But now his fuel was running low so Khlobystov decided to ram a second time, thinking he'd be very lucky if he came out alive. As soon as one opponent veered aside, he struck at the other's tail, using his shorter, damaged wing. Again his fighter bounced dizzily and he temporarily lost control. The foe had crashed. To Khlobystov's amazement his own plane was still navigable and he was able to land despite the partially sawn-off wing.

A short time later Khlobystov rammed a third enemy plane. But this time his opponent succeeded in hitting the engine of Khlobystov's fighter and he himself received two wounds. Thinking it was impossible to return to the airfield, he put on speed and rammed a Messerschmitt 109, which was sliced in half by the impact. Khlobystov's fighter was also smashed but he parachuted to safely. In his hospital bed he was decorated for bravery and exceptional flying skill.

DID JAPAN COPY THE RUSSIANS?

Up until the dropping of nuclear weapons, nothing was more punishing to the Japanese mainland than the blows delivered by the American Flying Fortresses, the four-engined heavy bombers, called B-29s. How to cope with this increasing menace from the air was constantly on the minds of the Imperial High Command. Actually, all Army flying corps pilots were routinely receiving instructions on how to ram incoming bombers.

The ramming of the Flying Fortresses quite naturally made American pilots uneasy. On November 25, 1944 an American pilot, the commander of the 21st Bomber Command, Heywood Hansen, saw one of his own planes demolished in front of his eyes. Hansen said that when his unit reached the skies over the sea area near Japan one enemy plane was seen pursuing a B-29 from the rear.

> The gunners on our plane at once opened fire and others of our unit followed so that the intruder was subjected to a cross-fire. But suddenly the gunners of the B-29 stopped firing as the Japanese fighter rammed the tail of the B-29 which was smashed to pieces. The next moment the B-29 started its fatal plunge.

Hansen's report ended: 'The Tokyo raid was not satisfactory to us. We see difficulties ahead.'

The Flying Fortresses first appeared over the main Japanese islands flying from Saipan on November 1, 1944. They rained bombs on the western and southern sections of the island of Kyushu. The bombers usually flew at an altitude over 10,000 metres so that the Japanese fighters were incapable of intercepting them. It was humiliating for them not to be able to deter the US bombers while the residents of Tokyo watched. But there was only one way for the interceptors to engage the B-29s flying at such a high altitude: If all cannons and protective armour were removed from the fighter to lighten its weight, it could crash into the enemy. Consequently, officials formally decided to adopt suicide tactics against the heavy bombers.

NOTES

[1] A reliable British account of the 'Russian Rambo' may be found in Hubert Griffith's *This is Russia*, published in London in 1943.

[2] Reports say that German skill managed to create at least five dummy Berlins around the German capital to confuse British pilots at the beginning of the air war. There were also a few fake Hamburgs built as well as duplicates of some chemical works.

21

. . . AND HITLER'S

In March 1945 Luftwaffe pilots were asked to volunteer for virtual suicide missions, entering the *Sondercommando* (or Special Forces) units to be used against American and British bombers that were delivering punishing blows to German cities. Eventually 300 pilots enrolled in these units. But the German 'Kamikaze pilots', who received their instruction in aircraft-ramming techniques over a ten-day period at a Luftwaffe air base near Magdeburg, had little effect against the massive Allied bomber raids against Hitler's Reich.

The name of German test pilot Hanna Reitsch is closely associated with this eleventh-hour strategy to convert a group of ordinary pilots into a Kamikaze-style operation. Reitsch, who had the ear of Adolf Hitler, records in a memoir that in a meeting with Hitler in early 1945 she mentioned the Kamikaze plan to him and that Hitler appeared to be perplexed, neither approving nor disapproving. But there are other reports – easily dismissable – which say Hitler opposed Reitsch's idea on 'humanitarian grounds'. In any case, Hitler's reaction must have been muted because the plan was put into practice and is mentioned several times in Dr Joseph Goebbels's diary.

The German suicide pilots went into action on April 7, at approximately the same time that Japanese crash-dive planes in the Okinawan area damaged a US battleship, an aircraft carrier and two destroyers, causing heavy casualties on the carrier. It is unclear how many German pilots were killed on that date but reports said that almost 170 Luftwaffe fighters were shot down by the US Air Force.

While it is unlikely that the Germans simply copied Kamikaze ramming tactics, it is undeniable that the widespread use of such tactics against ships and planes by Japanese pilots was closely watched by Nazi military aviation authorities in Tokyo and Berlin.

Reitsch, the first woman awarded the Iron Cross (First Class) for bravery, was a German hero of the skies as well as an ardent patriot. During the war she tested every type of plane that Hitler's regime produced, including the rocket-powered Me262 and a prototype of the V1 'flying bomb' that was launched against London and other cities from sites in France. She set many aviation records during her career, became a world-famous glider pilot, and survived several air crashes. During the 1930s she risked her life testing a small aircraft which landed on a 'bed of ropes' – actually wires strung together aboard a ship, making a unique but highly risky sea-going landing pad. Known as Germany's 'flying missionary' and unquestionably the leading German woman pilot of the twentieth century, Hanna Reitsch sought to get as many men (and women) as possible interested in aviation. Her popularity helped as she was the first German woman to win a captain's licence and the first person to fly a glider over the Alps. But her last claim to fame as a war pilot occurred close to the end of hostilities when she became a driving force behind the setting up of a German suicide unit within the Luftwaffe as a means of hindering and possibly restraining massive Anglo-American bombing raids on Germany. But the unit was too late and too small to be effective.

The first official conference to study and plan a German 'Kamikaze project' was held in November 1943 at the Air Ministry's guesthouse near Wannsee Lake in Berlin, attended by military and aviation specialists. Hitler's Vice Air Admiral officiated at the meeting. Those in attendance included Reitsch and the designer of the V1 missile, which was being readied for mass production and called the Fi103 missile.

At the meeting the Me328B jet fighter, which was under development, was chosen as the first candidate and Fi103 as the second candidate for suicide attack craft. Prior to the conference, Reitsch made known her idea of a 'self-sacrificial attack' among Luftwaffe pilots, and in response hundreds of pilots volunteered to fly such missions. Finally, 70 pilots were selected to fly the missions while the rest were kept in service.

However, the Me328B plane was dropped because of technical difficulties. Consequently the V1 was converted into a piloted missile. The first prototype, Fi103A-1R, was completed towards the end of August 1944. V1, launched from a pad, developed 17G force at its take-off. Hence, the piloted V1 was to be carried by the Heinkel-111 bomber and to be released in the air. The craft was tested in September. Reitsch herself flew the craft ten times. In the meantime, the SS selected the first batch of 30 suicide pilots. One hundred and fifty manned V1s were produced while the 200th Luftkrieg Air Wing, a special unit of piloted V1s, was formed. Through Albert Speer, Hitler's armaments minister, Hitler is said to have learned about the existence of the unit. There are some published photographs of the manned V1, one of them showing American GIs inspecting a V1 with a cockpit.

In the first half of 1945, the Luftwaffe formed an 'Elbe Special Commando' air unit, specializing in suicide crash attacks against Allied bombers. On April 7, 183 fighters, the bulk of them Me109G jet fighters, challenged some 1,300 American bombers, accompanied by about 850 fighters. They were headed for Desau along the Elbe River. The German suicide unit engaged the Allied formations at 11.45 a.m. over Steinhude, near Hannover and the aerial duel lasted 45 minutes. Only 15 'Elbe Special Commando' planes survived. Only a few smashed into the enemy bombers but most were shot down. The suicide unit was moved to a base near Passau in southern Germany but all planes were later destroyed by the Allied bombings.

Goebbels, who was Hitler's Propaganda Minister, makes several diary entries about the suicide pilots. On April 4, 1945 he mentions the attempted use of 'suicide fighters' but suggests that inclement weather apparently worked against a favourable outcome. Four days later Goebbels wrote: 'Yesterday . . . our fighters conducted crash attacks on enemy bombers. Results are yet to be confirmed but it seems that the attack did not meet our expectation. However . . . we should not give up.' Goebbels it seems was adopting a wait-and-see attitude regarding the idea of suicide units. In his diary entry he notes with dismay the lack of success of Germany's suicide volunteers in their contact with American heavy bombers and fighters and explains the failure, saying that the US planes did not fly in a tight formation, making the German pilots engage the enemy individually. Moreover, the resulting heavy counter-fire was so devastating to the German attackers that only in a few cases were they able to ram the US bombers.

Reitsch, incidentally, was one of the last people to see Hitler alive in his underground Berlin bunker when, in April 1945, she piloted the last light aircraft into the beleaguered city and reported to the Nazi leader whose moods of lucidity in the final days were interspersed with half-crazed ramblings. Hitler in the presence of Reitsch was heard denouncing the treachery of Hermann Goering, the Luftwaffe Commander-in-Chief. This concerned a message received from Goering about taking over the Reich leadership from Hitler. Reitsch recorded Hitler's remarks when she was interrogated by the US Army, on October 8, 1945. According to her testimony Hitler said at the time: 'Now nothing remains. Nothing is spared to me. No allegiances are kept, no honour lived up to, no disappointments that I have not had, no betrayals that I have not experienced – and now this above all else. Nothing remains. Every wrong has already been done me.'

That same night Hitler summoned Hanna Reitsch and handed her a vial of poison. According to her interrogation, Hitler said: 'Hanna, you belong to those who will die with me. Each of us has a vial of poison such as this. I do not wish that one of us falls into the hands of the Russians alive, nor do I wish our bodies to be found by them.' (Earlier Hitler had told his top generals and Albert Speer, his Armaments Minister, that he intended to shoot himself in his bunker to avoid falling into enemy hands.)

At another Hitler–Reitsch encounter, Hitler said reassuringly, if her report is to be believed: 'But, my Hanna, I still have hope.' Hitler's hope rested with the future success of his forces to the south and east of Berlin. Reitsch describes Hitler waving a road map that was fast coming to pieces from the sweat of his hands. Meanwhile, on the field of battle Hitler's forces were denied any success by swiftly advancing Allied armies.

A few days later Hitler ordered Reitsch to fly out of Berlin immediately with a top air force officer, Colonel-General Ritter von Greim (who was to replace Goering as the new head of the Luftwaffe) and arrest Heinrich Himmler whom he accused of treachery. In addition, Reitsch carried Hitler's orders to organize new bombing raids against the Allies. In what was to be the last flight out of Berlin, Reitsch and Greim left the city, which was being heavily shelled by the Russians, shortly after midnight on April 29, 1945. Within minutes their plane was hit by Russian flak, causing severe injury to Greim, but Reitsch was able to land safely, behind American lines. Himmler, arrested by the British Army, committed suicide on May 23, 1945. Hitler ended his life with a cyanide capsule three weeks earlier.

Hanna Reitsch was captured soon after by the US Army and incarcerated for 15 months. While being held, she gave the aforementioned account of Hitler's disintegration in his last days in his bunker. In later writings Reitsch sought to explain her activities as a loyal member of the Nazi regime. She has described in a memoir what she calls 'my offence': 'I was a German, well known as an aviator and as one who cherished an ardent love of her country and had done her duty to the last. Legends formed about my last flight into Berlin. Might I not perhaps have hidden Hitler away somewhere?'

Prison for this free spirit of aviation (her autobiography is entitled *The Sky My Kingdom*) was doubtless a bitter cup. She writes that she learned the 'degradation of captivity' as she lived through monotonous days behind walls, gazing at a patch of sky through a tiny barred window.

During her lifetime Reitsch set more than 40 endurance and high altitude records. She was accepted as a member of the American Test Pilots' Association after the war and was received by President John Kennedy in the White House. She died in Frankfort in 1979, aged 67.

22

BRITISH 'KAMIKAZES' . . . AND AMERICAN

BRITISH

All those who sailed in the Arctic regions risked finding an unmarked grave in the frigid waters. In the skies Nazi planes hovered like eagles searching for their prey; and beneath the waters lurked the deadly U-boats. Each Anglo-American convoy that entered the Arctic Ocean taking supplies to the beleaguered Russians had one special ship called a CAM which could launch a single Sea Hurricane fighter against marauding Luftwaffe bombers. CAM stands for Catapult Armed Merchant ships.

The Sea Hurricanes, flown by Royal Air Force pilots, were launched by rockets. Since the merchant ships had no flightdeck, a pilot's only chance of survival was to ditch in the icy sea and then hope for quick rescue by convoy escort ships. Consequently, the RAF pilots in the Arctic convoys accepted bravely the fact that their mission was almost as deadly as the Pacific crash-dive tactics of Japanese Kamikaze pilots. If still alive after engaging the enemy, it was impossible for the RAF pilot, flying the Hurricane, to return to the mother CAM ship. For these reasons, says Commander Ed Grenfell, Royal Navy (Rtd), 'it would have been more appropriate to call them KAM ships, that is, Kamikaze Armed Merchant ships'.

But there was a major difference between the Japanese Kamikazes and the CAM pilots: there was nothing suicidal about the CAM pilots; their senses were tuned to achieving a certain objective and they were very much aware of what they were doing. Moreover, they were not governed by emotion but by cold logic.

The CAM ships were first used in the Atlantic to counter the threat of the German long-range FW200 Condor reconnaissance bombers, and each carried a single Sea Hurricane fighter which could be shot off by rockets from a catapult on the bow. Most of the pilots were British, although there were also some Canadians and South Africans. Then in March 1942, the Germans, seeing the importance to the Allies of the Arctic route to Russia, concentrated a large air fleet in northern Norway, thus putting the Arctic convoys with their valuable cargoes at great risk. At this point, it was decided to sail CAM ships with some of the convoys to engage either German shadowers or attacking bombers. (But some Allies convoys continued to suffer. One, called PQ17, lost 24 of its 35 merchant ships to Nazi air and naval power.)

Grenfell remembers the fateful day in May 1942 when German torpedo-bombers were detected by the long-range warning radar on the 12,000 ton CAM ship *Empire Lawrence*, part of convoy PQ16, and it was decided to shoot off the Sea Hurricane. Grenfell was then in charge of the RDF (radio direction finder, or radar) crew and equipment on *Empire Lawrence*. There was almost a stand-up fight between the two RAF pilots, Bruce McPherson, a Canadian, and Ian Hay, a South African, for the honour of facing the Luftwaffe. Ian Hay won this war of words. Says Grenfell, '*Empire Lawrence*, soon to be blown to pieces close to the Arctic ice pack, slightly altered course into the wind and, like a roaring dragon spitting an orange flame, the Sea Hurricane was propelled along the catapult by the fourteen rockets attached to the cradle. Dipping a little as it left the ship and nearly hitting the surface of the sea, it raced off in the direction of the German intruder.'

Pilot Officer Hay quickly dived on the German planes and sent one crashing down in flames, but had just come back at them, damaging a second enemy plane to the extent that it limped back home trailing flames and smoke, when he was hit himself. He broke off the fight and flew towards the convoy, intending to parachute in a convenient position for a speedy rescue from a very cold sea. The sky was pockmarked from anti-aircraft bursts and slashed by tracer bullets when one of the merchant ships, mistaking him for an enemy plane, fired its guns and hit Hay a second time. Badly wounded, he came down in the sea near the British destroyer, HMS *Volunteer*, and was quickly rescued before he succumbed to the cold. He was later decorated for bravery but would be killed in action in the Normandy invasion in June 1944.

Meanwhile, the tremendous anti-aircraft barrage from the ships of the convoy had also sent two German Junkers-88 dive-bombers crashing into the sea. The ships had achieved a result similar to Pilot Officer Hay's without risking the loss of a fighter plane and, needless to say, the life of a Royal Air Force pilot. But the Sea Hurricane was gone. 'I thought about the futility of it all,' says Grenfell. 'What had Ian Hay achieved? His success was but a pinprick to the Germans. One thing was certain: the next attacks would concentrate on finding and destroying the CAM ship.' This they did with a vengeance. It seems that, in those early days, the Germans were not sure that a CAM ship carried only one aircraft.

On May 27, 1942 *Empire Lawrence*, loaded with ammunition, planes and tanks destined for Russia, exploded when hit by five bombs from Junkers-88 bombers 280 miles east of Bear Island. Grenfell and Neil Hulse, the only deck officer to survive, were thrown into the icy sea by the blast but were fortunately rescued by the British corvette, HMS *Hyderabad*. *Empire Lawrence* had disappeared in a matter of seconds.

In summing up, Grenfell was as critical of the CAM ships as some Japanese are about the use of Kamikaze pilots. He says:

> In my opinion CAM ships had a pointless task. Whoever thought of the idea, sitting back in a comfortable leather chair somewhere in London, no doubt spent so much time tickled pink with his brainless idea that he had little time to think of the brave men who suffered from it. It was the mad sort of thing thought up by chair-bound generals on the Western Front during the First World War, whose stupid ideas sent tens of thousands of men to their deaths in just one day. Catapult-Armed Ships carried only one aircraft, and there was no way it could land back on the ship for further use. On the Kola run to Russia, there were certainly no friendly land bases in the vicinity where the aircraft could land, and even if the pilot shot down a shadowing German plane, his action was an unacceptable risk. The German base in nearby Norway would have a replacement on the spot within a short period of time. If catapulted off to deal with a massive attack from German bombers, one aircraft was next to useless.

On the other hand, there is the equally strong argument that the Germans feared the Sea Hurricane because of its excellence as a fighter and because they didn't always know where it came from. Moreover, the Allied authorities had put a great deal of thought into creating the CAM ships. No doubt they were thinking it was the best thing they could provide for the convoys at that time and place.

Grenfell goes on to say that one or two of the massed enemy aircraft might be destroyed in a dogfight but that the Sea Hurricane would probably be shot down or forced to ditch through lack of fuel. In any case, whether shot down or crash-landed on the sea, the CAM pilots had very little chance of survival in the ice-cold Arctic. On the CAM ships, Grenfell gets support from Dr John Bullen, a British military historian, who says:

> The Hurricane pilots on board the CAM ships in the Arctic waters were almost on suicide missions. But if their chances of survival were slim they were never non-existent. The pilots were very brave men and true volunteers, never being coerced as was the case with many of Japan's Kamikaze pilots in the Pacific, especially in the final months of the war.

Grenfell said that about 35 CAM ships were used in the war and that 17 were lost at sea. All of the planes carried by these ships were lost, as were many of the pilots. In the opinion of many Arctic veterans, little value was gained by catapulting aircraft from CAM ships in the Arctic, and that deploying them was a 'dreadful waste of men and material'.

. . . AND AMERICAN

A group of Japanese ex-Imperial Navy officers have come up with an interesting hypothesis. The first Kamikaze operation (they say) was staged not in the Pacific Ocean but in the Mediterranean Sea; and not in the twentieth century but the nineteenth.

Specifically, the officers say, the operation took place during US naval warfare against the Barbary coast pirates in the Mediterranean on September 4, 1804; and the Kamikazes were American sailors. The place where the action occurred was Tripoli harbour, North Africa.[1]

The roots of the conflict were first observed in 1711 when a soldier of the old Turkish footguards established a dynasty, under which Tripolitania (together with the rest of Libya) became virtually autonomous. As one of the Barbary States, it made a practice of piratical attacks against the shipping of several maritime countries and the levying of tribute against these countries. This resulted in a war with the United States between 1801 and 1805.

The conflict between America and Tripoli (now part of Libya) arose after a sudden American refusal to continue payment of tribute to the piratical rulers of the North African Barbary States of Algiers, Tunis, Morocco, and Tripoli. The practice of paying sums for tribute had long been the custom among European nations, and the young American state went along with the practice in exchange for immunity from attack on its merchant vessels in the Mediterranean. But then a demand from the pasha of Tripoli for higher tribute and his improbable 'declaration of war' on the United States in 1801 coincided with a decision by President Thomas Jefferson's administration to show American resolve. Jefferson soon dispatched a US naval squadron to Tripolitanian waters. During the following years, American warships fought in the waters around Tripoli, and in 1803, when Commodore Edward Preble became commander of the Mediterranean squadron, greater successes ensued. The intrepid Preble sailed into Tangier to rescue a number of American prisoners and, in February 1804, he ordered his 25-year-old lieutenant, Stephen Decatur, to undertake a spectacular raid in the harbour of Tripoli.

Edward Preble commanded a squadron during the Tripolitanian War (1761–1807). Stephen Decatur later held important commands during the war of 1812. (Replying to a toast after returning from successful engagements abroad, in 1815, he replied with the famous remark: 'Our country! In her intercourse with foreign nations may she always be in the right; but our country, right or wrong.')

In 1804 Decatur led an expedition into the harbour of Tripoli, in North Africa, to burn the US frigate *Philadelphia*, which had grounded and fallen into Tripolitanian hands. During a night in February 1804 he sailed on a disguised warship into Tripoli harbour and alongside the frigate. His men swarmed aboard, drove the surprised pirate crew overboard, set fire to the ship, and were off in less than 30 minutes. This exploit earned him his captain's commission and a sword of honour from the US Congress.

The so-called American Kamikaze operation came at the end of September 1804. The facts are contained in a document entitled, *A History of the War Between the United States and Tripoli and other Barbary Powers*:

On the 4th of September [1804], a boat in Tripoli harbour was filled with 100 barrels of powder . . . and 300 shells, the command of which was given to [American] Lieut. Somers, accompanied by Lieuts Wadsworth and Israel, and about 10 men. His orders were to get in as near the town and batteries as possible, and then set fire to the train. He had with him a small boat, to make his escape from Tripoli harbour, on board the *Syren*, Capt. Stewart commanding, which was waiting for him. He obeyed his orders, and when all was ready, he set fire to the train.

But by accident, as was supposed, the train communicated to some dry powder. Accordingly, they had hardly got well in, when two gunboats full of men were sent to board him, which they effected. His boat being boarded by 100 Tripolitanians, he found that he must either fall into their hands, or blow himself up. He chose the latter alternative, and with his own hand put the match to the powder, which instantly dashed to pieces the boats and every person in them. About 100 shells fell into the town and castle, and spread consternation on all sides.

After this incident, a high officer in the British Navy sent a letter to the American squadron commander, Commodore Preble, as follows:

I beg leave to repeat my congratulations on the services you have rendered your country, and the hair-breadth escapes you have had in setting so distinguished an example to your countrymen, whose bravery and enterprise cannot fail to mark the character of a great and rising nation in a manner that will ultimately be attended with the best and most important consequences to your country. . . . A few brave men have been sacrificed, but they could not have fallen in a better cause; and I even conceive it better to risk more lives, than to submit to terms which might encourage the Barbary states in their demands and insults.

NOTE

[1] Ronald James Wren, who saw Kamikazes in action when he served with the Royal Navy in the Pacific War, makes an interesting point:

Any fellow can be a Kamikaze pilot. And many who never thought they were, eventually were. It's not a role set out for one group of people called Kamikaze. It's more a frame of mind that you get into at a certain point in your life; and you become a Kamikaze pilot, or you become a person who is willing to do so.

Wren cited the case of US Major Charles J. Loring, of Portland, Maine, who when his F-80 jet fighter was hit in November 1952, during the Korean War, decided to crash deliberately into enemy gun emplacements, destroying them and killing himself.

23

REPUTATIONS

A day after Japan surrendered, Vice Admiral Takijiro Onishi, who had staked his life on Kamikaze strategy, and was resolved not to survive the defeat of Japan, stripped himself to the waist at his official residence in Tokyo, unsheathed a borrowed sword, and stabbed himself in the abdomen, employing the traditional cross-cuts of ritual suicide. Refusing the *coup de grâce* and offers of medical relief from pain, he remained in agony for 12 hours, apparently a final act of expiation. His efforts to continue the war relying on the use of Special Attack pilots had failed; he had wept openly as his appeals against surrender to the two or three highest military officers, and to Prince Takamatsu, brother of the Emperor, were rejected.

Another officer who was closely involved in Kamikaze affairs was Kyoji Tominaga, a soft-spoken, well-educated general, who as the former Army Air Force commander in the Philippines had planned the Army's first suicide attacks. Ten years after the war, he sat down in his residence in Tokyo and began work on a thousand-page statement in which he described the war. Most of the pages were dictated to his son, Shigeru. The general passed sentence on his own conduct of Kamikaze operations, blaming himself for various excesses and failures. He also defended himself against suspicions that he was guilty of desertion, of fleeing from a battlefield. (In this case, his post in the Philippines, when it was under attack by General MacArthur's invasion force.) In addition, he wrote a set of extraordinary recommendations, highly confidential in nature, dealing with a future scenario in which Japan finds herself once more at war and obliged to resort to Kamikaze methods. Tominaga died in 1960 at the age of 68. Onishi was 55 when he committed suicide.

Less than three months before his suicide, Onishi had been appointed Vice-Chief of the Naval General Staff, a position he had long sought so he could have a voice in the overall direction of the war. But, despite his talent as leader and strategist (he had demonstrated his abilities during the planning and research conducted before the Pearl Harbor attack), he was aware that Japan was in a hopeless position. In his opinion, which he sometimes told to his aides, the best thing for Japan to do was to give a good account of herself. This he was doing with his Kamikaze tactics.

Onishi, the son of a farmer, had spent two years in England from November 1918 to October 1920. He was fluent in English. (After he returned from England a friend of his argued that the British House of Lords should be abolished while keeping the House of Commons. Onishi told him that the lords provided stability in politics because they were 'less moved by public opinion'.) Although he was known as a short-tempered hard-drinking man he was also noted for his quick intelligence and composure in the midst of difficulties.

As an officer Onishi was outspoken, fearless, impulsive, arrogant, sometimes highly unconventional. He was also full of fighting spirit and was fond of social drinking. But when he was on the job he was highly disciplined. He would not tolerate grumbling. After arriving in the Philippines in October 1944 to become commander of the First Air Fleet with the authority to commence Kamikaze operations, he lost no time in showing what he thought of those who might air dissenting opinions:

> We will tolerate no criticism of any kind of the operations about to get under way. Younger men do not complain or gripe. But it seems the old-timers are often given to objecting to decisions of their superiors. From this moment, anyone who speaks against orders or fails to carry them out will receive stern discipline. In the worst cases there will be no hesitation in ordering the extreme penalty.

When he later transferred his command to Taiwan, Onishi told his staff that Japan's salvation lay in the hands of young men whom he called 'the treasure of the nation'. When he addressed young flyers on Taiwan, and earlier in the Philippines, who were about to take off on suicide missions against warships of the American, British and Australian navies, he told them: 'You are already gods without earthly desires.' In Taiwan and on Kyushu it would be largely student pilots and young, unmarried men who would be called on to give up their lives. This wasn't enough for Onishi. Every able-bodied citizen, he said, should 'adopt the Kamikaze spirit'.

Not surprisingly, Onishi's heroes were Admiral Togo and General Nogi, Japan's war gods of the Russo-Japanese War at the beginning of the twentieth century. But if Onishi was a warrior of the old do-or-die school, he was also highly respected by many of the top admirals as well as young Navy officers who regarded him as a man of uncommon talent who was meticulous in mapping out plans. Bad planning or poor execution of suicide attacks could result in complete failure of an operation, leading to a lowering of morale. Morale never sagged when Onishi took over a command, according to Captain Rikihei Inoguchi, who was his Chief of Staff.

The admiral's view of life, or at least its transient nature, may be found in a short poem which Onishi wrote (in highly regarded calligraphy) for his Special Attack pilots. Thus:

> Blossoming today, then scattered,
> Life resembles a delicate flower.
> Can one expect its fragrance to last for ever?

Early in the new year, 1945, Onishi had revealed his innermost thoughts, saying that even if Japan were defeated, 'the noble spirit of the Kamikaze will keep our homeland from ruin'. Without this spirit, he continued, ruin would follow on the heels of defeat. One officer who knew Onishi well said that the reason he was so devoted to Kamikaze tactics was that only such unalloyed patriotism and willingness to die for the nation would perpetuate the essence of Japan, even in defeat.

As a man of action who was opposed to surrender, he had visited a friend's home on the evening the capitulation was announced and was so torn by emotion that his friend guessed the admiral's intention to kill himself. In his agitation, Onishi unashamedly burst into tears. Surrender was an intolerable humiliation and he wondered aloud why everyone wasn't weeping also. It was a warm, summer evening and Onishi's friend took in the incongruity of the scene: while inside the house a leading admiral was pent up with emotion and distress, outside the cicadas were chanting noisily; and the primroses, much admired by Onishi, were opening in the darkness of the garden.

On the following day, the admiral took his own life. Reflecting on the suicide, an aide believed that Onishi would have taken his own life even if Japan had won the war.

General Tominaga makes an interesting contrast to Admiral Onishi, who had marshalled the first Special Attack squadrons in the Philippine theatre of war. The two men were almost opposites. While Onishi was robust, virile and impulsive, Tominaga was urbane, even-tempered, reflective. However, as noted earlier, on occasion Tominaga could display showmanship, even the flamboyance of an actor when he saw off Kamikaze pilots. (But Onishi's top aides who knew their admiral well said that in difficult situations, Onishi could be counted on to act with composure.) Whereas Onishi liked gambling and drinking in his leisure time, Tominaga preferred reading or taking a turn at the piano. The general was fond of Tolstoy (he considered his books masterfully written in simple prose) and read him in the original Russian. He disliked traditional martial arts such as judo or kendo (Japanese fencing), believing they were 'not practical'. Unlike Onishi, Tominaga was a teetotaller and did not smoke. (But he knew the value of cigarettes: when he was an intelligence officer in Manchuria, while interrogating spies, he discovered they would start talking sooner after a cigarette was offered.) The Tominaga family lived rather modestly, the general often saying jokingly, 'Lack of money is not a disgrace but is inconvenient.' Before he was given command of the Fourth Air Army in the Philippines, Tominaga had no experience with aviation. After the Navy launched Japan's first suicide attack, Tominaga was ordered by the Army High Command to raise volunteers for crash-dive missions. On the other hand, Onishi had a solid background in aviation. As a young officer he had observed aerial warfare as far back as 1915 and had flown some of the first planes produced in Japan. He also had close ties with people in the nation's aircraft production industry. During the fighting in China, Onishi had personally led many sorties. Thereafter he served in the Navy's air force throughout his career. Before the attack on Pearl Harbor, Onishi had been in Hawaii for some time, clandestinely observing that US naval base. Like America's General Billy Mitchell, he was a lobbyist for greater air power. He said during the war that without control of the air the nation could not assume command of the seas.

General Tominaga served as the War Ministry's Director of the Personnel Bureau (1941–43), as Vice War Minister (1943–44), as Commander-in-Chief of the Fourth Air Army in the Philippines (August 1944–January 1945), as a member of the Army Reserve List on Taiwan in May 1945, and as commander of the hastily formed 139th Division in Manchuria (July–August 1945).

After returning to Japan from Taiwan in the spring of 1945, Tominaga suffered two misfortunes on the same day: news of the the death of his eldest son and the razing of his home in Tokyo by American fire bombs. Yasushi, a 20-year old Kamikaze pilot, had been a promising student at Tokyo's Keio University. According to his surviving younger brother, Shigeru, who saw him before his final mission, Yasushi was in 'jovial spirits' when he took off for the last time. ('He acted as calmly as if he was going on an outing.') Tominaga's eldest child and daughter, Hiroko, graduated from the prestigious Musashino Music School and became a pianist. Hiroko was born in 1920. Shigeru has recalled that his mother, Setsu, used to tell people during and after the war that people should not only praise fallen Kamikaze flyers; that those pilots who perished on regular missions deserved the same recognition as heroes. She often said: 'I believe that the Special Attack flyers who knew when they would die suffered less than ordinary pilots who had to fly many combat missions.'

Only minutes before the Tominaga home was hit by bombs, the general and his wife just barely managed to escape by walking to the wooded and spacious Meiji Shrine to take shelter. Tominaga was saddened at the loss of his upright piano which had given him many hours of enjoyment. After the raid, the family was evacuated to Fuji Yoshida, a town on the slopes of Mount Fuji.

A few weeks after the loss of his son and his home, Tominaga received orders to take command of a division in Manchuria comprised of old men raised from Japanese residents in the area. The new division (the 139th) was very poorly equipped, it being a division in name only. His new assignment was tantamont to a demotion but, anyhow, Tominaga was highly pleased to be restored to active service. (In the Philippines he had been commander of an Air army.) It was his fourth assignment in Manchuria since 1925. At one time he was the head of an Army tank training school in Manchuria. But, in addition to the pressure of Chinese armies, Moscow had now entered the lists and, in a swift campaign, the Russians captured Tominaga as well as 150 other generals. He was tried as a spy, apparently because he had served as an intelligence officer in Manchuria, spoke fluent Russian, and had once been an assistant military attaché at the Japanese Embassy in Moscow. Six years earlier, after Japanese troops clashed with Russian forces at the Outer Mongolian border along the Khalkin River (in the summer of 1939), Tominaga, who was then serving at the Imperial High Command in Tokyo, had correctly predicted that a major Russian offensive would soon start because General (later Marshal) Georgi Zhukov had arrived at the scene. Tominaga knew Zhukov personally from his days at the embassy in Moscow. After his trial, Tominaga was given a punitive sentence of 75 years presumably because of his intelligence links. But two years after Stalin's death he was released after being incarcerated in Siberia for ten years.

Tominaga returned to Japan in 1955. There is a black-and-white photograph of him standing on the deck of a repatriation ship as it enters the Japanese port of Maizuru on the Japan Sea coast. The ordeal of war and long captivity are over. In the photo the ageing general, seeing his homeland for the first time in ten years, is choked with tears.

Home at last, Tominaga spent countless hours preparing hundreds of pages of personal war history and reminiscences. The general's lengthy statement is dated August 13, 1955. There are passages in it in which the general does not spare himself in expressing remorse, even admitting guilt over the expenditure of Kamikaze lives. The manuscript has numerous sentences beginning 'I should have . . .' (*shinakereba naranakatta*) and a few that begin 'I am deeply ashamed that . . .' (*watakushiwa fukaku hajiteiru*), with occasional variations. But Tominaga does not actually object to Kamikaze tactics. His misgivings are directed against his own deeds or failures.

The following passage shows that Tominaga is far from being the stereotype of a tough soldier without sympathy for his men:

> The majority of the Special Attack flyers were young and unmarried. But there was a unit composed of assistant instructors of flight schools. Some were married and had children and some were over thirty years old. I felt my heart was on the verge of breaking whenever I received a new group of Special Attack flyers, or was giving orders to them, or was dining with them and seeing them taking off from the airfield. It was almost unbearable to bid farewell to those who were married and had children. I felt a deep sense of grief and asked myself: 'Can't we stop sending these men on these missions?'

There is no evidence that the general took any action other than to ask himself the question. Actually some Special Attack units in Japan firmly refused to allow men to join their ranks if they had children. As for the Navy, high-ranking officers of the First Air Fleet (presumably including Admiral Onishi) knew that the first Kamikaze pilot, Lieutenant Yukio Seki, was married. He was even asked if he was married by two high Navy officers who thought he was a bachelor. But when they learned he had a wife, they still accepted him as the first official Kamikaze pilot, even though they really had wanted an unmarried pilot for the first sortie.

In this key paragraph in Tominaga's lengthy statement, the general is clearly repentant:

> The commanding officer should not kill his men wastefully. He must be courageous and spare only the minimum number of men required for the [suicide] mission. He should not have stood aloof but should have prevented every one who wanted to go from boarding the [Kamikaze] planes. I must take the blame for my failure to convey my thoughts more clearly to the [Kamikaze] corps.

This waste of lives occurred, he explains, because at his base in the Philippines every one of the bomber crews begged to join in the Kamikaze missions, calling out 'Let me take part! Let me take part!' The general relented and let more men take part in the sorties than were necessary.

Here is another quotation from the manuscript:

> The brave men of the Special Attack units were so pure-hearted and sublime; they were almost divine. They were also dignified. However, there was a tendency among them to sally at the earliest opportunity to unload the heavy burden cast upon them and to fulfil their noble wishes. At the same time, the commanding officer who was tormented day and night as how best to utilize the Special Attack units, tended to use them prematurely. I sensed such a tendency in myself and felt other commanding officers shared a similar mentality.

In this connection, Tominaga has received the support of a well-known war correspondent (Takashi Muramatsu of the big-circulation *Mainichi Shimbun*) who knew the general well. The correspondent says that Tominaga would invariably tell newly arrived Kamikaze pilots not to waste their lives needlessly. In the correspondent's words:

> General Tominaga would always tell the men, 'Though you are members of *tokko-tai*, you should not necessarily die. Your mission is to annihilate enemy vessels. If you judge confidently that you can sink or severely damage your target by releasing the bomb, then bomb the target and come back. If you fail to attack the enemy successfully, return to the base. Do not waste your life!'

The general's remorse also covers the failure to notify the families of the deceased pilots:

> Many Special Attack heroes went to their death without themselves notifying the members of their family of their decision to sally on the [one-way] mission. I am sure that many families felt discontented and also experienced deep sadness at the lack of tangible articles left behind by the pilots. I should have taken good care of the men, have had their photographs taken, have collected their articles they were leaving behind and delivered them to members of the family. I am deeply ashamed that I failed to do so.

The High Command itself appears to have had a bad conscience about organizing and executing as a desperate measure the Kamikaze operations. In the event, for half a year or so it kept these operations at arm's length, so that at least some of the Special Attack-related guidance materials and classified manuals for Kamikaze pilots were not compiled or distributed by the High Command until late spring of 1945, although the suicide sorties were officially launched in October of the previous year.

General Tominaga also expressed regret at not having obtained an audience with Emperor Hirohito, and not giving the pilots the freedom to choose the names for their Special Attack suicide units. Says Tominaga:

> I should have sent in a request to the War Minister to allow members of *tokko* units formed in the Tokyo area to be granted an audience with His Majesty. I should have made an effort to let all *tokko* flyers be given the honour of being presented to His Majesty, not only those limited to or formed in the Tokyo area. After the audience, the War Minister and the Army Chief of Staff should have met the men and encouraged them. . . . I am convinced that *Tenshi-sama* [the Son of Heaven, i.e. the Emperor] would have agreed to grant audiences to the Special Attack flyers. It is my deep chagrin that I failed to submit such a request.

The Tominaga papers reveal that after mid-November, 1944, the suicide attacks 'became the mainstay' of his aerial attacks against the Americans. In a parallel case, on Okinawa, in the spring of 1945, Americans were apparently unaware that the big-scale sea and air Kamikaze attacks were meant to carry the full burden, initially, of destroying the US invasion armada. When landings began, the Americans had to learn the hard way; they had thought the going would be easy.

The first suicide attack by Tominaga's Army pilots was carried out on November 7, 1944. The general himself named the Army's first Kamikaze attack Fugaku (another name for Mount Fuji):

I selected the names of all Special Attack units, such as Fugaku or Banda [cherry blossoms in full bloom]. I recall that for the first unit, there was an instruction from the Imperial High Command that the Commander-in-Chief should give a suitable name to the unit. In any case, it was presumptuous of me to have named all units. I should have let the men who flew the missions select the names of their units themselves. Of course, if such freedom were allowed to the men, they may [mistakenly] choose the same name used by other units.

The Tominaga papers, which at length cover the war situation during the Philippine campaign, also dealt with the nasty incident involving the general's flight from the Philippines to Taiwan when rumours circulated that he had 'deserted' his post. He was the only general who fell under this stigma during the war. Tominaga refers to the incident in a 20-page statement, 'To My Beloved Son, Shigeru: The Truth About My Retreat from the Philippines'. (An abridged version of it can be found in Chapter 7.)

Ten years after the war, when Tominaga returned from captivity, he was asked to write a confidential report about his experiences and the lessons he felt would be of use for the future. Tominaga also added recommendations at his own initiative on the possibility of Japan's military having to resort to future Kamikaze tactics. Tominaga's report was made at the request of a Defence Agency think-tank. In it Tominaga freely admits that an attempt to adopt such 'pathetic tactics' (the general's own words) in peacetime would meet strong opposition due to the 'change in mentality of the people'.

Whatever his inner feelings, Tominaga appears unrepentant about the wartime use of suicide pilots, meanwhile providing suggestions about 'future' crash-dive operations: 'Commanders must guard against pessimistic tendencies. The units must be used at the most effective moment.'

At times the tone of the Tominaga report seems offhand, even mechanical: 'In the future, officers and non-commissioned officers should be appointed at the headquarters to administer such a task.' Furthermore, the report says that the commanding general of an army in the field should be expected to 'gladly carry out the order' [to execute Kamikaze attacks] of the High Command if and when such an order is issued. However, the report admits that uncertainties may exist about military leaders in the field. Tominaga's conclusion:

> It would be difficult to send units to the front line with orders simply stating, 'Dispatching to your command as Special Attack units'. For undertaking the extraordinary tactics [Kamikaze tactics], a qualified staff officer must be sent out in order to convince the C-in-C to undertake such tactics. In case the C-in-C is not persuaded, he should be removed from command and replaced by a general officer with an unswerving willpower, who would not develop nervous prostration, suffering physically and mentally from directing such pathetic tactics.

Here Tominaga was recalling his own bungling exit from the Philippines in early 1945, when he left without orders. In his 'Retreat from the Philippines' statement he says: 'The presence and departures of heroic Special Attack flyers was mentally gruelling and deprived me of sleep. Consequently I contracted a febrile disease.' Also: 'I was suffering from an extreme case of nervous prostration.'

How would future generations regard Onishi and Tominaga? Both men gave serious thought to this question.

Tominaga wrote a lengthy statement to explain himself, but asked that it not be published in his lifetime. Until now it has never been published. Onishi rationalized his deeds and disembowelled himself, believing he had helped save Japan's eternal spirit. In one of the last letters he left behind, the admiral wrote this verse:

> Now all is done,
> And I can take a nap for a million years.

Nevertheless, there is evidence that Onishi felt uneasy about the judgement of history, once remarking to an aide that even when he had been in his coffin a hundred years there would be no one to honour his intentions or even remember what he had tried to accomplish in his various commands.

But he was wrong by fifty-odd years – and he need not have worried about his reputation.

On August 15, 2001, a banquet commemorating Onishi's death and attended by more than 1,000 people was held at Tokyo's Imperial Hotel. The banquet opened with a female soprano singing 'Ave Maria' in honour of the Allied sailors who perished in the Kamikaze attacks. Those present at the banquet included a former prime minister (Yoshiro Mori), dozens of members of Parliament, business leaders, editors, writers and entertainers. Many invited guests delivered speeches praising the 'Father of Special Attack Strategy'. Newsreel films of Onishi were shown and young men dressed in the attire of Kamikaze flyers – the youths who were regarded as 'hero gods of the war' – mounted the stage, singing a series of war songs of bygone days. The evening closed with everyone standing and singing the words of an old patriotic song, '*Umi Yukaba*' ('If You Go to Sea'). They stood because it is traditional for one to stand up when singing '*Umi Yukaba*' since the word *Okimi* (the Sovereign) is mentioned.

This popular ditty, often sung by young and old, was written by a warrior in the eighth century and contains these lines:

> If you go to sea
> Your corpse will be brine-soaked.
> If duty calls you to the hills,
> Your pall will be mossy green.
>
> If I perish for the glory of our Sovereign
> I shall have no regrets.

The well-attended banquet offered a clear signal that the man known as 'the Father of the Kamikaze' might yet attain iconic status.

APPENDIX 1

IMPERIAL RESCRIPT ON WAR

Hirohito's Rescript declaring war on the United States and Britain, released on December 8, 1941:

We, by grace of heaven, Emperor of Japan, seated on the Throne of a line unbroken for ages eternal, enjoin upon ye, Our loyal and brave subjects:

We hereby declare war on the United States of America and the British Empire. The men and officers of Our Army and Navy shall do their utmost in prosecuting the war, Our public servants of various departments shall perform faithfully and diligently their appointed tasks, and all other subjects of Ours shall pursue their respective duties; the entire nation with a united will shall mobilize their total strength so that nothing will miscarry in the attainment of Our war aims.

To insure the stability of East Asia and to contribute to world peace is the far-sighted policy which was formulated by Our Great Illustrious Imperial Grandsire and Our Great Imperial Sire succeeding Him, and which We lay constantly to heart. To cultivate friendship among nations and to enjoy prosperity in common with all nations has always been the guiding principle of Our Empire's foreign policy. It has been truly unavoidable and far from Our wishes that Our Empire has now been brought to cross swords with America and Britain. More than four years have passed since China, failing to comprehend the true intentions of Our Empire, and recklessly courting trouble, disturbed the peace of East Asia and compelled Our Empire to take up arms. Although there has been re-established the National Government of China, with which Japan has effected neighbourly intercourse and co-operation, the regime which has survived at Chungking, relying upon American and British protection, still continues its fratricidal opposition.

Eager for the realization of their inordinate ambition to dominate the Orient, both America and Britain, giving support to the Chunking regime, have aggravated the disturbances in East Asia. Moreover, these two Powers, inducing other countries to follow suit, increased military preparations on all sides of our Empire to challenge us. They have obstructed by every means our peaceful commerce, and finally resorted to a direct severance of economic relations, menacing gravely the existence of Our Empire. Patiently have We waited and long have We endured, in the hope that Our Government might retrieve the situation in peace. But our adversaries, showing not the least spirit of conciliation, have unduly delayed a settlement; and in the meantime, they have intensified the economic and political pressure to compel thereby Our Empire to submission. This trend of affairs would, if left unchecked, not only nullify Our Empire's efforts of many years for the sake of the stabilization of East Asia, but also endanger the very existence of Our nation. The situation being such as it is, Our Empire for its existence and self-defence has no other recourse but to appeal to arms and to crush every obstacle in its path.

The hallowed spirits of Our Imperial Ancestors guarding us from above, We rely upon the loyalty and courage of Our subjects in Our confident expectation that the task bequeathed by Our forefathers will be carried forward, and that the sources of evil will be speedily eradicated and an enduring peace immutably established in East Asia, preserving thereby the glory of Our Empire.

[Imperial Sign Manual]

[Imperial Seal]

The 8th day of the 12th month
of the 16th year of Showa
[December 8, 1941]

Japanese historians say the sentence beginning 'It has been truly unavoidable and far from Our wishes' was inserted at Hirohito's insistence.

APPENDIX 2

IMPERIAL RESCRIPT ON SURRENDER

The Imperial Rescript of August 14, 1945, which accepted the terms of the Allies for the surrender of Japan:

To Our good and loyal subjects:

After pondering deeply, the general trends of the world and the actual conditions obtaining in Our Empire today, We have decided to effect a settlement of the present situation by resorting to an extraordinary measure.

We have ordered Our Government to communicate to the Governments of the United States, Great Britain, China and the Soviet Union that Our Empire accepts the provisions of their Joint Declaration.

To strive for the common prosperity and happiness of all nations as well as the security and well-being of Our subjects is the solemn obligation which has been handed down by Our Imperial Ancestors, and which We lay close to heart. Indeed, We declared war on America and Britain out of Our sincere desire to ensure Japan's self-preservation and the stabilization of East Asia, it being far from Our thought either to infringe upon the sovereignty of other nations or to embark upon territorial aggrandizement. But now the war has lasted for nearly four years. Despite the best that has been done by everyone – the gallant fighting of military and naval forces, the diligence and assiduity of Our servants of the State and the devoted service of Our one hundred million people, the war situation has developed not necessarily to Japan's advantage, while the general trends of the world have all turned against her interest. Moreover, the enemy has begun to employ a new and most cruel bomb, the power of which to do damage is indeed incalculable, taking the toll of many innocent lives. Should We continue to fight, it would not only result in an ultimate collapse and obliteration of the Japanese nation, but also would lead to the total extinction of human civilization. Such being the case, how are We to save the millions of our subjects; or to atone Ourselves before the hallowed spirits of Our Imperial Ancestors? This is the reason why We have ordered the acceptance of the provisions of the Joint Declaration of the Powers.

We cannot but express the deepest sense of regret to our Allied nations of East Asia, who have consistently co-operated with the Empire towards the empancipation of East Asia. The thought of those officers and men as well as others who have fallen in the fields of battle, those who died at their posts of duty, or those who met with untimely death and all their bereaved families, pains Our heart night and day. The welfare of the wounded and the war-sufferers, and of those who have lost their home and liveli-hood, are the objects of Our profound solicitude. The hardships and sufferings to which Our nation is to be subjected here-after will be certainly great. We are keenly aware of the inmost feelings of all ye, Our subjects. However, it is according to the dictate of time and fate that We have resolved to pave the way for a grand peace for all the generations to come by enduring the unendurable and suffering what is insufferable.

Having been able to safeguard and maintain the structure of the Imperial State, We are always with ye, Our good and loyal subjects, relying upon your sincerity and integrity. Beware most strictly of any outbursts of emotion which may engender need-less complications, or any fraternal contention and strife which may create confusion, lead ye astray and cause ye to lose the confidence of the world. Let the entire nation continue as one family from generation to generation, ever firm in its faith of the imperishableness of its divine land, and mindful of its heavy bur-den of responsibilities, and the long road before it. Unite your total strength to be devoted to the construction of the future. Cultivate the ways of rectitude; foster nobility of spirit; and work

with resolution so as ye may enhance the innate glory of the
Imperial State and keep pace with the progress of the world.

[Imperial Sign Manual]

The 14th day of the 8th month   [Imperial Seal]
of the 20th year of Showa
[August 14, 1945]

RECOMMENDED READING

Adams, Andrew (ed.) (1973), *The Hagoromo Society of Kamikaze Divine Thunderbolt Corps Survivors: The Cherry Blossom Squadrons Born to Die*, Los Angeles, CA.

Axell, Albert (1971), *Gunkokushugi* (Militarism), in Japanese, Tokyo.

Benedict, Ruth (1946), *The Chrysanthemum and the Sword*, Boston, MA.

Bennett, Geoffrey (1975), *Naval Battles of World War II*, New York.

Bergamini, David (1971), *Japan's Imperial Conspiracy*, London.

Bix, Herbert (2000), *Hirohito and the Making of Modern Japan*, New York.

Breen, John and Mark Teeuwen (1999), *Shinto in History: Ways of the Kami*, Richmond.

Butow, Robert J.C. (1954), *Japan's Decision to Surrender*, Palo Alto, CA.

Butow, Robert J.C. (1961), *Tojo and the Coming of the War*, Princeton, NJ.

Bywater, Hector (1991), *The Great Pacific War*, New York.

Chiran Tokko Kichi (Chiran Tokko Base) (1979), Chiran Kojo Nadeshikokai (edited by Chiran Women's High School Pink Fringe Society), Tokyo.

Clostermann, Pierre (1952), *Flames in the Sky*, London.

Costello, John (1981), *The Pacific War*, London.

Craig, William (1967), *The Fall of Japan*, New York.

Deacon, F.W. and G.R. Storry (1966), *The Case of Richard Sorge*, New York.

Fane, Francis Douglas (1985), *The Naked Warriors*, New York.

Farago, Ladislas (1967), *The Broken Seal: The Story of Operation Magic and the Pearl Harbor Disaster*, New York.

Feifer, George (2001), *The Battle of Okinawa: The Blood and the Bomb*, Guildford, CT.

Feis, Herbert (1961), *Japan Subdued: The Atomic Bomb and the End of the War in the Pacific*, Princeton, NJ.

Grew, Joseph C. (1944), *Ten Years in Japan*, New York.

Hayashi, Saburo (1959), *Kogun: The Japanese Army in the Pacific War* (in collaboration with Alvin D. Coox), Quantico, VA.

Hearings Before the Joint Committee on the Investigation of the Pearl Harbor Attack (1946), Washington, DC.

Hersey, John (1989), *Hiroshima*, New York.

Hoyt, Edwin Palmer (1983), *The Kamikazes*, New York.

Ickes, Harold L. (1954), *The Secret Diary*, New York.

Ienaga, Saburo (1978), *The Pacific War: World War II and the Japanese, 1931–45*, New York.

Ikuta, Atsushi (1977), *Rikugun Koku Tokubetsu Kogekitaishi* (History of the Army Special Attack Squadrons), Tokyo.

Inoguchi, Rikihei and Tadashi Nakajima and Roger Pineau (1959), *The Divine Wind*, London.

Kase, Hideaki (1975), *Tennoke no Tatakai* (Struggle of the Tenno Family), Tokyo.

Kase, Hideaki (2001), *Korehodo Gunka ga Utawareteiru Kuniwanai, Watshi no Hanseiki* (There is no other country where military songs are so popular), Tokyo.

Kirihara, Hisashi (1988), *Tokko ni Chitta Chosenjin* (Koreans Who Dedicated Their Lives as Tokko Flyers), Tokyo.

Kolko, Gabriel (1984), *Main Currents in Modern American History*, New York.

Kusayanagi, Taizo (1972), *Tokko no Shiso: Onishi Takijiro Den* (Philosophy of Tokko: Biography of Takijiro Onishi), Tokyo.

Lamont-Brown, Raymond (1999), *Kamikaze: Japan's Suicide Samurai*, London.

Leckie, Robert (1987), *Delivered From Evil: The Saga of World War II*, New York.

Maeda, Masahiro (1985), *Kaiten no Shiso* (The Philosophy of Kaiten), Tokyo.

Manchester, William (1980), *Goodbye, Darkness: A Memoir of the Pacific War*, Boston, MA.

Manchester, William (1978), *American Caesar*, New York.

Matsushita, Ryuichi (2000), *Shihei Tokko* (Private Tokko Unit), Tokyo. (This is the description that the author gave to Admiral Ugaki's suicide mission inasmuch as it was a private undertaking.)

Millot, Bernard (1971), *Divine Thunder: The Life and Death of the Kamikazes*, New York.

Morison, Samuel Eliot (1958), *History of US Naval Operations in World War II*, London.

Morris, Ivan (1975), *The Nobility of Failure: Tragic Heroes in the History of Japan*, New York.

Munson, Kenneth (1969), *Aircraft of World War II*, London.

Naemura, Hichiro (1993), *Rikugun Saigo no Tokkokichi* (The Army's Last Kamikaze Base), Tokyo.

Nagatsuka, Ryuji (1973), *I Was a Kamikaze*, London.

Nagasawa, Michio (2001), *Gakuto Shutsujin no Kiroku: Kaigun Yobigakusei, Seishun no Kiroku* (Records of College Students at War; College Students Drafted by the Navy and the Saga of Their Passion as Youth), Tokyo.

Naito, Hatsuho (1989), *Thunder Gods: The Kamikaze Pilots Tell Their Story*, New York.

Nitobe, Inazo (2001 – originally published in 1905), *Bushido: the Soul of Japan*, Tokyo.

O'Callaghan, Father Joseph, SJ (1985), *I Was Chaplain on the* Franklin, New York.

Okuma, Shigenobu (1895), *Okuma Haku Kajitsutan* (Autobiography of Count Okuma), Tokyo.

Okumiya, Masake and Jiro Horikoshi (1956), *Zero*, New York.

O'Neill, Richard (1981), *Suicide Squads: Axis and Allied Special Attack Weapons of World War II*, New York.

Pacific War Research Society (1968), *Japan's Longest Day*, Tokyo.

Papers Relating to the Foreign Relations of the United States, Japan, 1931–1941, Vol. II (1943), Washington, DC.

Reischauer, Edwin O. (1974), *Japan: The Story of a Nation*, New York.

Rolling, B.V.A. and Antonio Cassese (1993), *The Tokyo Trial and Beyond*, London.

Roskill, Captain S.W. (1960), *The Navy at War, 1939–45*, London.

Ross, Bill (1986), *Iwo Jima: Legacy of Valor*, New York.

Sherman, Frederick C. (1950), *Combat Command: the American Aircraft Carriers in the Pacific War*, New York.

Sherrod, Robert (1952), *History of Marine Corps Aviation in World War II*, New York.

Slim, Sir William (1956), *Defeat into Victory*, London.

Sora no Kanatani: Tokko Obasan no Kaisho (Beyond the Blue Sky: Recollections of 'Aunty Tokko') (1995), Tokyo.

Spector, Ronald H. (1985), *Eagle Against the Sun: the American War With Japan*, New York.

Storry, Richard (1957), *The Double Patriots*, London.

Tagata, Takeo and others (1991), *Hien yo! Kessen no Ozora ni Habatake* (Hien! Fly to the Sky for the Decisive Battle), Tokyo.

Takagi, Toshiro (1973), *Tokko Chiran Kichi* (Chiran Tokko Base), Tokyo.

Ugaki, Matome (1968), *Sensouroku* (Records of the weeds of war), Tokyo.

Vidal, Gore (1994), *United States: Essays 1952–1992*, New York.

Warner, Denis and Peggy Warner (1983), *Kamikaze: The Sacred Warriors 1941–1945*, Oxford.

Whymant, Robert (1996), *Stalin's Spy, Richard Sorge and the Tokyo Espionage Ring*, London.

INDEX

Abele, US destroyer, 194
Afghanistan, 23–4
Ahtisaari, Martti, 2
Air Self-Defense Force, 135
Al-Qaeda, xi–xiii, 1, 78, 119, 192
Ancestor worship, 6
Anti-Comintern Pact (1936), 21–2
Anti-Japanese prejudice, 76
Aoyama Gakuin College, 123
Arima, Admiral Masafumi, 36–7
Arita, Foreign Minister Hachiro, 22
Asahi newspaper, 38, 76, 108
Australia, x, 108
  navy at war, 184
Australia, cruiser, 181
Austrian Crisis, 31
Average life span, 1, 17
Axell, Albert, 45, 210

Babarossa, Operation, 24
Bansei Air Base, 111
Barbary Coast pirates, 245
Barbey, Rear Admiral Daniel, 224
Baring, Maurice, 222
Baucus, US Senator Max, xiii
Beijing, 95
Berlin, 25–6, 30
  five dummy Berlins, 236
Biak Island, 37
Bigart, US reporter Homer, 169
Bismarck, German statesman Otto von, 13
Blackburn, Lt.-Commander Tom, 224
British Blenheim bombers, 97
British Conservatives, 20
Brooke, Sub-Lt. Geoffrey, xii
Brown, Vice Admiral C.R., 178, 225

Brunetière, Ferdinand, 8
Buddhism, 5–8
Buddhist proverbs, 8
Bullen, Dr John, 245
Bungei Shunju, 47
Bunker Hill, US carrier, 184
Burma, 41, 96
Bushido, 4, 7, 9
Bushido: The Soul of Japan, 7–8

Caldwell, Erskine, 231
Callaghan, US destroyer, 173–4
Caroline Islands, 192
Cassese, Antonio, 18
Catholic rebellion (in Japan), 7
Chamberlain, Prof. Basil Hall, 5
Chennault, Gen. Claire, 21
Chechnya, x
Chiang Kai-shek, 21, 25, 31, 96, 203
China, xiii, 20–1, 30, 94, 163
Chiran, 55, 57
  Air Base, 56, 64
Chiran Peace Museum, 66
Chiyoda, carrier, 34
Cho, Gen. Isamu, 214
Christianity, 2, 6
Christians in Japan, 7, 122
  as Kamikaze pilots, 118–24
Christian pilgrims in Holy Land, x
Churchill, Winston, 26, 29, 71, 204
Code of the Samurai, 6–7
Communism, 2
Compton, Karl T., US scientist, 205
Confucianism, 96
Consensus in Japan, 1–2, 11
Coral Sea, Battle of (1942), 30
Crash boats, 193